DESCENT INTO DREAD

*FOR ALEXIS SHANNON
AND BRIANNA LEBOEUF*

*BEST OF WIVES AND
BEST OF WOMEN*

DESCENT INTO DREAD. Volume 1. Published by Caliber Comics, a division of Caliber Entertainment LLC. Copyright 2020 Dalton Shannon and Wells Thompson. All Rights Reserved. No part of this book may be copied or retransmitted without the express written permission of the copyright holder and publisher. Limited use of art may be used for journalistic or review purposes. Any similarities to individuals living or dead is purely coincidental and unintentional except where fair use laws apply. For more information visit the Caliber Comics website: www.calibercomics.com

CONTENTS

ALL COMICS WRITTEN BY
DALTON SHANNON AND WELLS THOMPSON

EDITED BY ANDREA LORENZO MOLINARI

THE MYTH OF TOMORROW	DRAWN AND LETTERED BY ANTONIO RUSSO TANTARO	1
THE BEAST RETURNED	DRAWN BY ANDREA MODUGNO LETTERED BY ANTONIO RUSSO TANTARO	9
AWASH	DRAWN AND LETTERED BY SERG ACUÑA	17
THE FINAL SCREAM	DRAWN AND LETTERED BY SLEIGHT	25
THE BEAST AVENGED	DRAWN BY ANDREA MODUGNO LETTERED BY ANTONIO RUSSO TANTARO	33
DREAMS OF THE DROWNED	DRAWN AND LETTERED BY LEONARDO MARCELLO GRASSI	41
RUBBING ELBOWS	DRAWN AND LETTERED BY KATH LOBO	49
THE BEAST DISPLAYED	DRAWN BY ANDREA MODUGNO LETTERED BY ANTONIO RUSSO TANTARO	57
THE FLY TRAP	DRAWN BY MIA STRIZZI LETTERED BY ANTONIO RUSSO TANTARO	65
TERRITORIAL IMPERATIVE	DRAWN AND LETTERED BY MR. FISH LEE	73
CHASING THE SUN	DRAWN AND LETTERED BY MARY LANDRO	81
THE BEAST DENIED	DRAWN BY ANDREA MODUGNO LETTERED BY ANTONIO RUSSO TANTARO	89

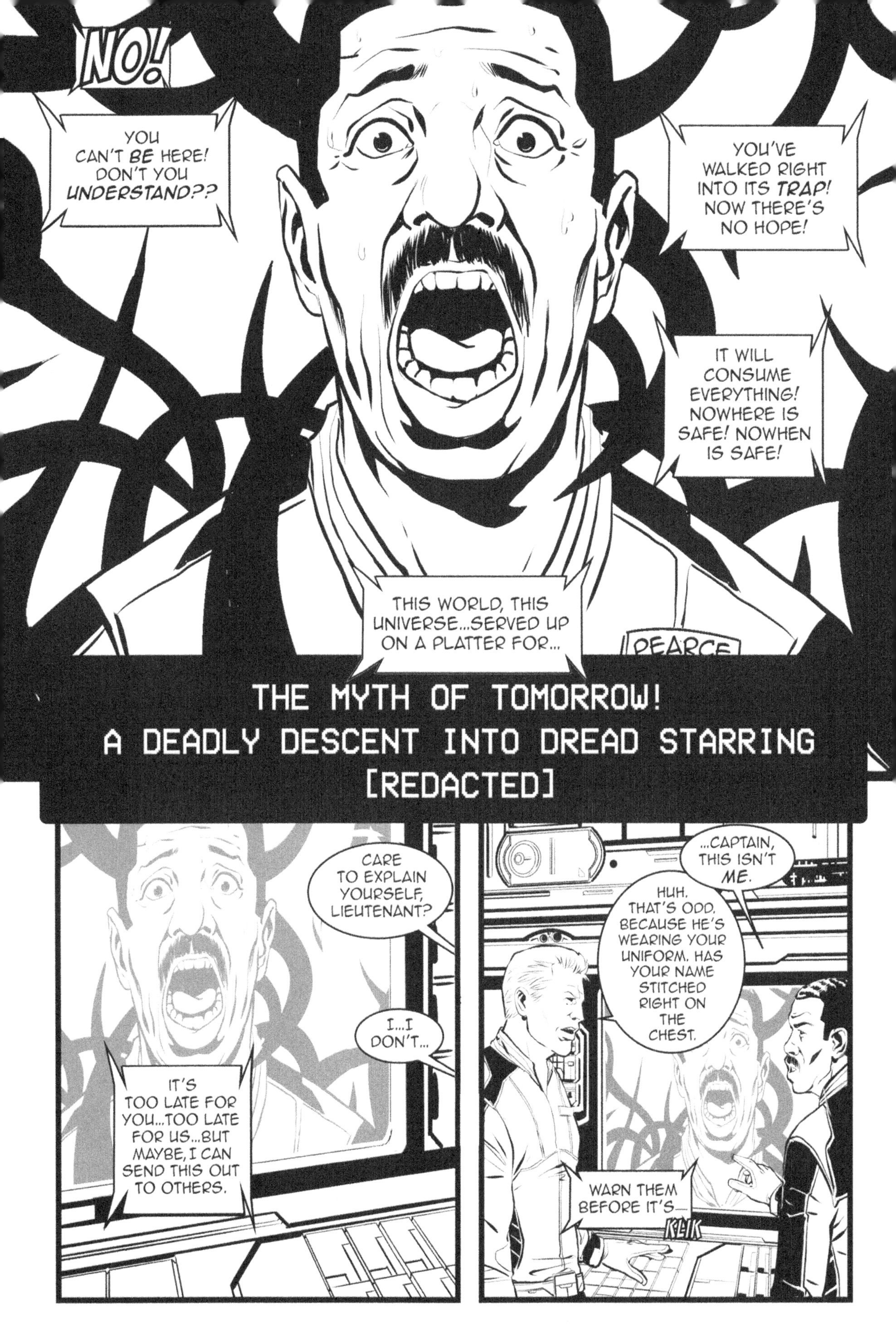
NO!
YOU CAN'T BE HERE! DON'T YOU UNDERSTAND??
YOU'VE WALKED RIGHT INTO ITS TRAP! NOW THERE'S NO HOPE!
IT WILL CONSUME EVERYTHING! NOWHERE IS SAFE! NOWHEN IS SAFE!
THIS WORLD, THIS UNIVERSE...SERVED UP ON A PLATTER FOR...
PEARCE
THE MYTH OF TOMORROW!
A DEADLY DESCENT INTO DREAD STARRING
[REDACTED]
CARE TO EXPLAIN YOURSELF, LIEUTENANT?
I...I DON'T...
IT'S TOO LATE FOR YOU...TOO LATE FOR US...BUT MAYBE, I CAN SEND THIS OUT TO OTHERS.
...CAPTAIN, THIS ISN'T ME.
HUH. THAT'S ODD. BECAUSE HE'S WEARING YOUR UNIFORM. HAS YOUR NAME STITCHED RIGHT ON THE CHEST.
WARN THEM BEFORE IT'S—
KLIK

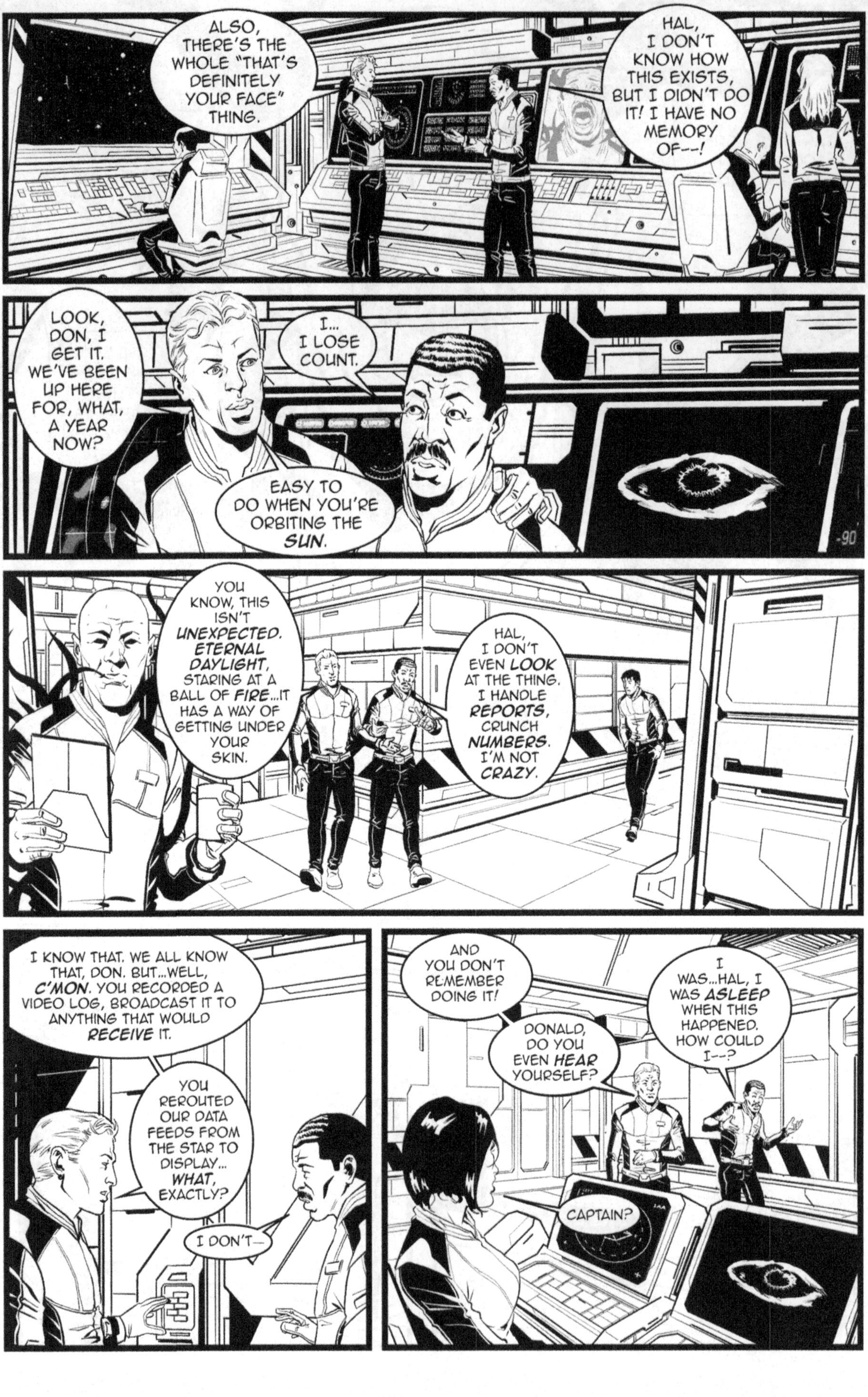

ALSO, THERE'S THE WHOLE "THAT'S DEFINITELY YOUR FACE" THING.
HAL, I DON'T KNOW HOW THIS EXISTS, BUT I DIDN'T DO IT! I HAVE NO MEMORY OF--!
LOOK, DON, I GET IT. WE'VE BEEN UP HERE FOR, WHAT, A YEAR NOW?
I... I LOSE COUNT.
EASY TO DO WHEN YOU'RE ORBITING THE SUN.
-90
YOU KNOW, THIS ISN'T UNEXPECTED. ETERNAL DAYLIGHT, STARING AT A BALL OF FIRE...IT HAS A WAY OF GETTING UNDER YOUR SKIN.
HAL, I DON'T EVEN LOOK AT THE THING. I HANDLE REPORTS, CRUNCH NUMBERS. I'M NOT CRAZY.
I KNOW THAT. WE ALL KNOW THAT, DON. BUT...WELL, C'MON. YOU RECORDED A VIDEO LOG, BROADCAST IT TO ANYTHING THAT WOULD RECEIVE IT.
YOU REROUTED OUR DATA FEEDS FROM THE STAR TO DISPLAY... WHAT, EXACTLY?
I DON'T—
AND YOU DON'T REMEMBER DOING IT!
DONALD, DO YOU EVEN HEAR YOURSELF?
I WAS...HAL, I WAS ASLEEP WHEN THIS HAPPENED. HOW COULD I--?
CAPTAIN?

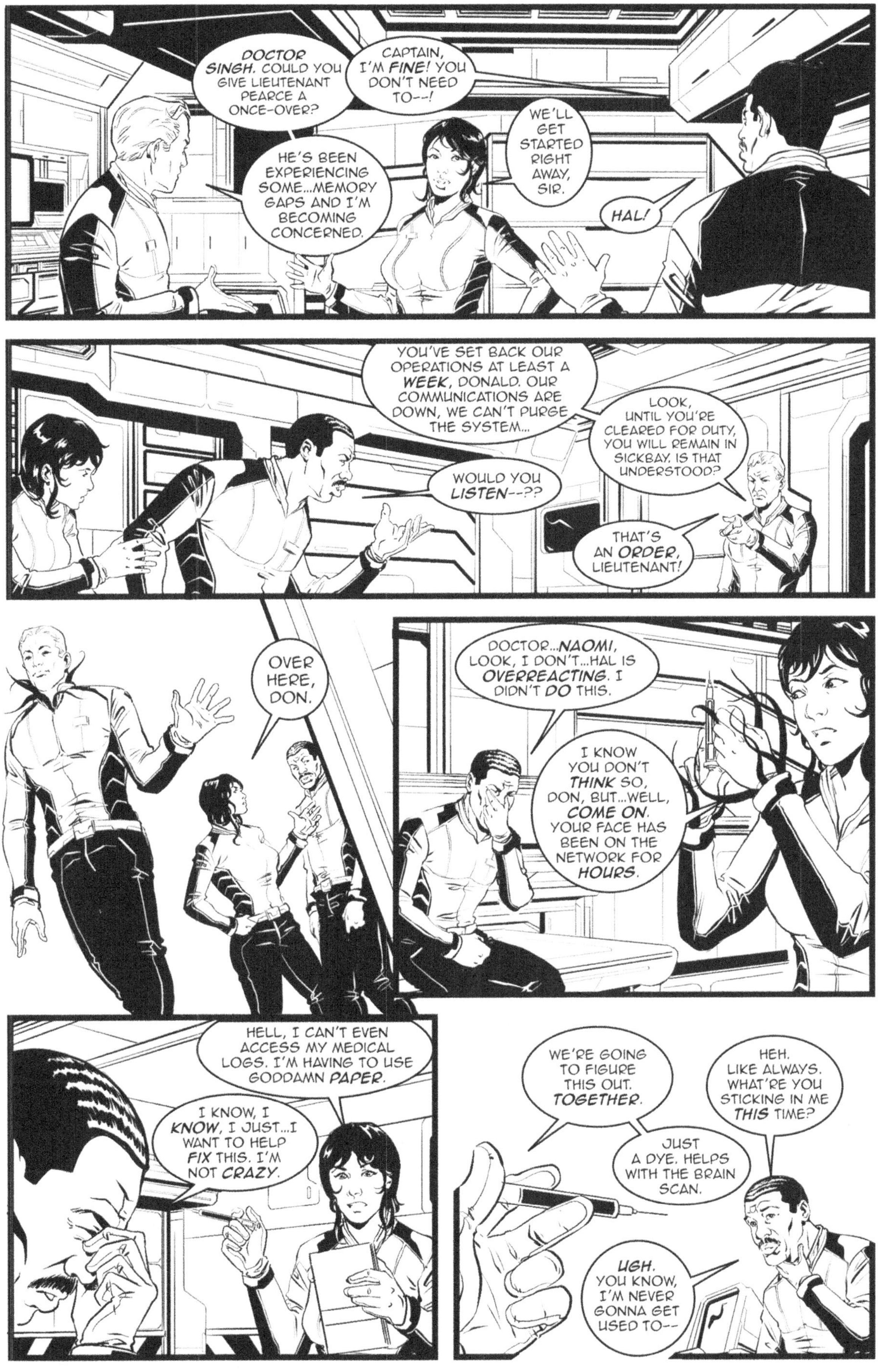
DOCTOR SINGH. COULD YOU GIVE LIEUTENANT PEARCE A ONCE-OVER?
CAPTAIN, I'M FINE! YOU DON'T NEED TO--!
HE'S BEEN EXPERIENCING SOME...MEMORY GAPS AND I'M BECOMING CONCERNED.
WE'LL GET STARTED RIGHT AWAY, SIR.
HAL!
YOU'VE SET BACK OUR OPERATIONS AT LEAST A WEEK, DONALD. OUR COMMUNICATIONS ARE DOWN, WE CAN'T PURGE THE SYSTEM...
WOULD YOU LISTEN--??
LOOK, UNTIL YOU'RE CLEARED FOR DUTY, YOU WILL REMAIN IN SICKBAY. IS THAT UNDERSTOOD?
THAT'S AN ORDER, LIEUTENANT!
OVER HERE, DON.
DOCTOR...NAOMI, LOOK, I DON'T...HAL IS OVERREACTING. I DIDN'T DO THIS.
I KNOW YOU DON'T THINK SO, DON, BUT...WELL, COME ON. YOUR FACE HAS BEEN ON THE NETWORK FOR HOURS.
HELL, I CAN'T EVEN ACCESS MY MEDICAL LOGS. I'M HAVING TO USE GODDAMN PAPER.
I KNOW, I KNOW, I JUST...I WANT TO HELP FIX THIS. I'M NOT CRAZY.
WE'RE GOING TO FIGURE THIS OUT. TOGETHER.
HEH. LIKE ALWAYS. WHAT'RE YOU STICKING IN ME THIS TIME?
JUST A DYE. HELPS WITH THE BRAIN SCAN.
UGH. YOU KNOW, I'M NEVER GONNA GET USED TO--

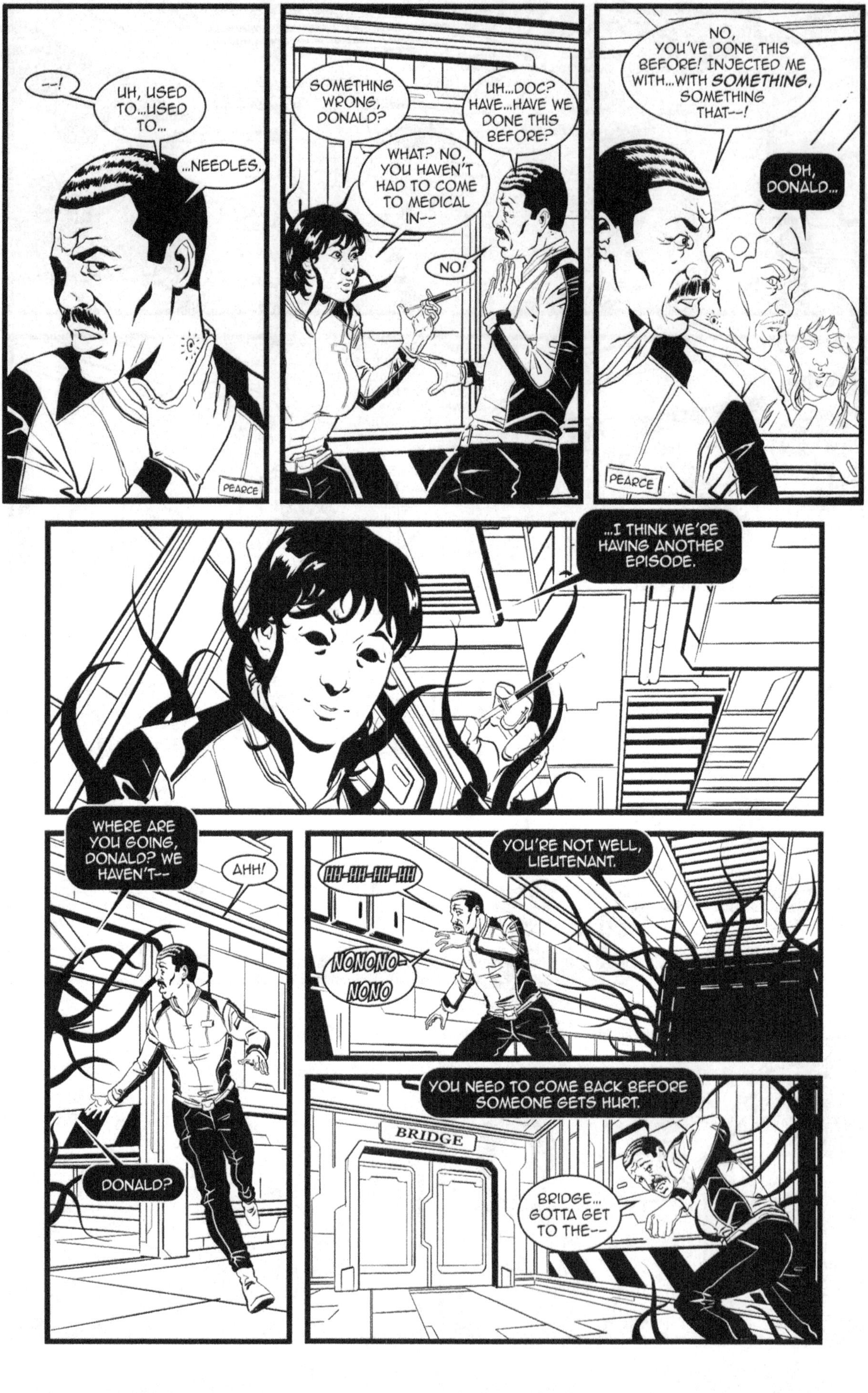
--!
UH, USED TO...USED TO...
...NEEDLES.
PEARCE
SOMETHING WRONG, DONALD?
UH...DOC? HAVE...HAVE WE DONE THIS BEFORE?
WHAT? NO, YOU HAVEN'T HAD TO COME TO MEDICAL IN--
NO!
NO, YOU'VE DONE THIS BEFORE! INJECTED ME WITH...WITH SOMETHING, SOMETHING THAT--!
OH, DONALD...
PEARCE
...I THINK WE'RE HAVING ANOTHER EPISODE.
WHERE ARE YOU GOING, DONALD? WE HAVEN'T--
AHH!
DONALD?
YOU'RE NOT WELL, LIEUTENANT.
HH-HH-HH-HH
NONONO-NONO
YOU NEED TO COME BACK BEFORE SOMEONE GETS HURT.
BRIDGE
BRIDGE... GOTTA GET TO THE--

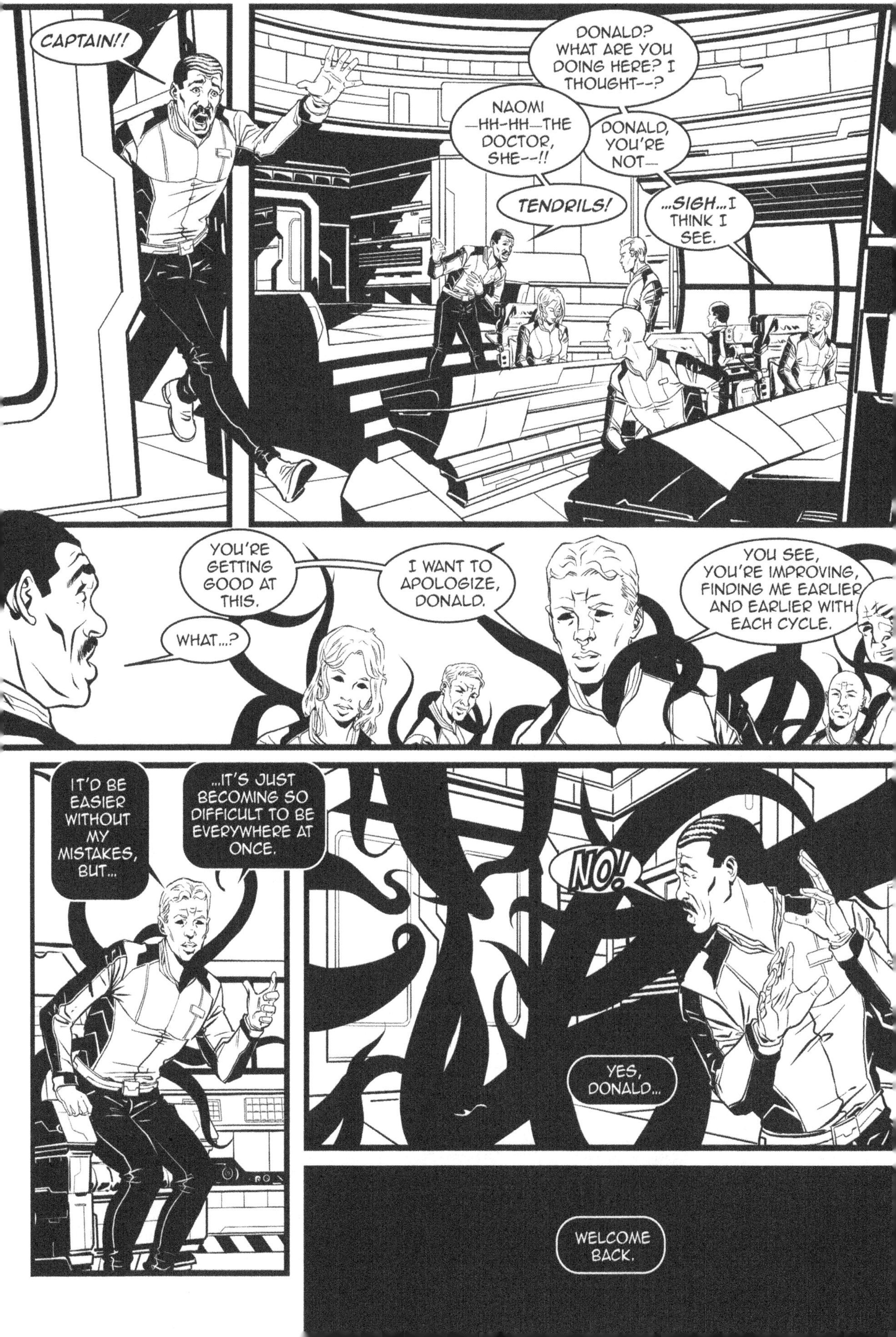
CAPTAIN!!
DONALD? WHAT ARE YOU DOING HERE? I THOUGHT--?
NAOMI —HH-HH— THE DOCTOR, SHE--!!
DONALD, YOU'RE NOT—
TENDRILS!
...SIGH...I THINK I SEE.
YOU'RE GETTING GOOD AT THIS.
WHAT...?
I WANT TO APOLOGIZE, DONALD.
YOU SEE, YOU'RE IMPROVING, FINDING ME EARLIER AND EARLIER WITH EACH CYCLE.
IT'D BE EASIER WITHOUT MY MISTAKES, BUT...
...IT'S JUST BECOMING SO DIFFICULT TO BE EVERYWHERE AT ONCE.
NO!
YES, DONALD...
WELCOME BACK.

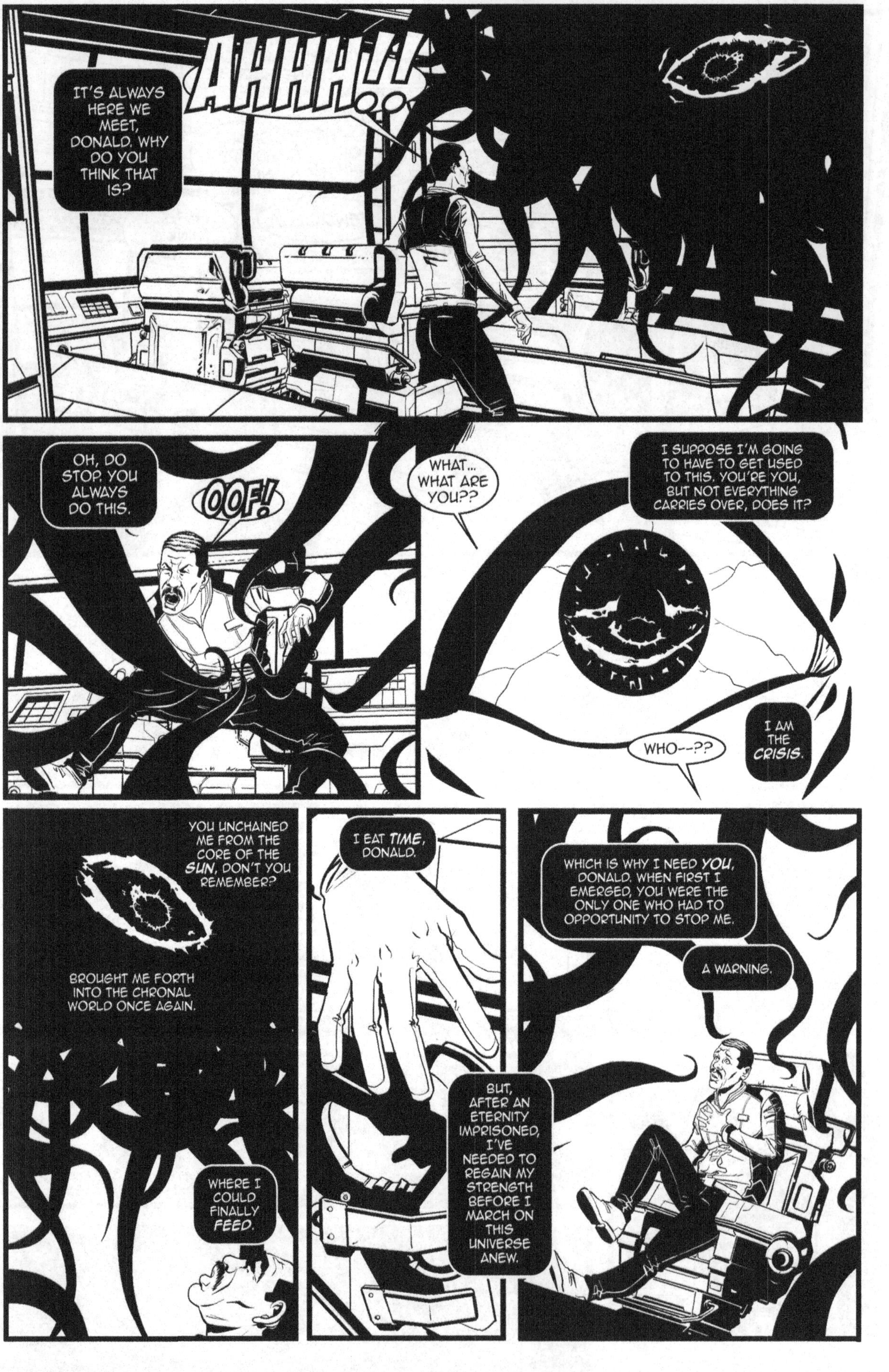
AHHH!!
IT'S ALWAYS HERE WE MEET, DONALD. WHY DO YOU THINK THAT IS?
OH, DO STOP. YOU ALWAYS DO THIS.
OOF!
WHAT... WHAT ARE YOU??
I SUPPOSE I'M GOING TO HAVE TO GET USED TO THIS. YOU'RE YOU, BUT NOT EVERYTHING CARRIES OVER, DOES IT?
WHO--??
I AM THE CRISIS.
YOU UNCHAINED ME FROM THE CORE OF THE SUN, DON'T YOU REMEMBER?
BROUGHT ME FORTH INTO THE CHRONAL WORLD ONCE AGAIN.
WHERE I COULD FINALLY FEED.
I EAT TIME, DONALD.
BUT, AFTER AN ETERNITY IMPRISONED, I'VE NEEDED TO REGAIN MY STRENGTH BEFORE I MARCH ON THIS UNIVERSE ANEW.
WHICH IS WHY I NEED YOU, DONALD. WHEN FIRST I EMERGED, YOU WERE THE ONLY ONE WHO HAD TO OPPORTUNITY TO STOP ME.
A WARNING.

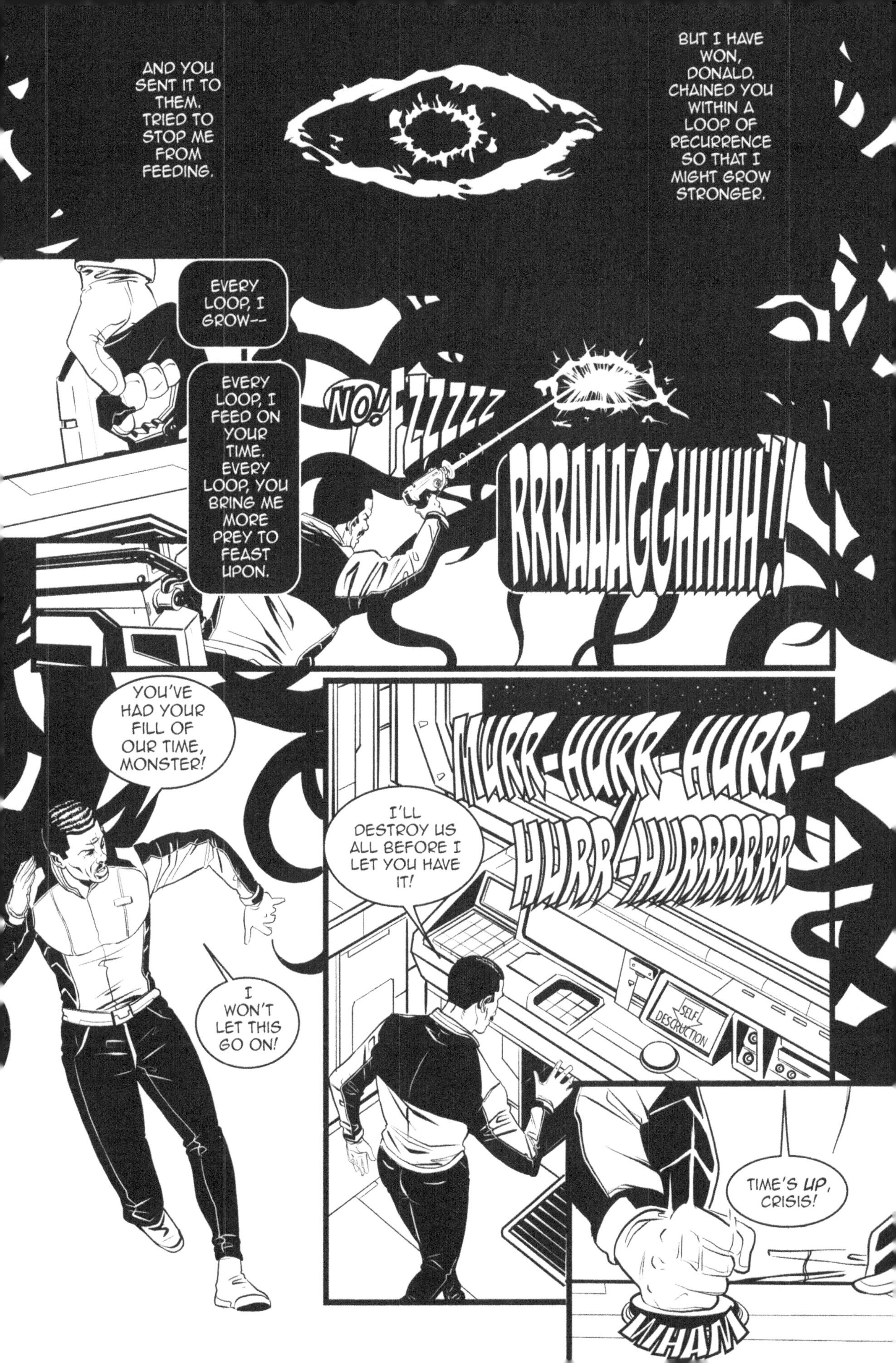
AND YOU SENT IT TO THEM. TRIED TO STOP ME FROM FEEDING.
BUT I HAVE WON, DONALD. CHAINED YOU WITHIN A LOOP OF RECURRENCE SO THAT I MIGHT GROW STRONGER.
EVERY LOOP, I GROW--
EVERY LOOP, I FEED ON YOUR TIME. EVERY LOOP, YOU BRING ME MORE PREY TO FEAST UPON.
NO!
FZZZZZ
RRRAAAGGHHHH!!
YOU'VE HAD YOUR FILL OF OUR TIME, MONSTER!
I WON'T LET THIS GO ON!
HURR-HURR-HURR-HURR-HURRRRRR
I'LL DESTROY US ALL BEFORE I LET YOU HAVE IT!
SELF DESCRUCTION
TIME'S UP, CRISIS!
WHAM

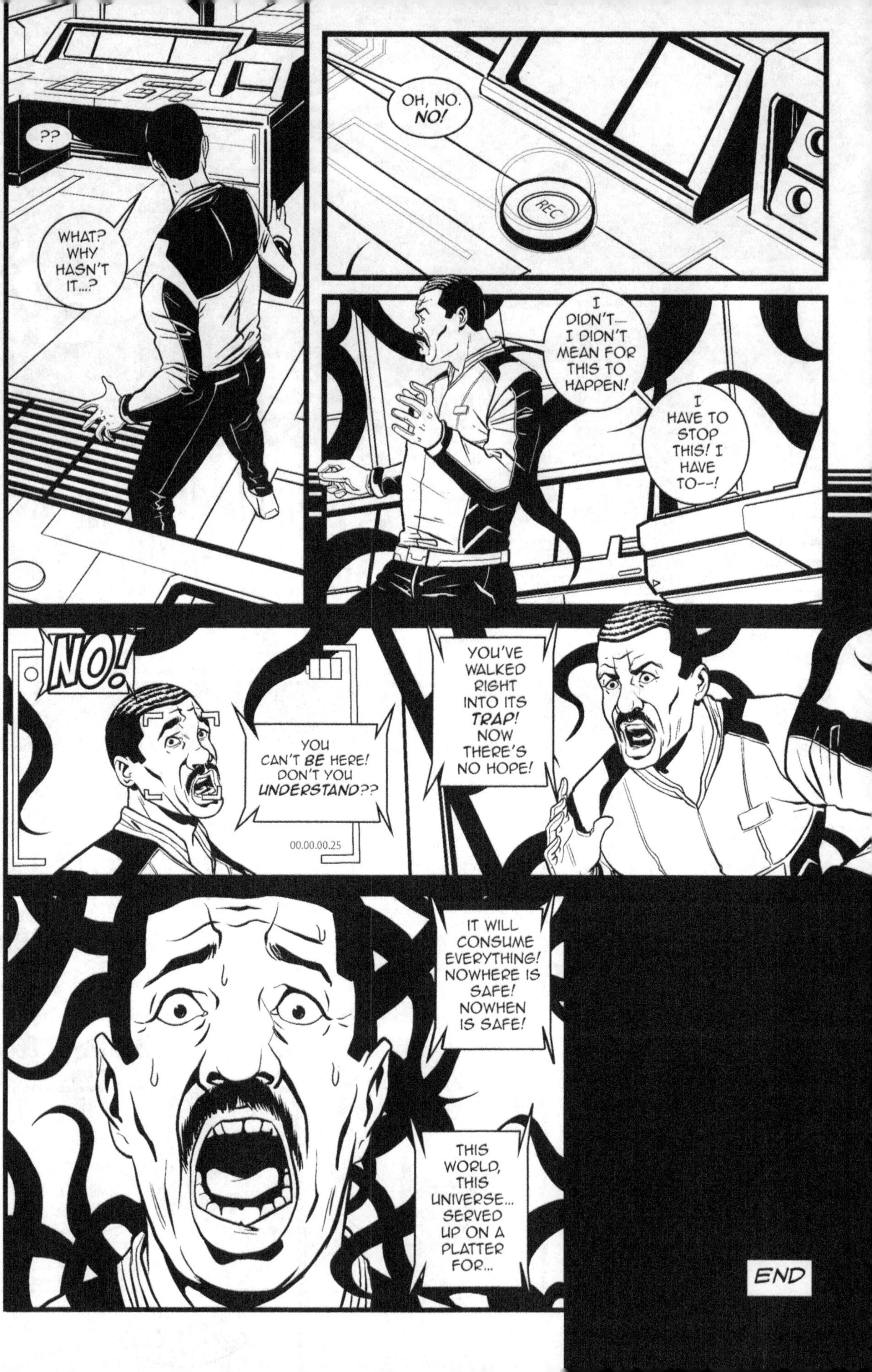
??
WHAT? WHY HASN'T IT...?
OH, NO. *NO!*
REC
I DIDN'T— I DIDN'T MEAN FOR THIS TO HAPPEN!
I HAVE TO STOP THIS! I HAVE TO--!
NO!
YOU CAN'T *BE* HERE! DON'T YOU *UNDERSTAND*??
00.00.00.25
YOU'VE WALKED RIGHT INTO ITS *TRAP!* NOW THERE'S NO HOPE!
IT WILL CONSUME EVERYTHING! NOWHERE IS SAFE! NOWHEN IS SAFE!
THIS WORLD, THIS UNIVERSE... SERVED UP ON A PLATTER FOR...
END

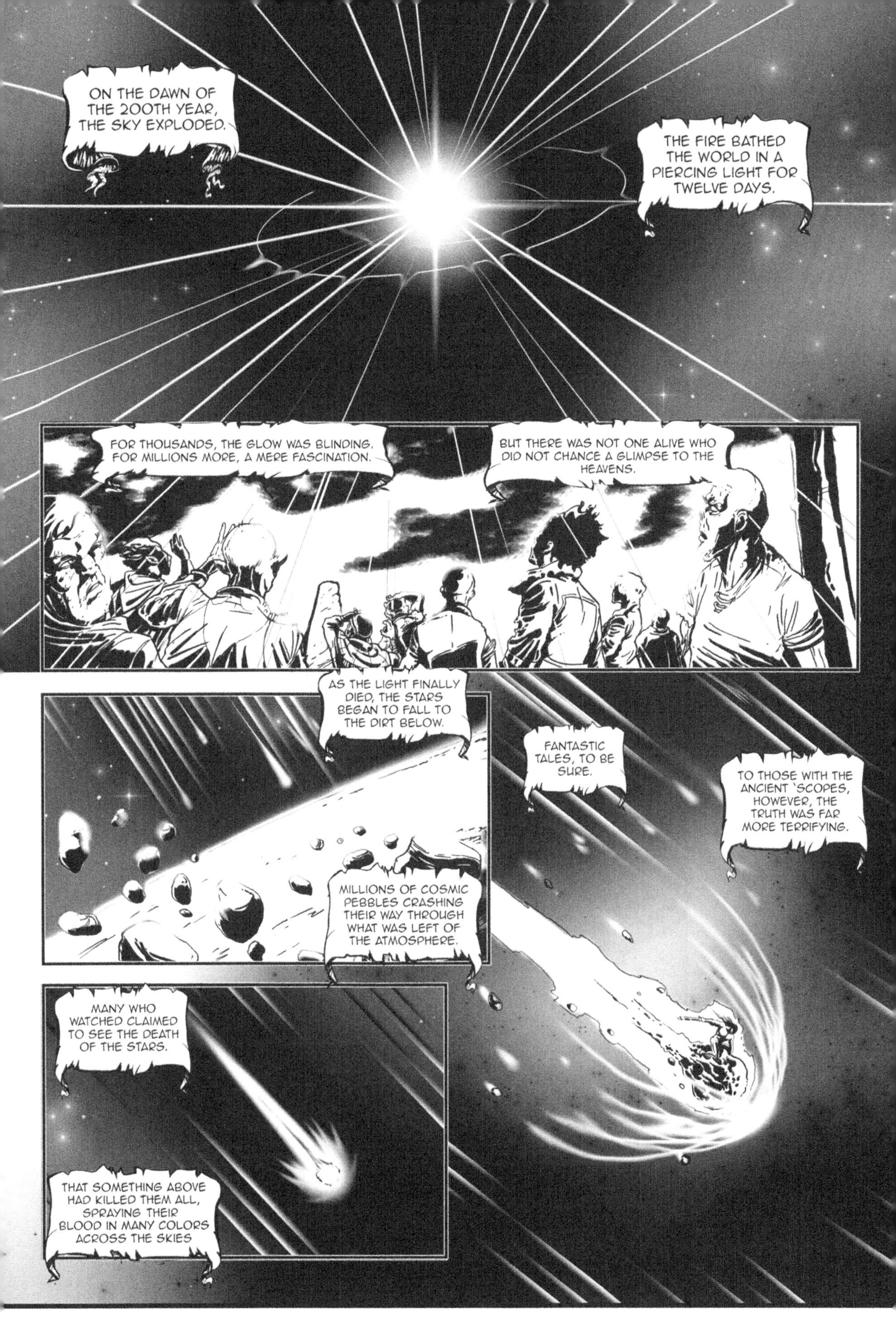
ON THE DAWN OF THE 200TH YEAR, THE SKY EXPLODED.
THE FIRE BATHED THE WORLD IN A PIERCING LIGHT FOR TWELVE DAYS.
FOR THOUSANDS, THE GLOW WAS BLINDING. FOR MILLIONS MORE, A MERE FASCINATION.
BUT THERE WAS NOT ONE ALIVE WHO DID NOT CHANCE A GLIMPSE TO THE HEAVENS.
AS THE LIGHT FINALLY DIED, THE STARS BEGAN TO FALL TO THE DIRT BELOW.
FANTASTIC TALES, TO BE SURE.
TO THOSE WITH THE ANCIENT 'SCOPES, HOWEVER, THE TRUTH WAS FAR MORE TERRIFYING.
MILLIONS OF COSMIC PEBBLES CRASHING THEIR WAY THROUGH WHAT WAS LEFT OF THE ATMOSPHERE.
MANY WHO WATCHED CLAIMED TO SEE THE DEATH OF THE STARS.
THAT SOMETHING ABOVE HAD KILLED THEM ALL, SPRAYING THEIR BLOOD IN MANY COLORS ACROSS THE SKIES

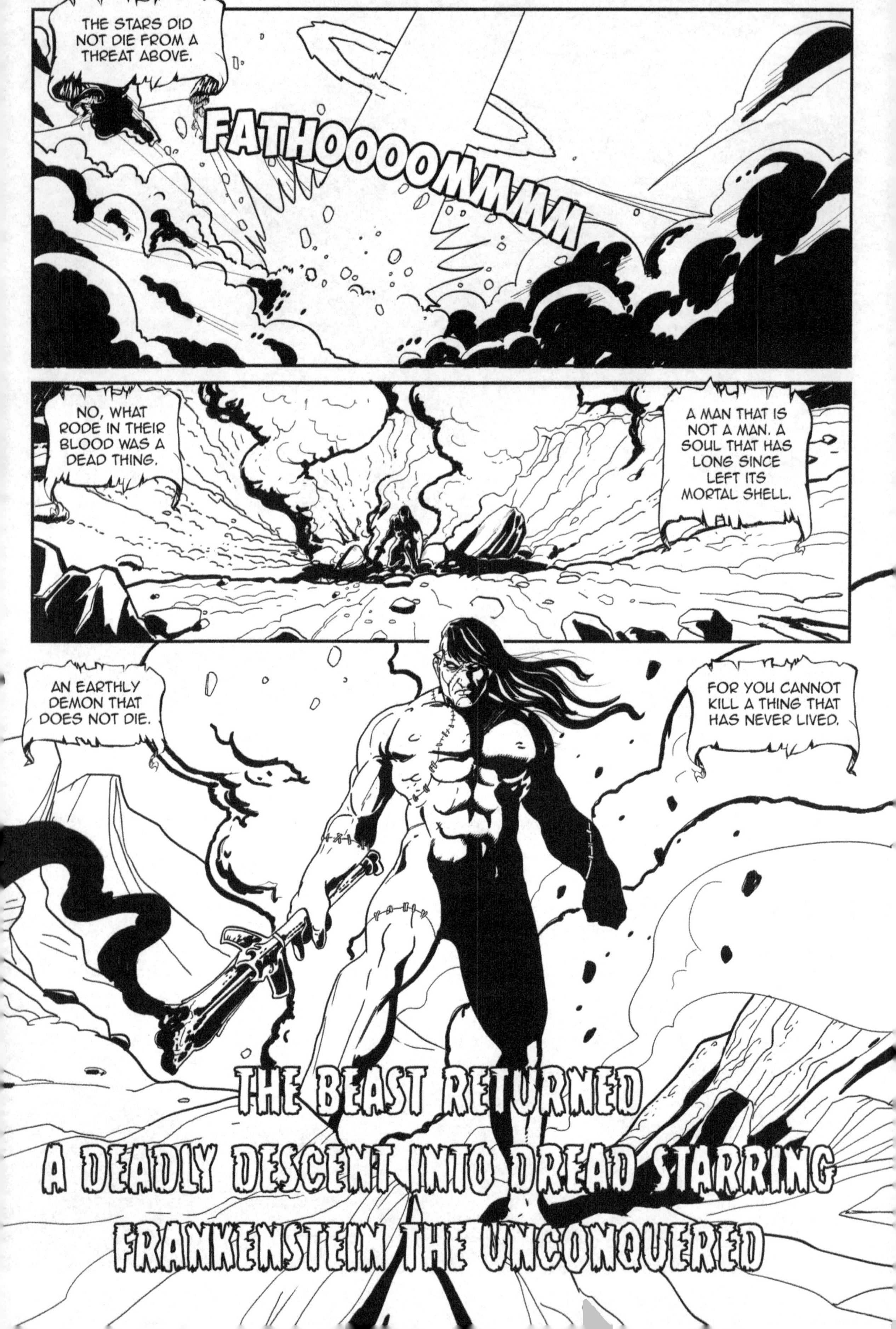
THE STARS DID NOT DIE FROM A THREAT ABOVE.
FATHOOOOOMMMMM
NO, WHAT RODE IN THEIR BLOOD WAS A DEAD THING.
A MAN THAT IS NOT A MAN. A SOUL THAT HAS LONG SINCE LEFT ITS MORTAL SHELL.
AN EARTHLY DEMON THAT DOES NOT DIE.
FOR YOU CANNOT KILL A THING THAT HAS NEVER LIVED.
THE BEAST RETURNED
A DEADLY DESCENT INTO DREAD STARRING
FRANKENSTEIN THE UNCONQUERED

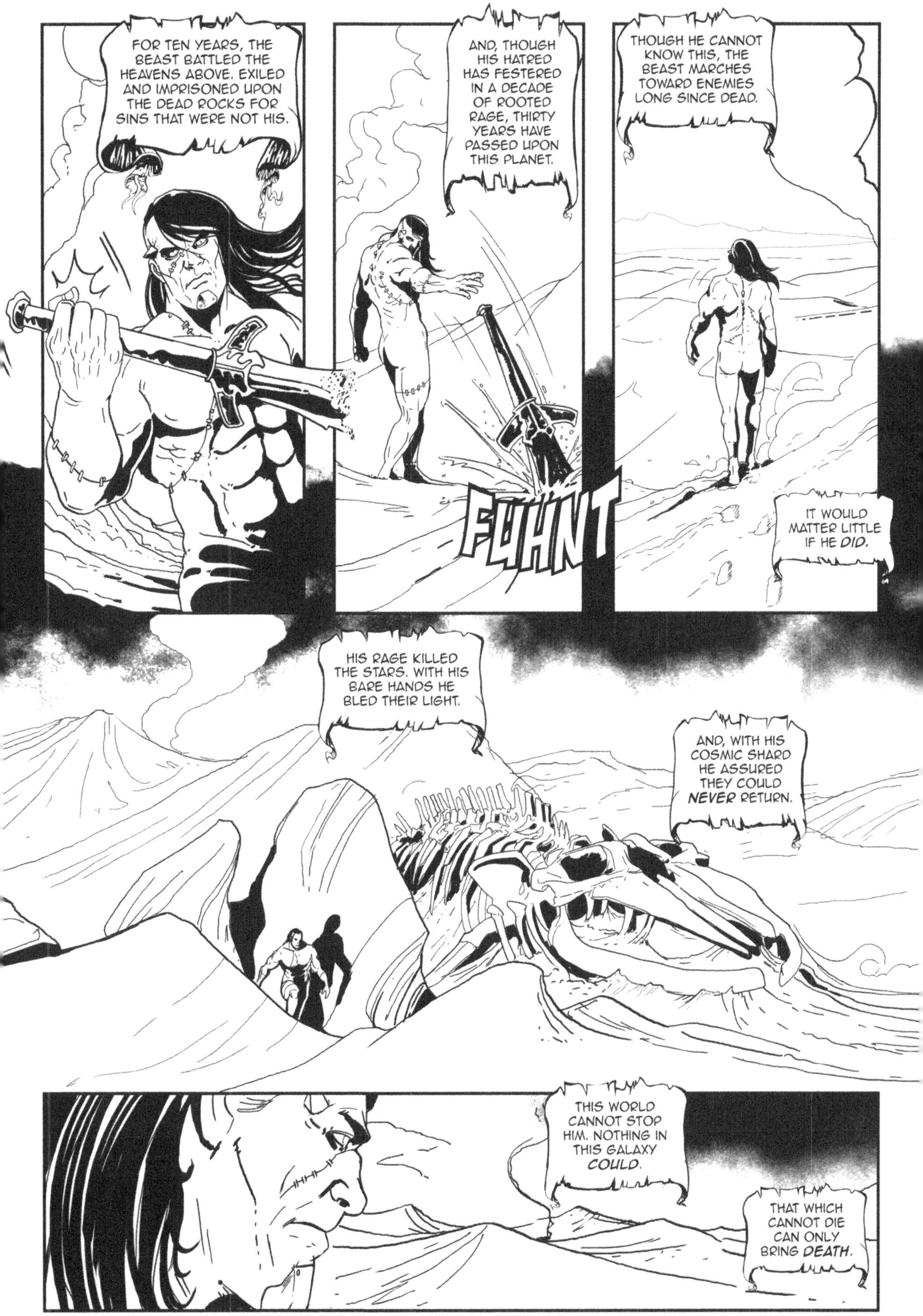
FOR TEN YEARS, THE BEAST BATTLED THE HEAVENS ABOVE. EXILED AND IMPRISONED UPON THE DEAD ROCKS FOR SINS THAT WERE NOT HIS.
AND, THOUGH HIS HATRED HAS FESTERED IN A DECADE OF ROOTED RAGE, THIRTY YEARS HAVE PASSED UPON THIS PLANET.
FUHNT
THOUGH HE CANNOT KNOW THIS, THE BEAST MARCHES TOWARD ENEMIES LONG SINCE DEAD.
IT WOULD MATTER LITTLE IF HE *DID.*
HIS RAGE KILLED THE STARS. WITH HIS BARE HANDS HE BLED THEIR LIGHT.
AND, WITH HIS COSMIC SHARD HE ASSURED THEY COULD ***NEVER*** RETURN.
THIS WORLD CANNOT STOP HIM. NOTHING IN THIS GALAXY ***COULD***.
THAT WHICH CANNOT DIE CAN ONLY BRING ***DEATH***.

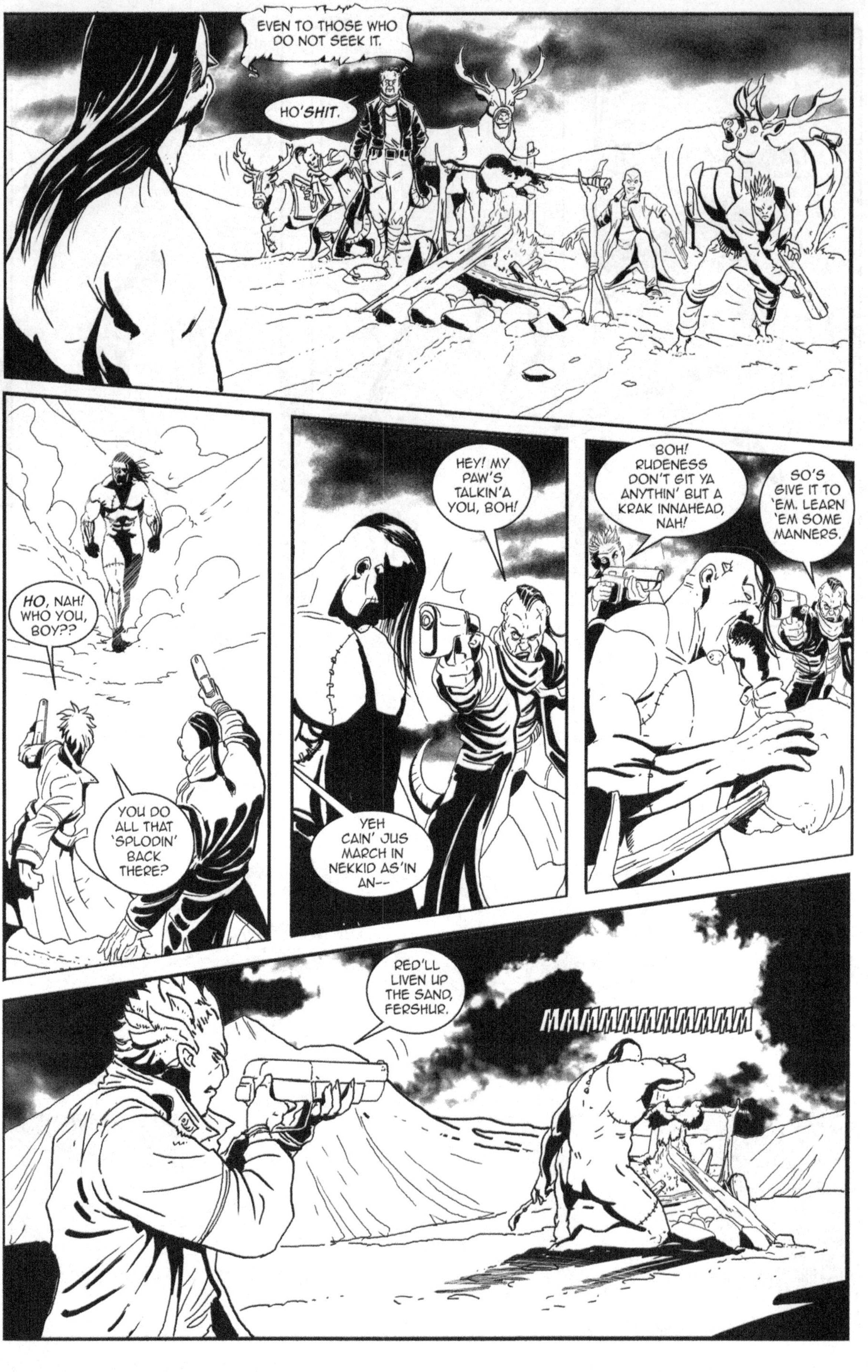
EVEN TO THOSE WHO DO NOT SEEK IT.
HO'SHIT.
HO, NAH! WHO YOU, BOY??
YOU DO ALL THAT 'SPLODIN' BACK THERE?
HEY! MY PAW'S TALKIN'A YOU, BOH!
YEH CAIN' JUS MARCH IN NEKKID AS'IN AN--
BOH! RUDENESS DON'T GIT YA ANYTHIN' BUT A KRAK INNAHEAD, NAH!
SO'S GIVE IT TO 'EM. LEARN 'EM SOME MANNERS.
RED'LL LIVEN UP THE SAND, FERSHUR.
MMMMMMMMMMMMM

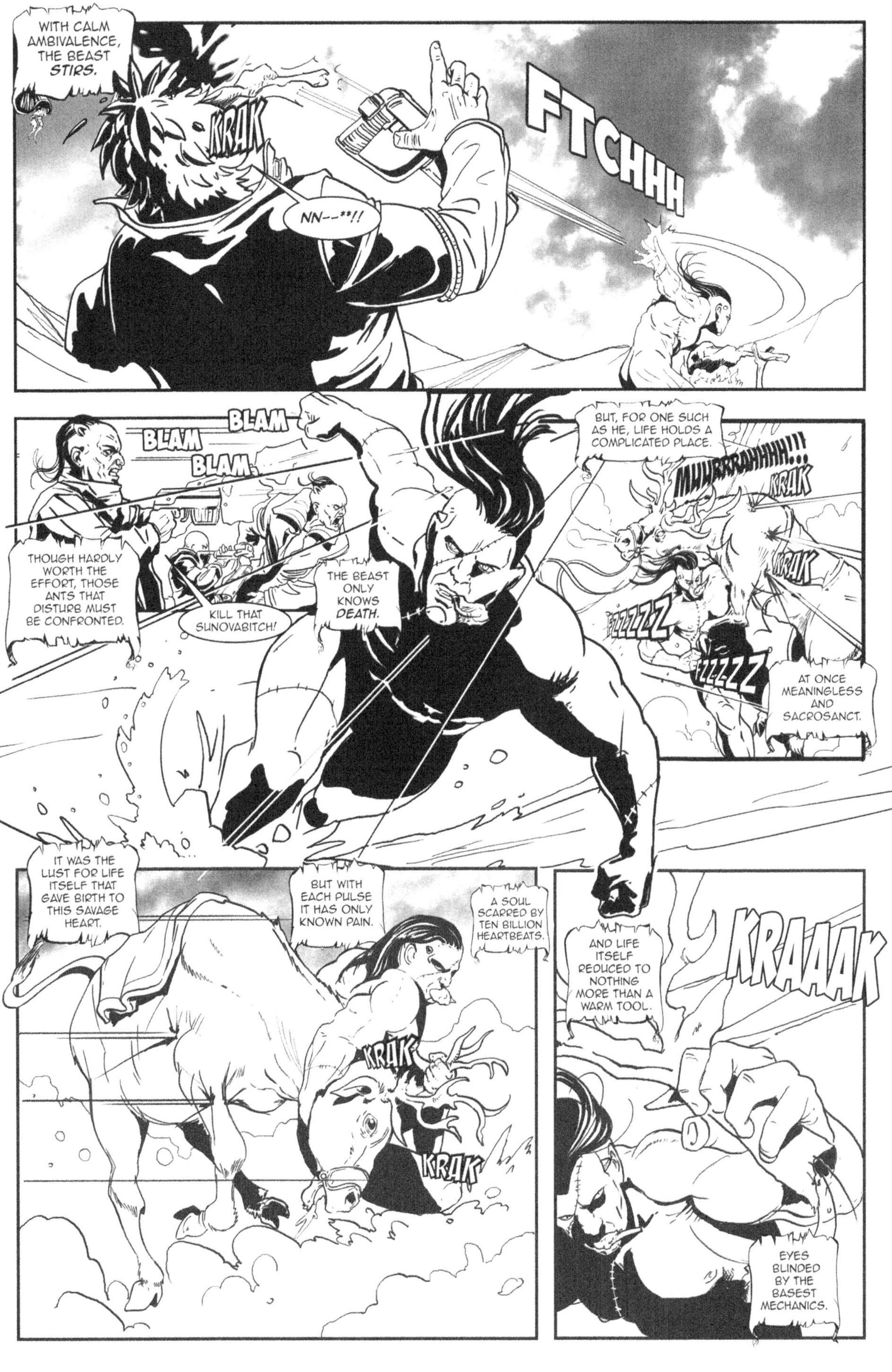

WITH CALM AMBIVALENCE, THE BEAST *STIRS.*
KRAK
FTCHHH
NN--**!!
BLAM
BLAM
BLAM
BUT, FOR ONE SUCH AS HE, LIFE HOLDS A COMPLICATED PLACE.
MUHRRRAHHHH!!!
KRAK
KRAK
THOUGH HARDLY WORTH THE EFFORT, THOSE ANTS THAT DISTURB MUST BE CONFRONTED.
THE BEAST ONLY KNOWS *DEATH.*
KILL THAT SUNOVABITCH!
FZZZZZ
FZZZZZ
AT ONCE MEANINGLESS AND SACROSANCT.
IT WAS THE LUST FOR LIFE ITSELF THAT GAVE BIRTH TO THIS SAVAGE HEART.
BUT WITH EACH PULSE IT HAS ONLY KNOWN PAIN.
A SOUL SCARRED BY TEN BILLION HEARTBEATS.
KRAK
KRAK
AND LIFE ITSELF REDUCED TO NOTHING MORE THAN A WARM TOOL.
KRAAAK
EYES BLINDED BY THE BASEST MECHANICS.

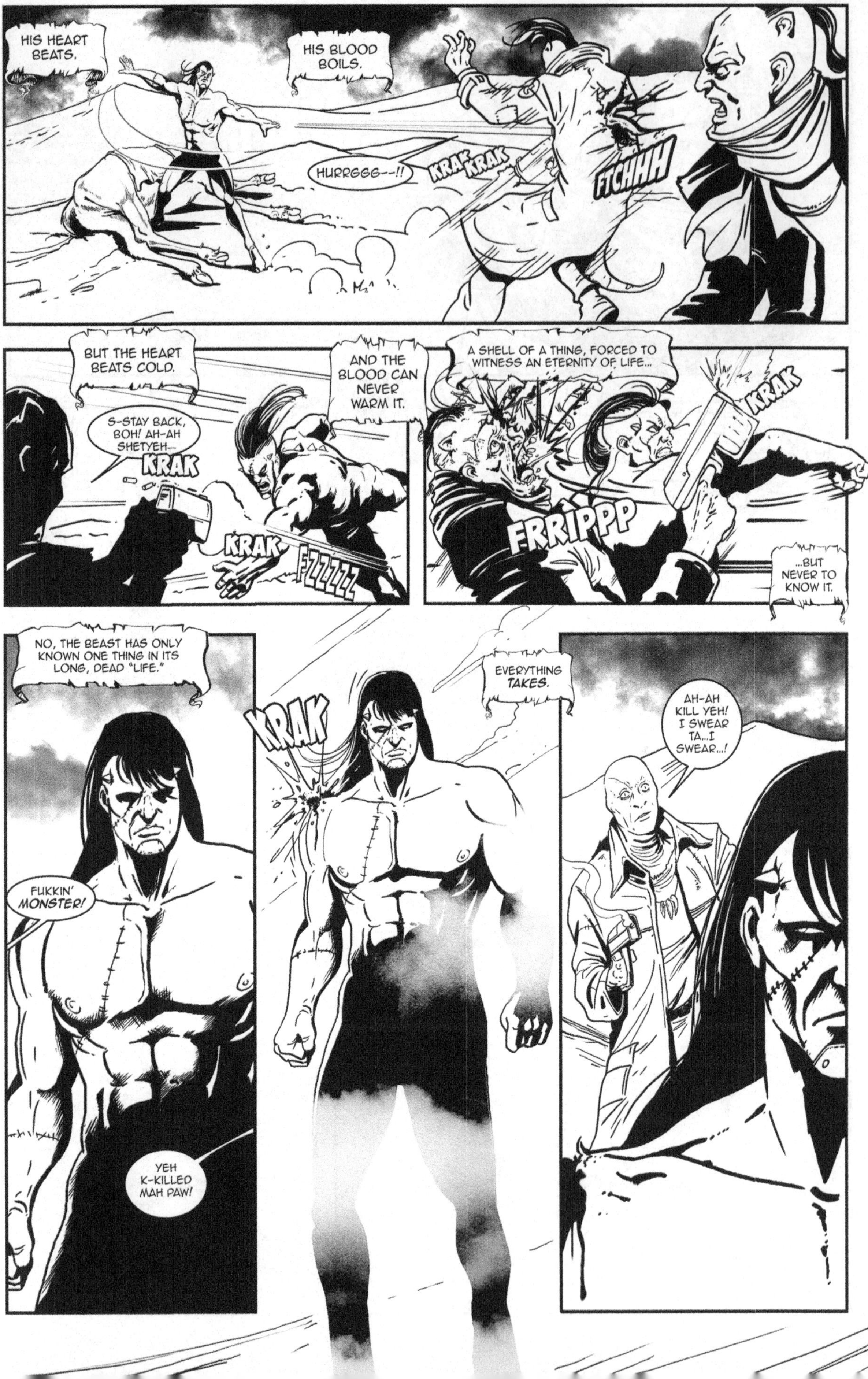
HIS HEART BEATS.
HIS BLOOD BOILS.
HURRGGG--!!
KRAK KRAK
FTCHHH
BUT THE HEART BEATS COLD.
S-STAY BACK, BOH! AH-AH SHETYEH--
KRAK
KRAK
FZZZZZ
AND THE BLOOD CAN NEVER WARM IT.
A SHELL OF A THING, FORCED TO WITNESS AN ETERNITY OF LIFE...
KRAK
FRRIPPP
...BUT NEVER TO KNOW IT.
NO, THE BEAST HAS ONLY KNOWN ONE THING IN ITS LONG, DEAD "LIFE."
FUKKIN' MONSTER!
YEH K-KILLED MAH PAW!
KRAK
EVERYTHING TAKES.
AH-AH KILL YEH! I SWEAR TA...I SWEAR...!

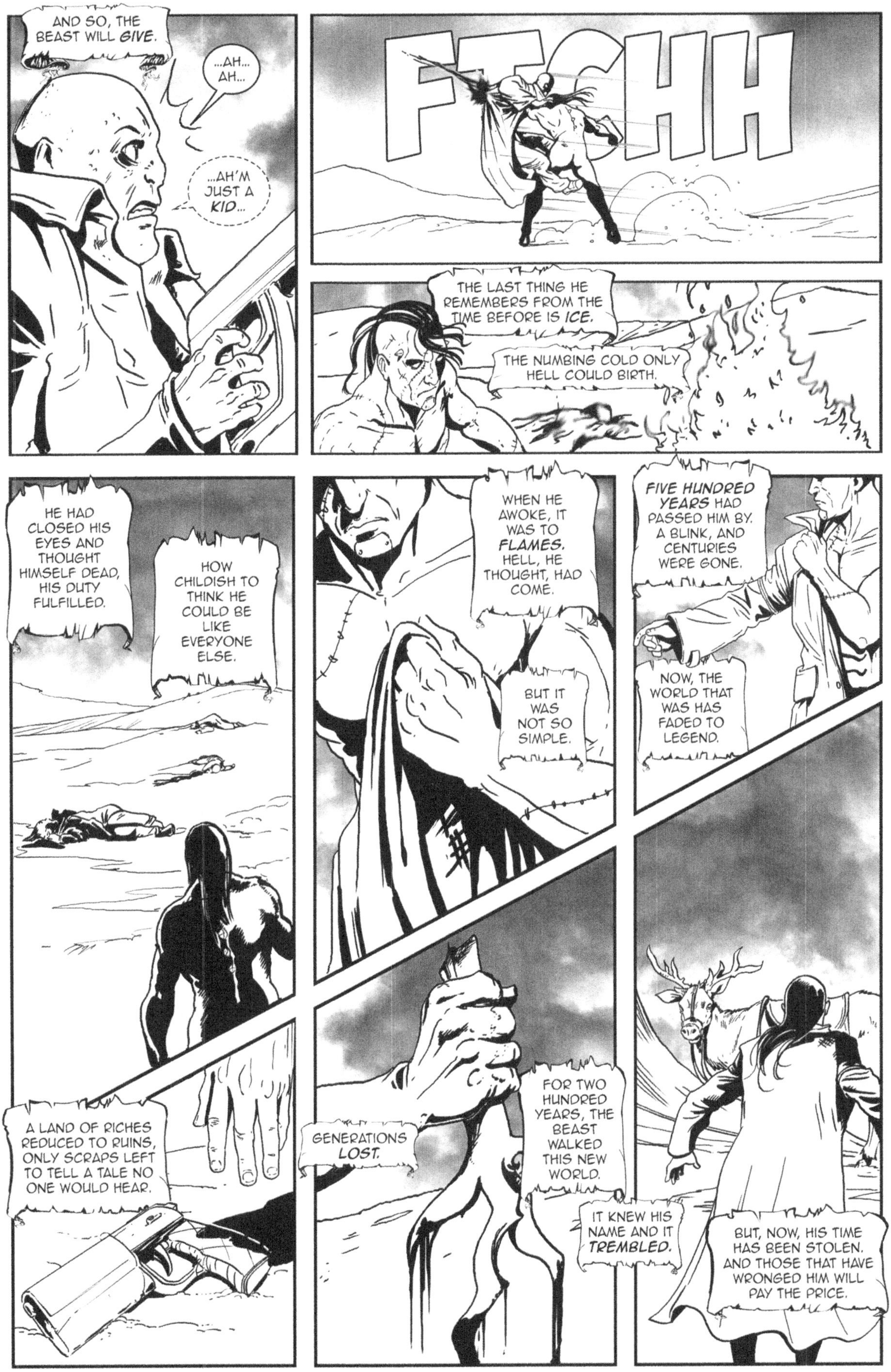
AND SO, THE BEAST WILL GIVE.
...AH... AH...
...AH'M JUST A KID...
FTCHH
THE LAST THING HE REMEMBERS FROM THE TIME BEFORE IS ICE.
THE NUMBING COLD ONLY HELL COULD BIRTH.
HE HAD CLOSED HIS EYES AND THOUGHT HIMSELF DEAD, HIS DUTY FULFILLED.
HOW CHILDISH TO THINK HE COULD BE LIKE EVERYONE ELSE.
WHEN HE AWOKE, IT WAS TO FLAMES. HELL, HE THOUGHT, HAD COME.
BUT IT WAS NOT SO SIMPLE.
FIVE HUNDRED YEARS HAD PASSED HIM BY. A BLINK, AND CENTURIES WERE GONE.
NOW, THE WORLD THAT WAS HAS FADED TO LEGEND.
A LAND OF RICHES REDUCED TO RUINS, ONLY SCRAPS LEFT TO TELL A TALE NO ONE WOULD HEAR.
GENERATIONS LOST.
FOR TWO HUNDRED YEARS, THE BEAST WALKED THIS NEW WORLD.
IT KNEW HIS NAME AND IT TREMBLED.
BUT, NOW, HIS TIME HAS BEEN STOLEN. AND THOSE THAT HAVE WRONGED HIM WILL PAY THE PRICE.

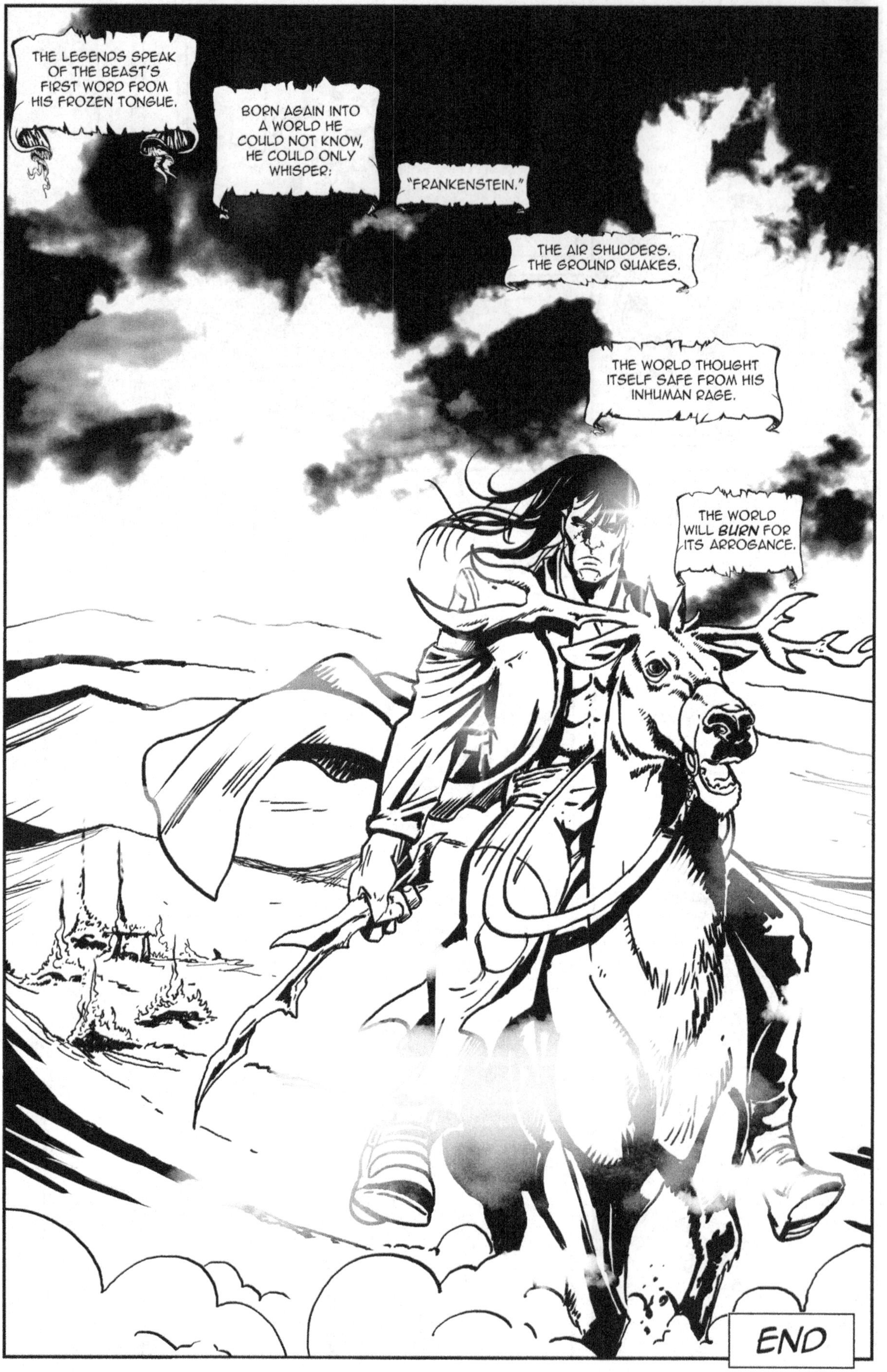
THE LEGENDS SPEAK OF THE BEAST'S FIRST WORD FROM HIS FROZEN TONGUE.
BORN AGAIN INTO A WORLD HE COULD NOT KNOW, HE COULD ONLY WHISPER:
"FRANKENSTEIN."
THE AIR SHUDDERS. THE GROUND QUAKES.
THE WORLD THOUGHT ITSELF SAFE FROM HIS INHUMAN RAGE.
THE WORLD WILL *BURN* FOR ITS ARROGANCE.
END

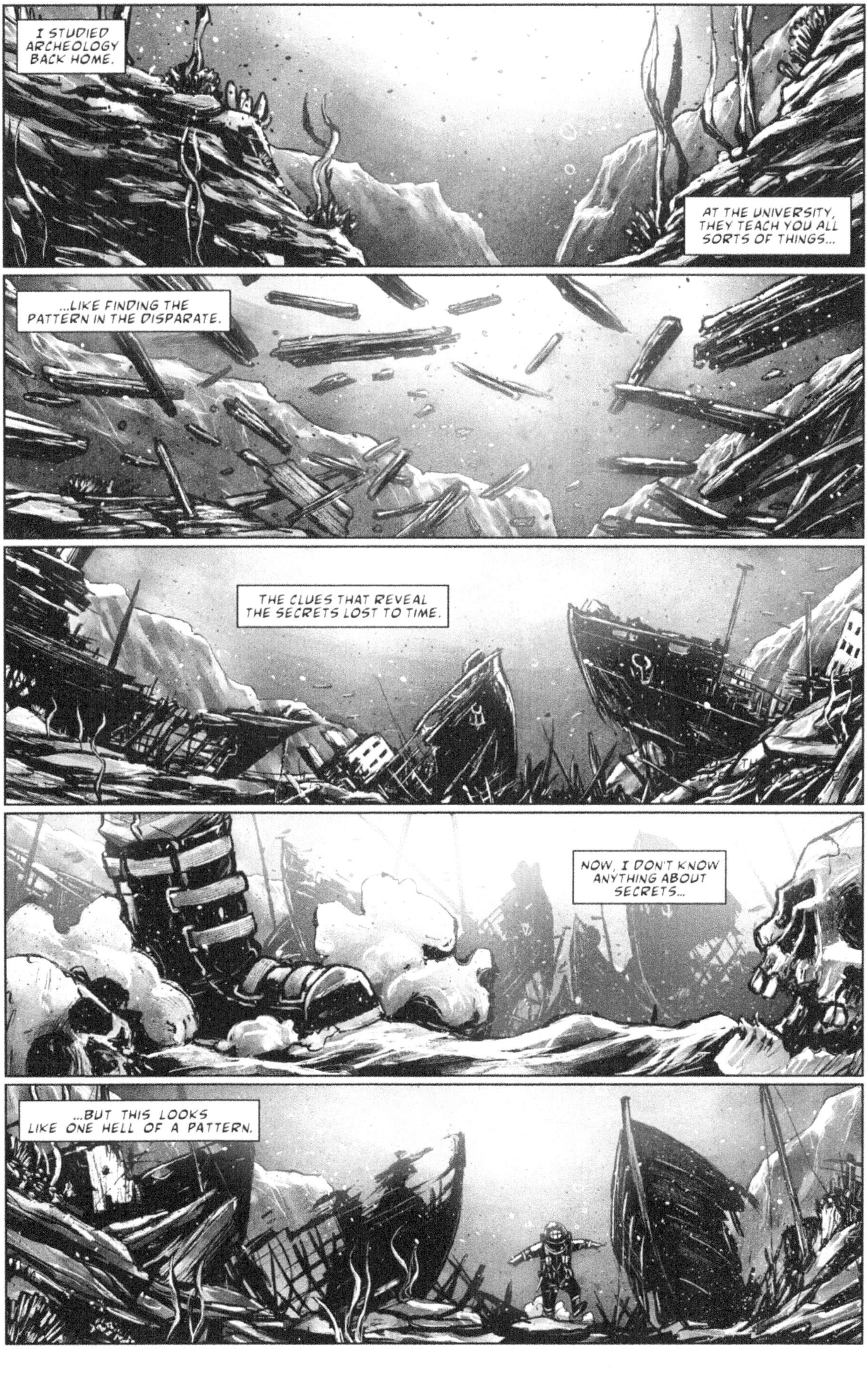
I STUDIED ARCHEOLOGY BACK HOME.
AT THE UNIVERSITY, THEY TEACH YOU ALL SORTS OF THINGS...
...LIKE FINDING THE PATTERN IN THE DISPARATE.
THE CLUES THAT REVEAL THE SECRETS LOST TO TIME.
NOW, I DON'T KNOW ANYTHING ABOUT SECRETS...
...BUT THIS LOOKS LIKE ONE HELL OF A PATTERN.

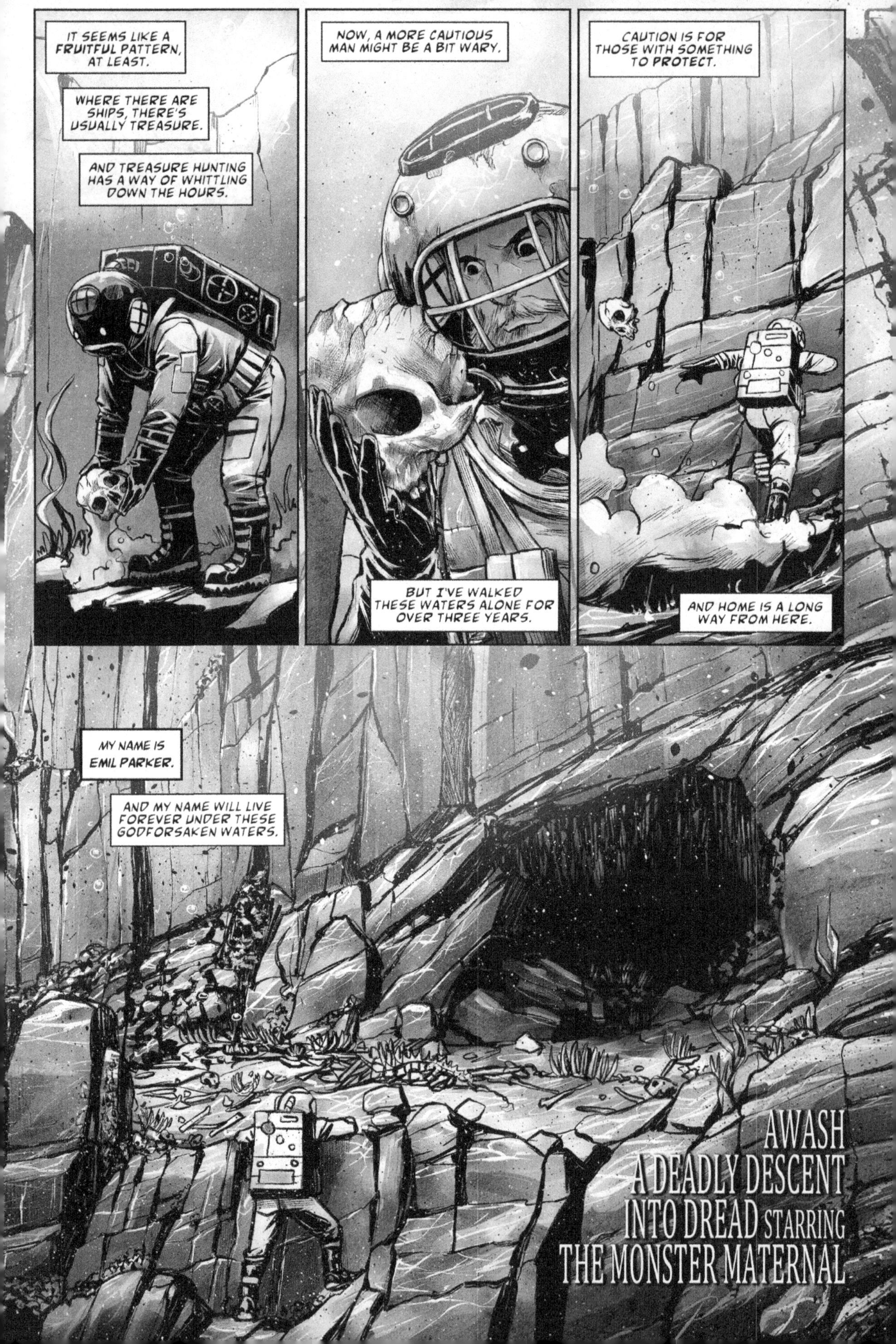
IT SEEMS LIKE A FRUITFUL PATTERN, AT LEAST.
WHERE THERE ARE SHIPS, THERE'S USUALLY TREASURE.
AND TREASURE HUNTING HAS A WAY OF WHITTLING DOWN THE HOURS.
NOW, A MORE CAUTIOUS MAN MIGHT BE A BIT WARY.
BUT I'VE WALKED THESE WATERS ALONE FOR OVER THREE YEARS.
CAUTION IS FOR THOSE WITH SOMETHING TO PROTECT.
AND HOME IS A LONG WAY FROM HERE.
MY NAME IS EMIL PARKER.
AND MY NAME WILL LIVE FOREVER UNDER THESE GODFORSAKEN WATERS.
AWASH
A DEADLY DESCENT
INTO DREAD STARRING
THE MONSTER MATERNAL

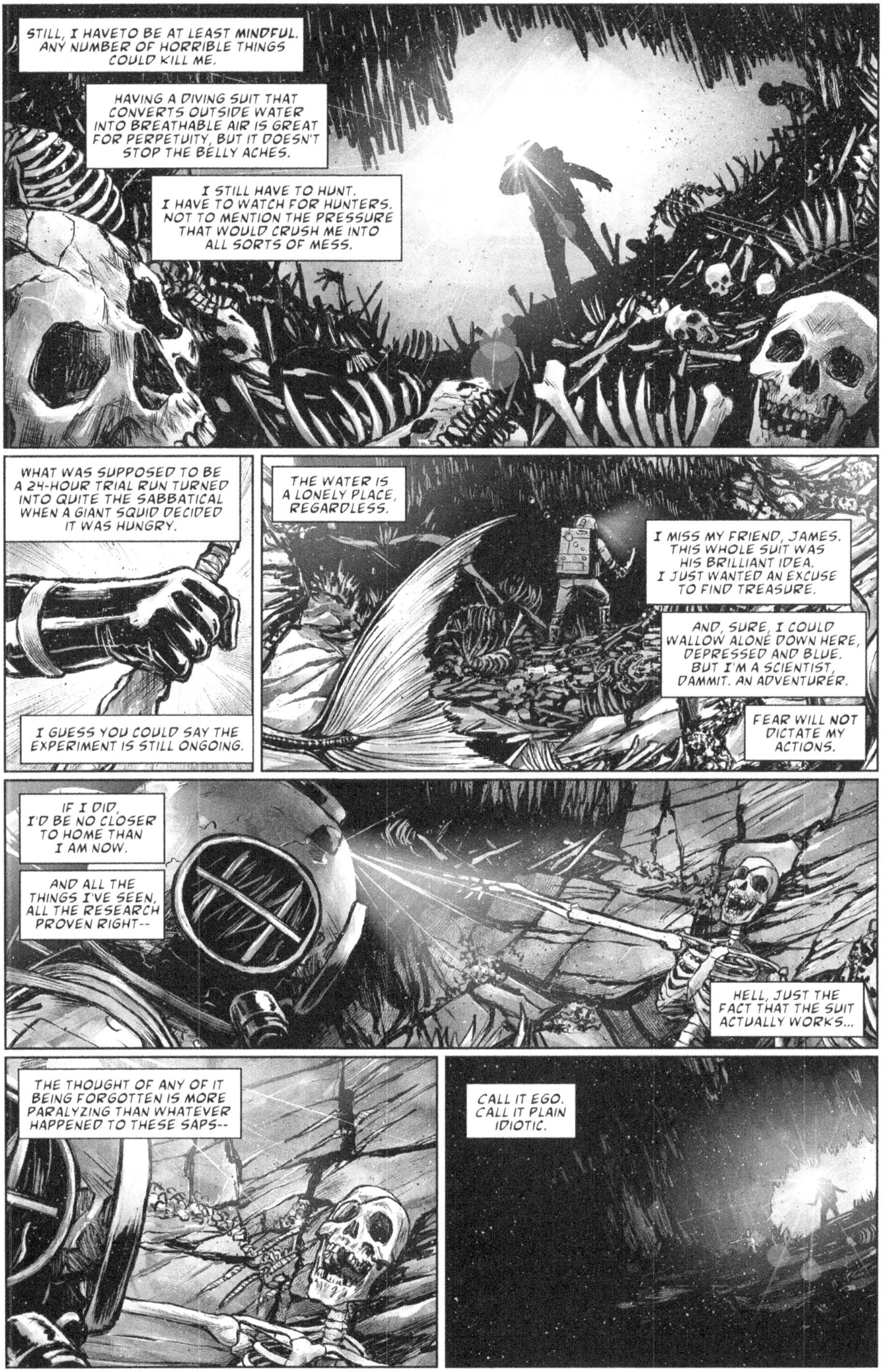
STILL, I HAVETO BE AT LEAST MINDFUL. ANY NUMBER OF HORRIBLE THINGS COULD KILL ME.
HAVING A DIVING SUIT THAT CONVERTS OUTSIDE WATER INTO BREATHABLE AIR IS GREAT FOR PERPETUITY, BUT IT DOESN'T STOP THE BELLY ACHES.
I STILL HAVE TO HUNT. I HAVE TO WATCH FOR HUNTERS. NOT TO MENTION THE PRESSURE THAT WOULD CRUSH ME INTO ALL SORTS OF MESS.
WHAT WAS SUPPOSED TO BE A 24-HOUR TRIAL RUN TURNED INTO QUITE THE SABBATICAL WHEN A GIANT SQUID DECIDED IT WAS HUNGRY.
I GUESS YOU COULD SAY THE EXPERIMENT IS STILL ONGOING.
THE WATER IS A LONELY PLACE, REGARDLESS.
I MISS MY FRIEND, JAMES. THIS WHOLE SUIT WAS HIS BRILLIANT IDEA. I JUST WANTED AN EXCUSE TO FIND TREASURE.
AND, SURE, I COULD WALLOW ALONE DOWN HERE, DEPRESSED AND BLUE. BUT I'M A SCIENTIST, DAMMIT. AN ADVENTURER.
FEAR WILL NOT DICTATE MY ACTIONS.
IF I DID, I'D BE NO CLOSER TO HOME THAN I AM NOW.
AND ALL THE THINGS I'VE SEEN, ALL THE RESEARCH PROVEN RIGHT--
HELL, JUST THE FACT THAT THE SUIT ACTUALLY WORKS...
THE THOUGHT OF ANY OF IT BEING FORGOTTEN IS MORE PARALYZING THAN WHATEVER HAPPENED TO THESE SAPS--
CALL IT EGO. CALL IT PLAIN IDIOTIC.

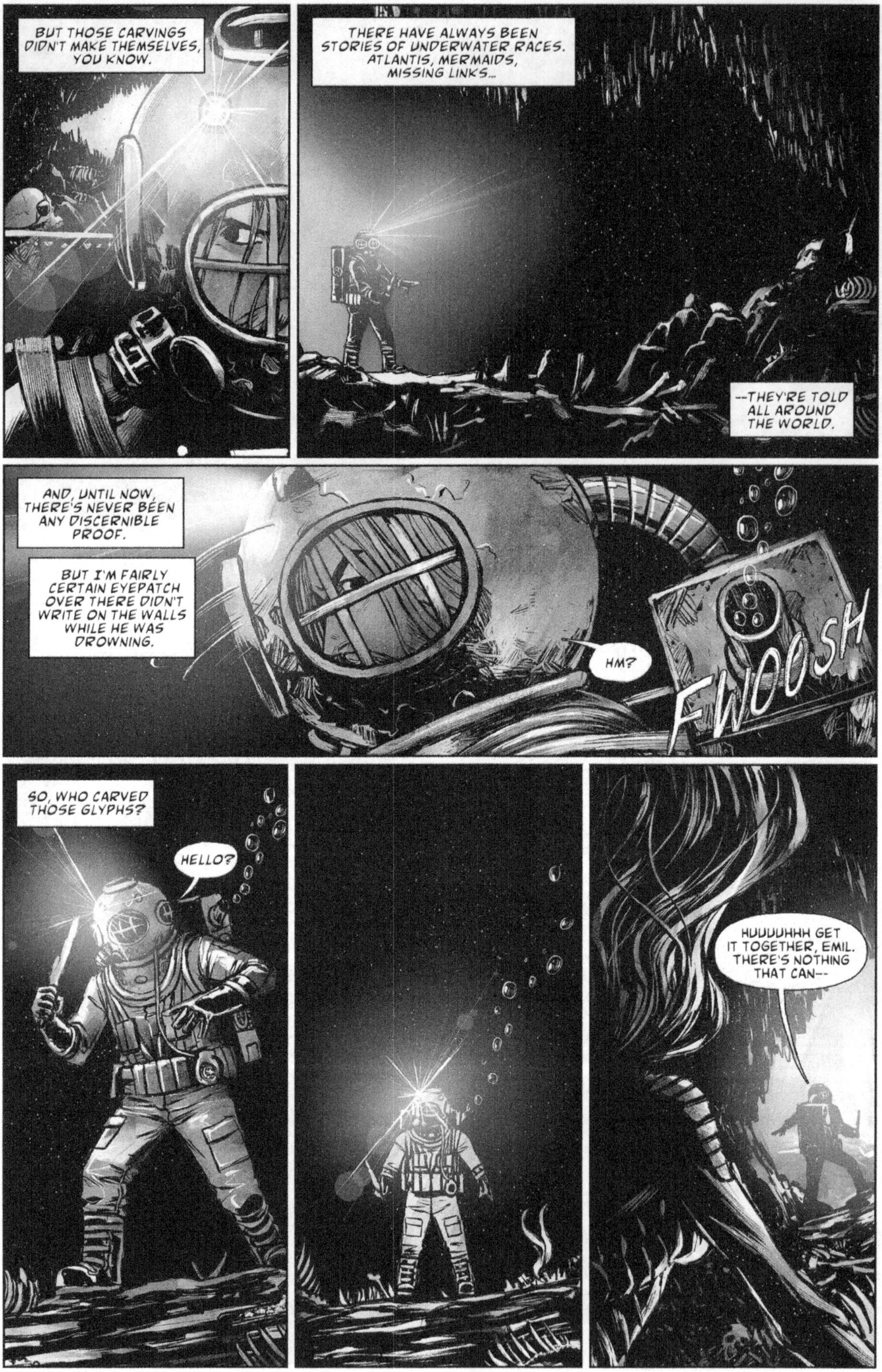
BUT THOSE CARVINGS DIDN'T MAKE THEMSELVES, YOU KNOW.
THERE HAVE ALWAYS BEEN STORIES OF UNDERWATER RACES. ATLANTIS, MERMAIDS, MISSING LINKS...
--THEY'RE TOLD ALL AROUND THE WORLD.
AND, UNTIL NOW, THERE'S NEVER BEEN ANY DISCERNIBLE PROOF.
BUT I'M FAIRLY CERTAIN EYEPATCH OVER THERE DIDN'T WRITE ON THE WALLS WHILE HE WAS DROWNING.
HM?
FWOOSH
SO, WHO CARVED THOSE GLYPHS?
HELLO?
HUUUUHHH GET IT TOGETHER, EMIL. THERE'S NOTHING THAT CAN--

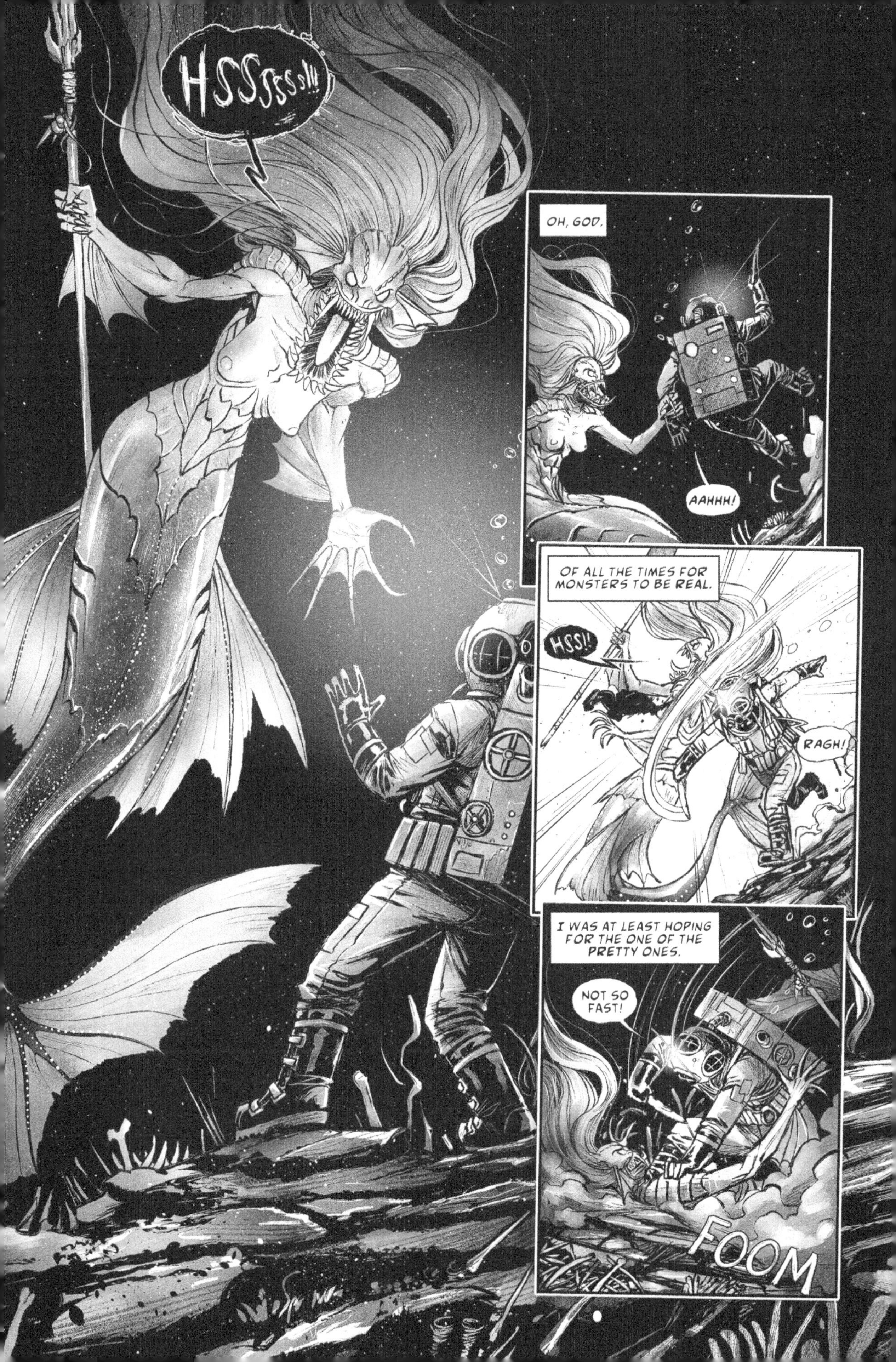
HSSsssss!!!
OH, GOD.
AAHHH!
OF ALL THE TIMES FOR MONSTERS TO BE REAL.
HSS!
RAGH!
I WAS AT LEAST HOPING FOR THE ONE OF THE PRETTY ONES.
NOT SO FAST!
FOOM

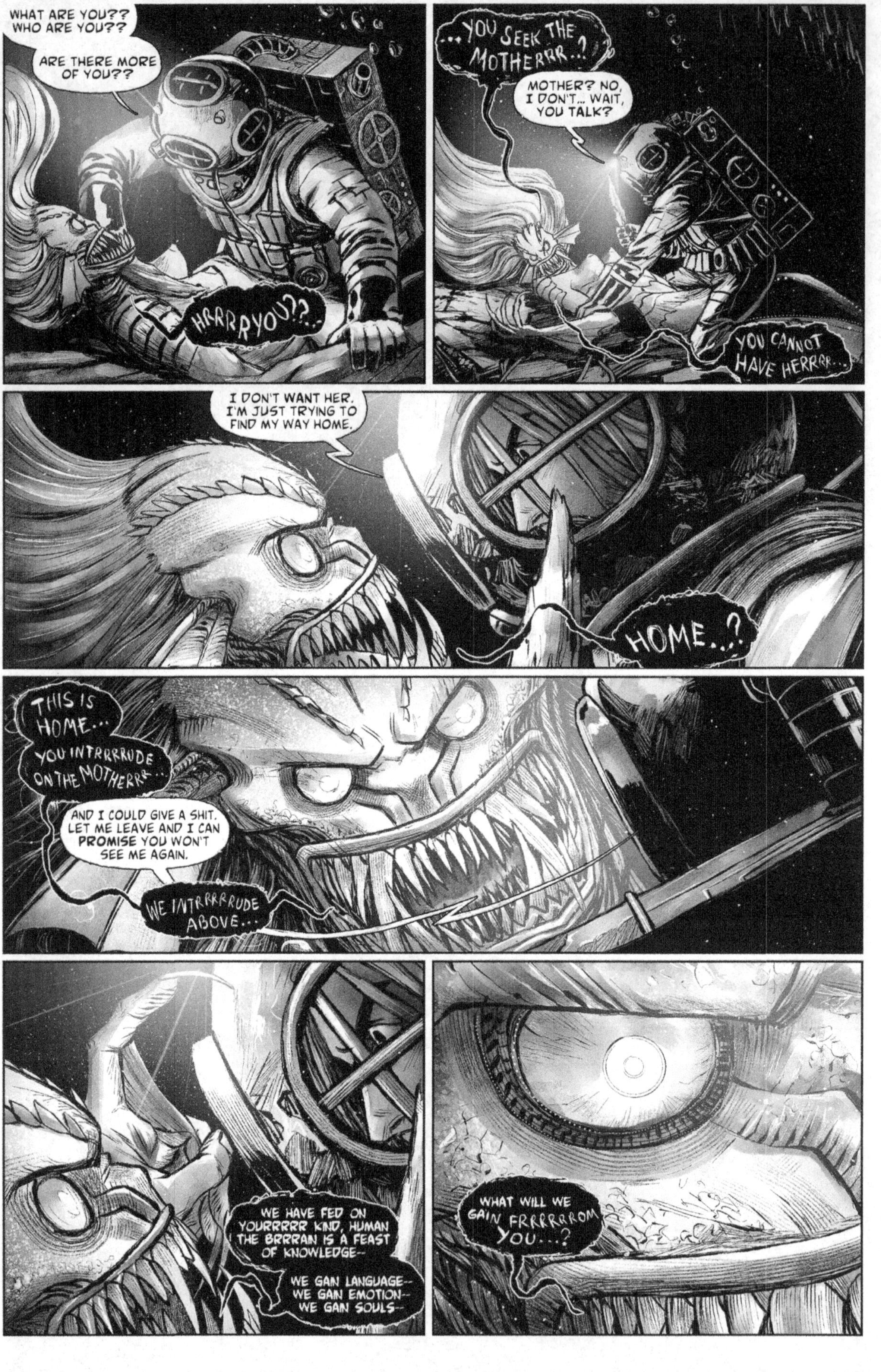
WHAT ARE YOU?? WHO ARE YOU??
ARE THERE MORE OF YOU??
HRRRRYOU??...
...YOU SEEK THE MOTHERRR..?
MOTHER? NO, I DON'T... WAIT, YOU TALK?
YOU CANNOT HAVE HERRRR...
I DON'T WANT HER. I'M JUST TRYING TO FIND MY WAY HOME.
HOME..?
THIS IS HOME...
YOU INTRRRRUDE ON THE MOTHERRR...
AND I COULD GIVE A SHIT. LET ME LEAVE AND I CAN PROMISE YOU WON'T SEE ME AGAIN.
WE INTRRRRRUDE ABOVE...
WE HAVE FED ON YOURRRRR KIND, HUMAN THE BRRRAN IS A FEAST OF KNOWLEDGE--
WE GAN LANGUAGE-- WE GAN EMOTION-- WE GAN SOULS--
WHAT WILL WE GAIN FRRRRRROM YOU...?

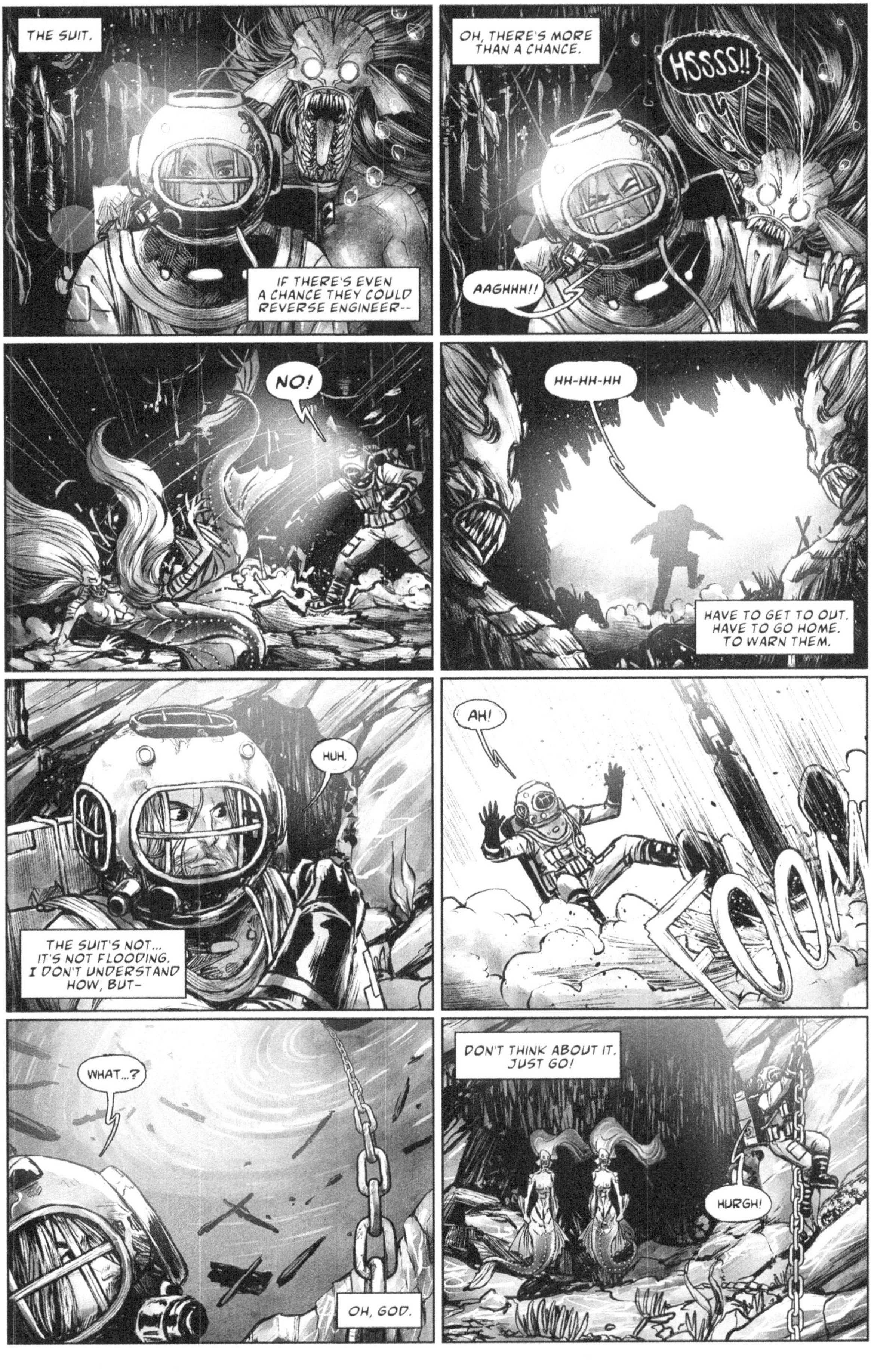
THE SUIT.
IF THERE'S EVEN A CHANCE THEY COULD REVERSE ENGINEER--
OH, THERE'S MORE THAN A CHANCE.
HSSSS!!
AAGHHH!!
NO!
HH-HH-HH
HAVE TO GET TO OUT. HAVE TO GO HOME. TO WARN THEM.
HUH.
THE SUIT'S NOT... IT'S NOT FLOODING. I DON'T UNDERSTAND HOW, BUT-
AH!
WHAT...?
OH, GOD.
DON'T THINK ABOUT IT. JUST GO!
HURGH!

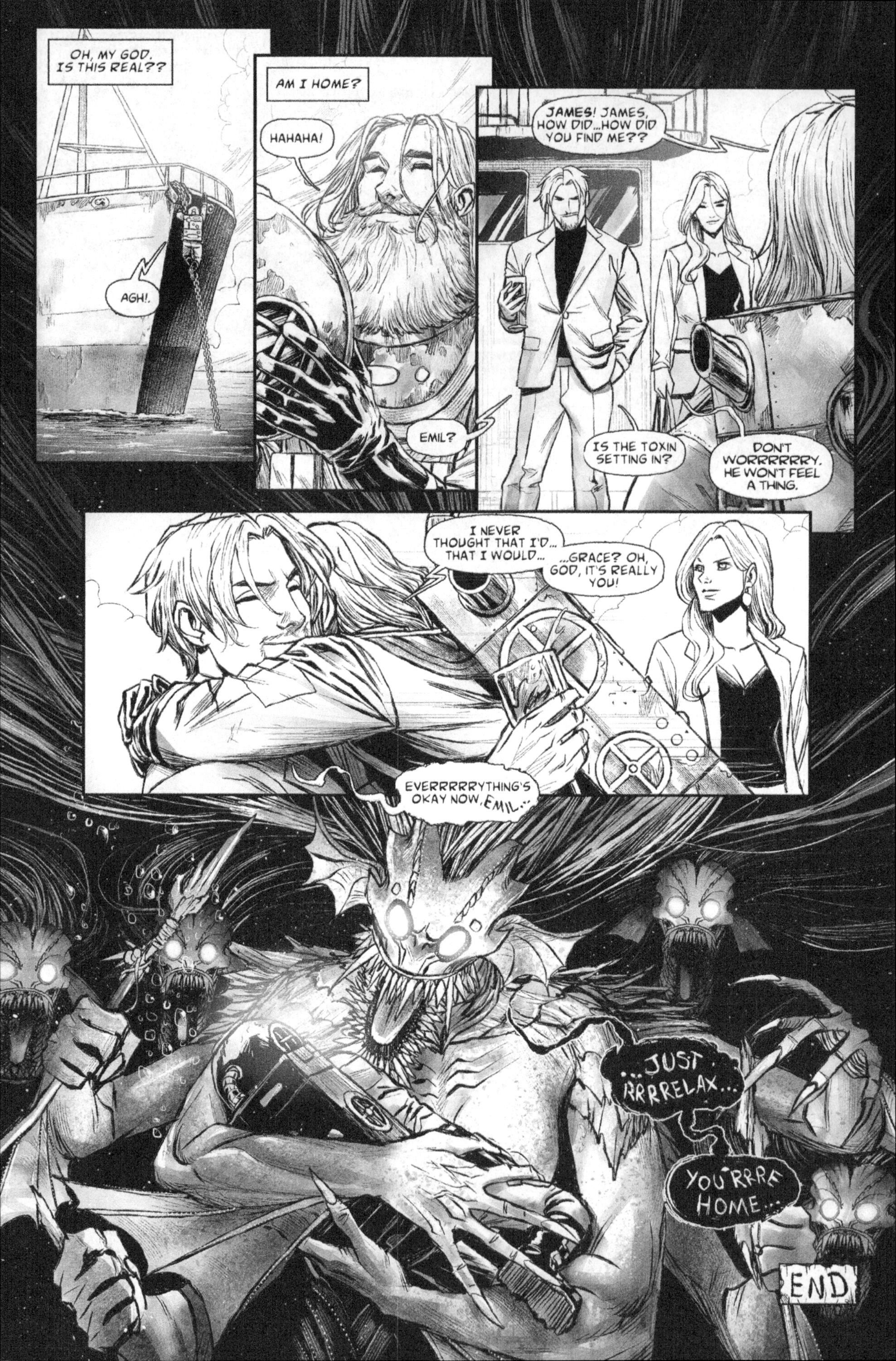
OH, MY GOD. IS THIS REAL??
AGH!.
AM I HOME?
HAHAHA!
EMIL?
JAMES! JAMES, HOW DID...HOW DID YOU FIND ME??
IS THE TOXIN SETTING IN?
DON'T WORRRRRRY. HE WON'T FEEL A THING.
I NEVER THOUGHT THAT I'D... THAT I WOULD...
...GRACE? OH, GOD, IT'S REALLY YOU!
EVERRRRRYTHING'S OKAY NOW, EMIL...
...JUST RRRRELAX...
YOU'RRRE HOME...
END

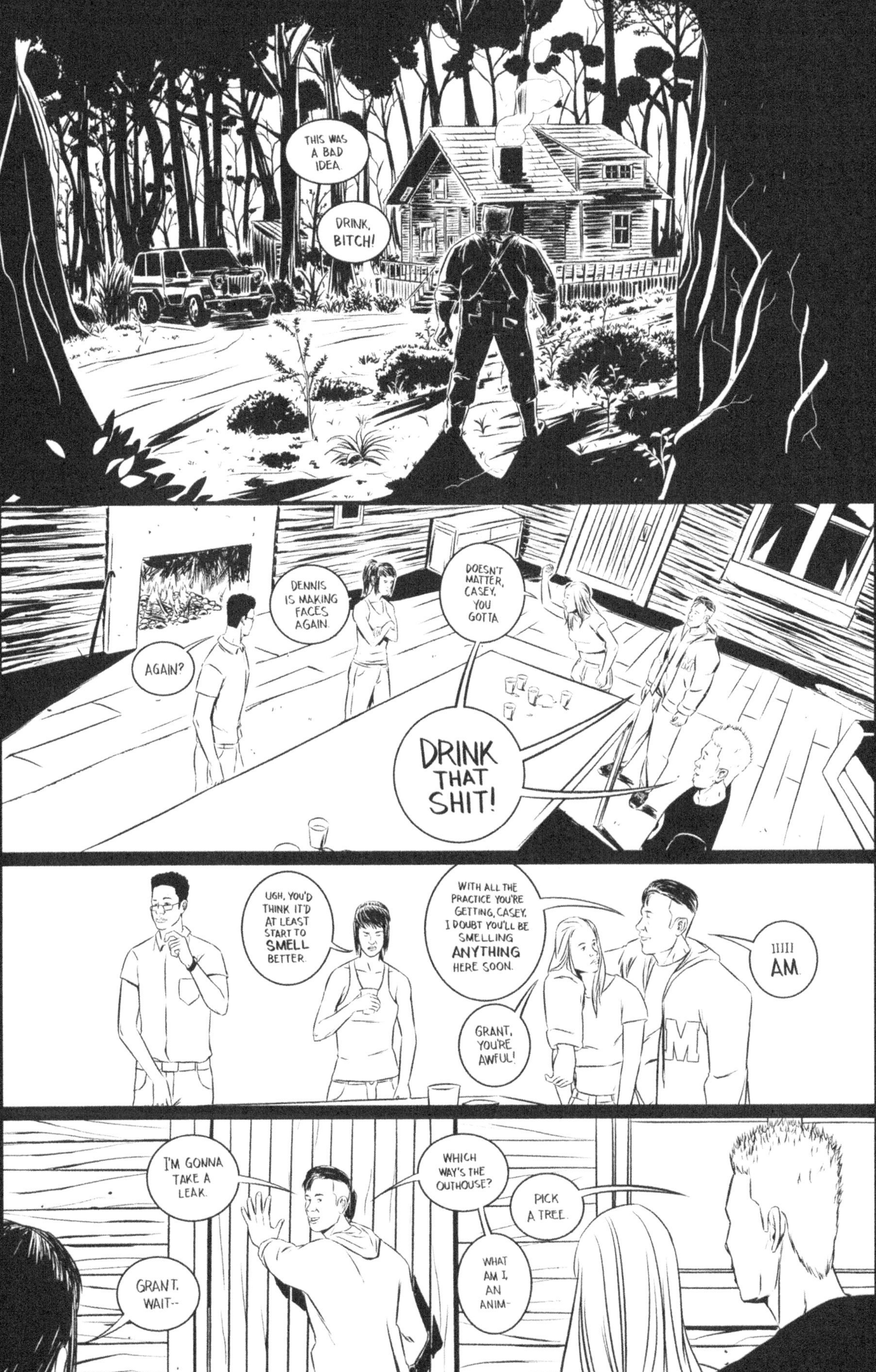
THIS WAS A BAD IDEA.
DRINK, BITCH!
DENNIS IS MAKING FACES AGAIN.
AGAIN?
DOESN'T MATTER, CASEY. YOU GOTTA
DRINK THAT SHIT!
UGH, YOU'D THINK IT'D AT LEAST START TO SMELL BETTER.
WITH ALL THE PRACTICE YOU'RE GETTING, CASEY, I DOUBT YOU'LL BE SMELLING ANYTHING HERE SOON.
GRANT, YOU'RE AWFUL!
IIIII AM.
I'M GONNA TAKE A LEAK.
WHICH WAY'S THE OUTHOUSE?
PICK A TREE.
WHAT AM I, AN ANIM-
GRANT. WAIT--

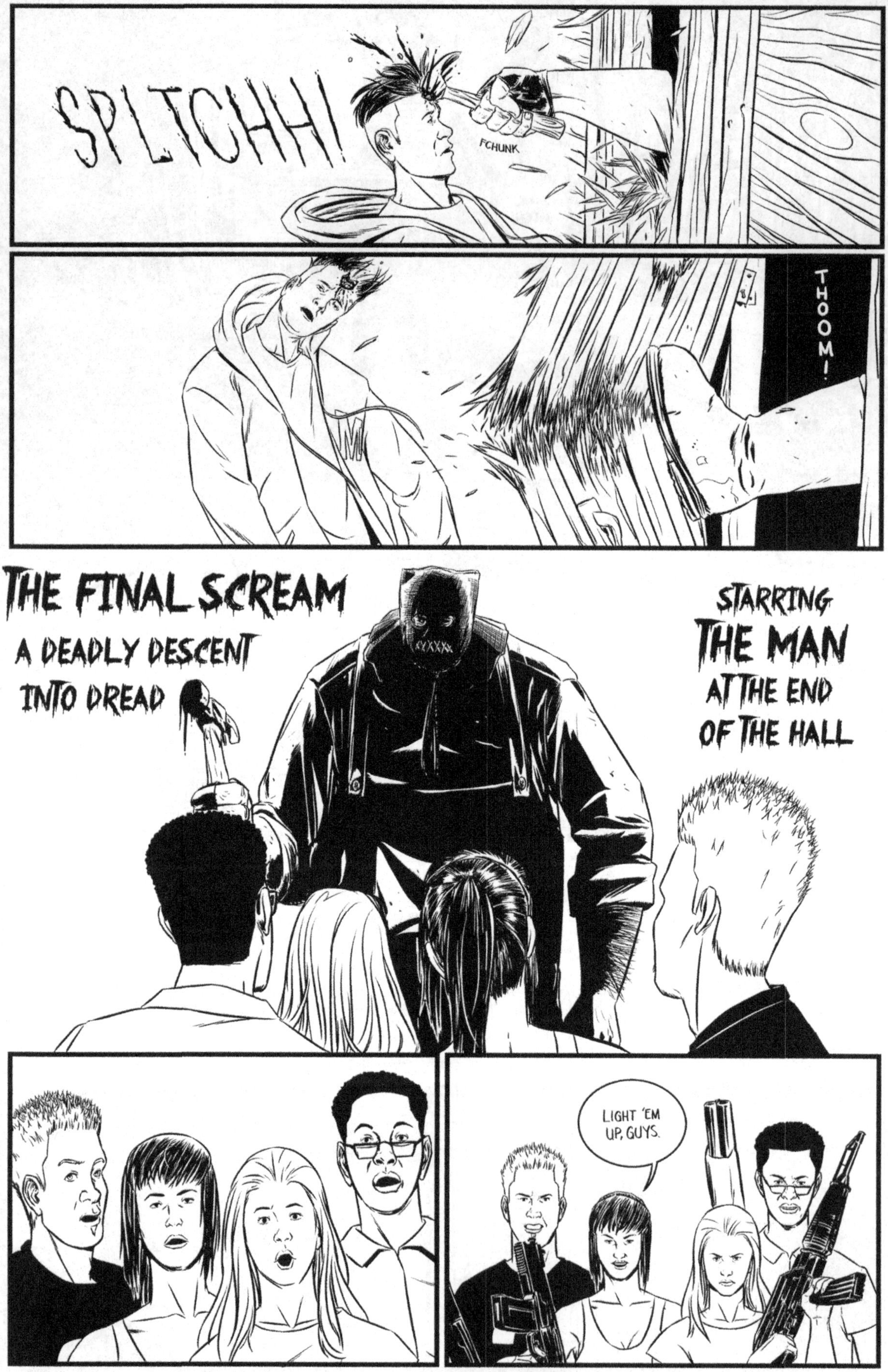
SPLTCHH!
FCHUNK
THOOM!
THE FINAL SCREAM
A DEADLY DESCENT INTO DREAD
STARRING THE MAN AT THE END OF THE HALL
LIGHT 'EM UP, GUYS.

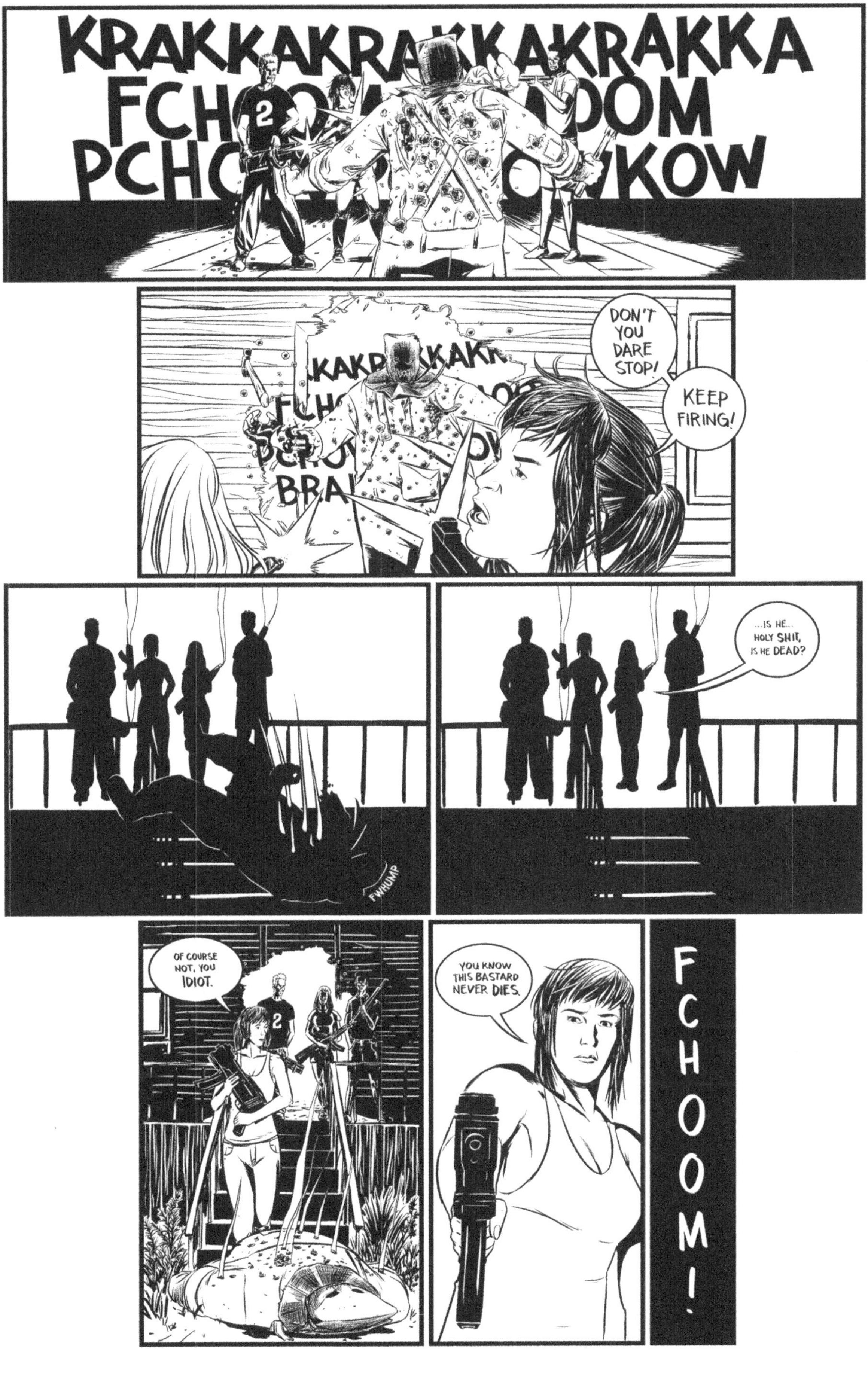
DON'T YOU DARE STOP!
KEEP FIRING!
FWHUMP
...IS HE... HOLY SHIT, IS HE DEAD?
OF COURSE NOT, YOU IDIOT.
YOU KNOW THIS BASTARD NEVER DIES.
FCHOOM!

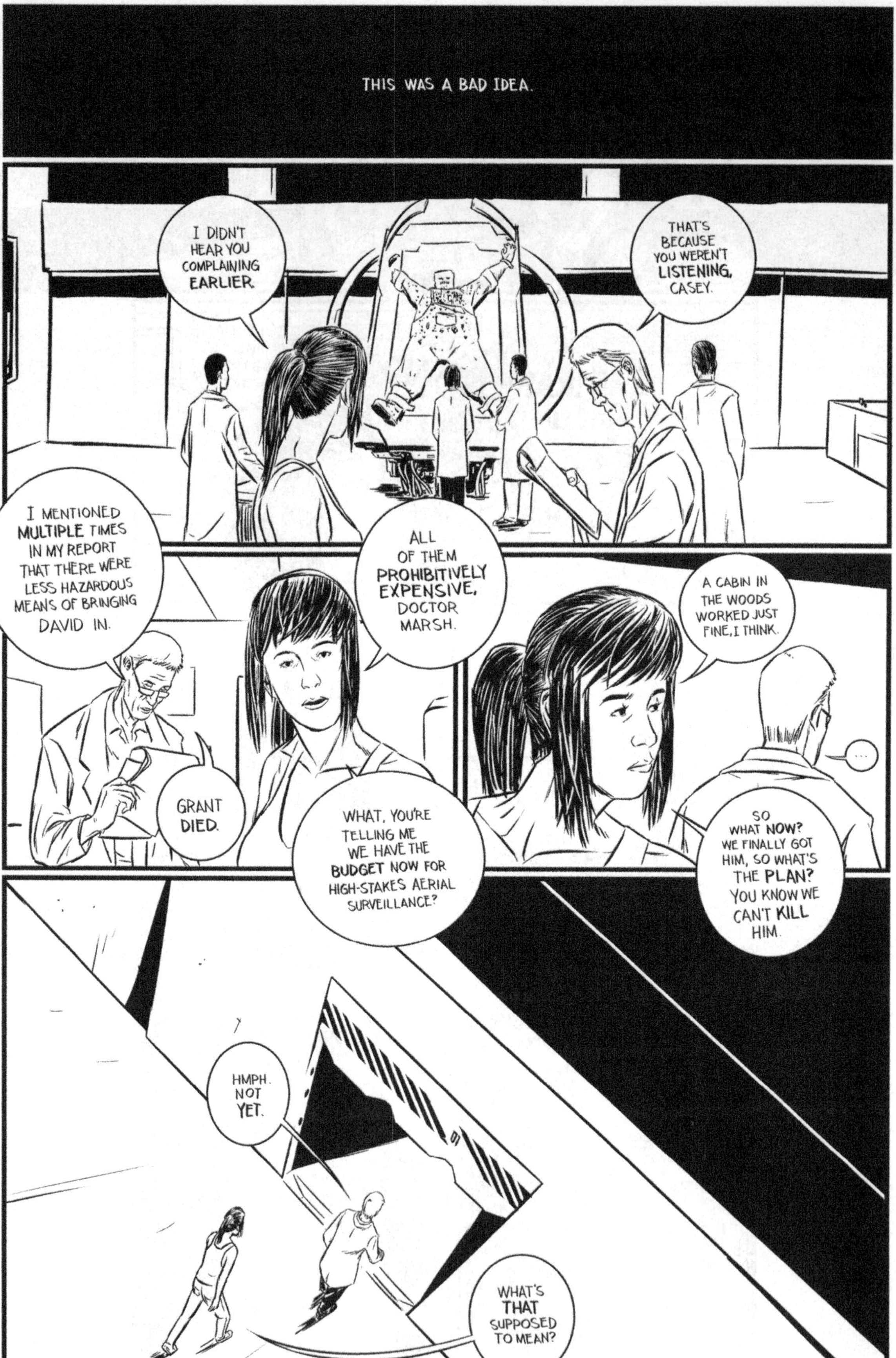
THIS WAS A BAD IDEA.
I DIDN'T HEAR YOU COMPLAINING EARLIER.
THAT'S BECAUSE YOU WEREN'T LISTENING, CASEY.
I MENTIONED MULTIPLE TIMES IN MY REPORT THAT THERE WERE LESS HAZARDOUS MEANS OF BRINGING DAVID IN.
ALL OF THEM PROHIBITIVELY EXPENSIVE, DOCTOR MARSH.
GRANT DIED.
WHAT, YOU'RE TELLING ME WE HAVE THE BUDGET NOW FOR HIGH-STAKES AERIAL SURVEILLANCE?
A CABIN IN THE WOODS WORKED JUST FINE, I THINK.
...
SO WHAT NOW? WE FINALLY GOT HIM, SO WHAT'S THE PLAN? YOU KNOW WE CAN'T KILL HIM.
HMPH. NOT YET.
WHAT'S THAT SUPPOSED TO MEAN?

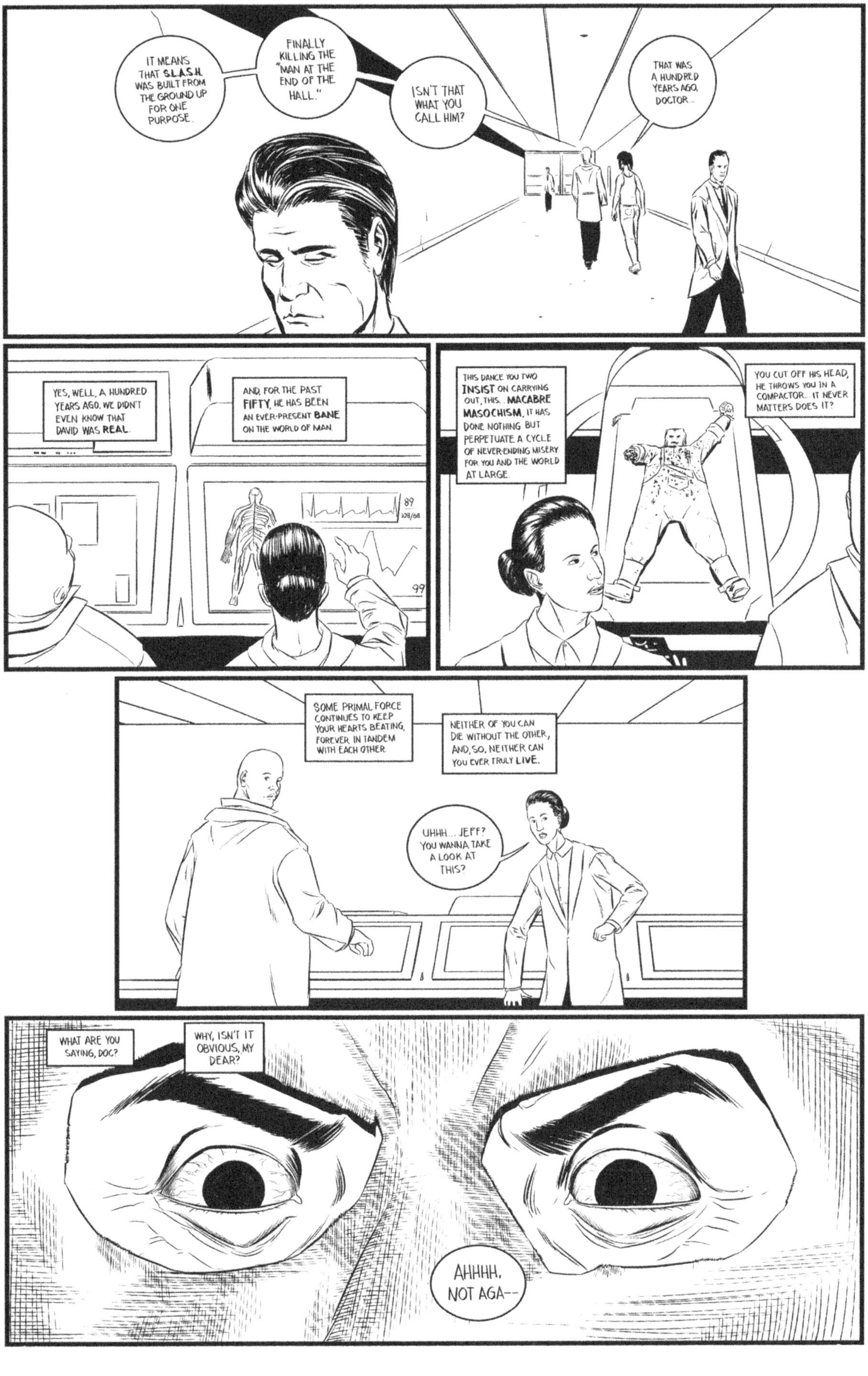
IT MEANS THAT S.L.A.S.H. WAS BUILT FROM THE GROUND UP FOR ONE PURPOSE.
FINALLY KILLING THE "MAN AT THE END OF THE HALL."
ISN'T THAT WHAT YOU CALL HIM?
THAT WAS A HUNDRED YEARS AGO, DOCTOR...
YES, WELL, A HUNDRED YEARS AGO, WE DIDN'T EVEN KNOW THAT DAVID WAS REAL.
AND, FOR THE PAST FIFTY, HE HAS BEEN AN EVER-PRESENT BANE ON THE WORLD OF MAN.
89
108/68
99
THIS DANCE YOU TWO INSIST ON CARRYING OUT, THIS...MACABRE MASOCHISM, IT HAS DONE NOTHING BUT PERPETUATE A CYCLE OF NEVER-ENDING MISERY FOR YOU AND THE WORLD AT LARGE.
YOU CUT OFF HIS HEAD, HE THROWS YOU IN A COMPACTOR... IT NEVER MATTERS DOES IT?
SOME PRIMAL FORCE CONTINUES TO KEEP YOUR HEARTS BEATING, FOREVER IN TANDEM WITH EACH OTHER.
NEITHER OF YOU CAN DIE WITHOUT THE OTHER, AND, SO, NEITHER CAN YOU EVER TRULY LIVE.
UHHH... JEFF? YOU WANNA TAKE A LOOK AT THIS?
WHAT ARE YOU SAYING, DOC?
WHY, ISN'T IT OBVIOUS, MY DEAR?
AHHHH, NOT AGA--

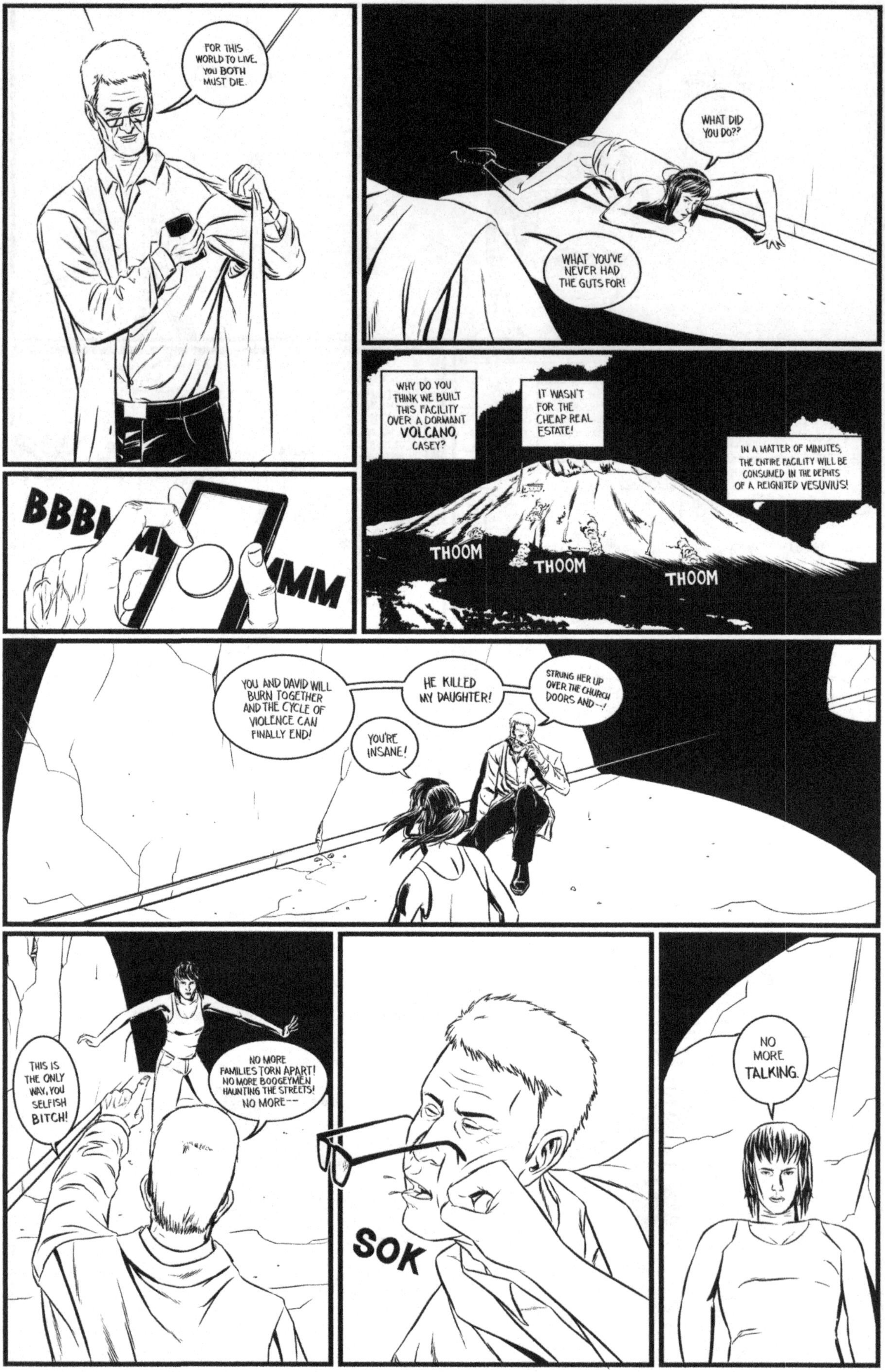
FOR THIS WORLD TO LIVE, YOU BOTH MUST DIE.
WHAT DID YOU DO??
WHAT YOU'VE NEVER HAD THE GUTS FOR!
BBBMMMMMM
WHY DO YOU THINK WE BUILT THIS FACILITY OVER A DORMANT VOLCANO, CASEY?
IT WASN'T FOR THE CHEAP REAL ESTATE!
IN A MATTER OF MINUTES, THE ENTIRE FACILITY WILL BE CONSUMED IN THE DEPTHS OF A REIGNITED VESUVIUS!
THOOM
THOOM
THOOM
YOU AND DAVID WILL BURN TOGETHER AND THE CYCLE OF VIOLENCE CAN FINALLY END!
HE KILLED MY DAUGHTER!
STRUNG HER UP OVER THE CHURCH DOORS AND--!
YOU'RE INSANE!
THIS IS THE ONLY WAY, YOU SELFISH BITCH!
NO MORE FAMILIES TORN APART! NO MORE BOOGEYMEN HAUNTING THE STREETS! NO MORE--
SOK
NO MORE TALKING.

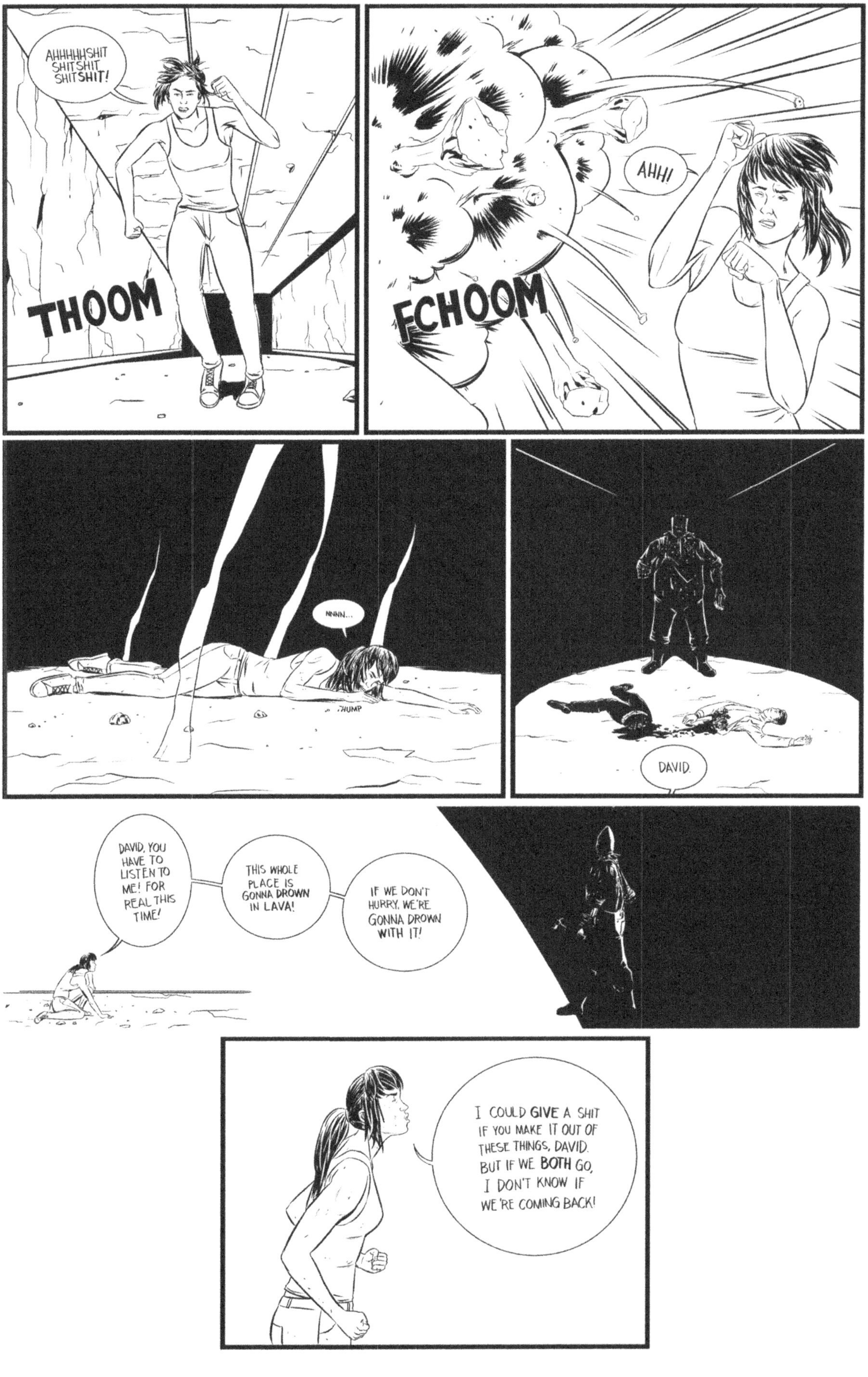
AHHHHHSHIT SHITSHIT SHITSHIT!
THOOM
FCHOOM
AHH!
NNNN...
THUMP
DAVID.
DAVID, YOU HAVE TO LISTEN TO ME! FOR REAL THIS TIME!
THIS WHOLE PLACE IS GONNA DROWN IN LAVA!
IF WE DON'T HURRY, WE'RE GONNA DROWN WITH IT!
I COULD GIVE A SHIT IF YOU MAKE IT OUT OF THESE THINGS, DAVID. BUT IF WE BOTH GO, I DON'T KNOW IF WE'RE COMING BACK!

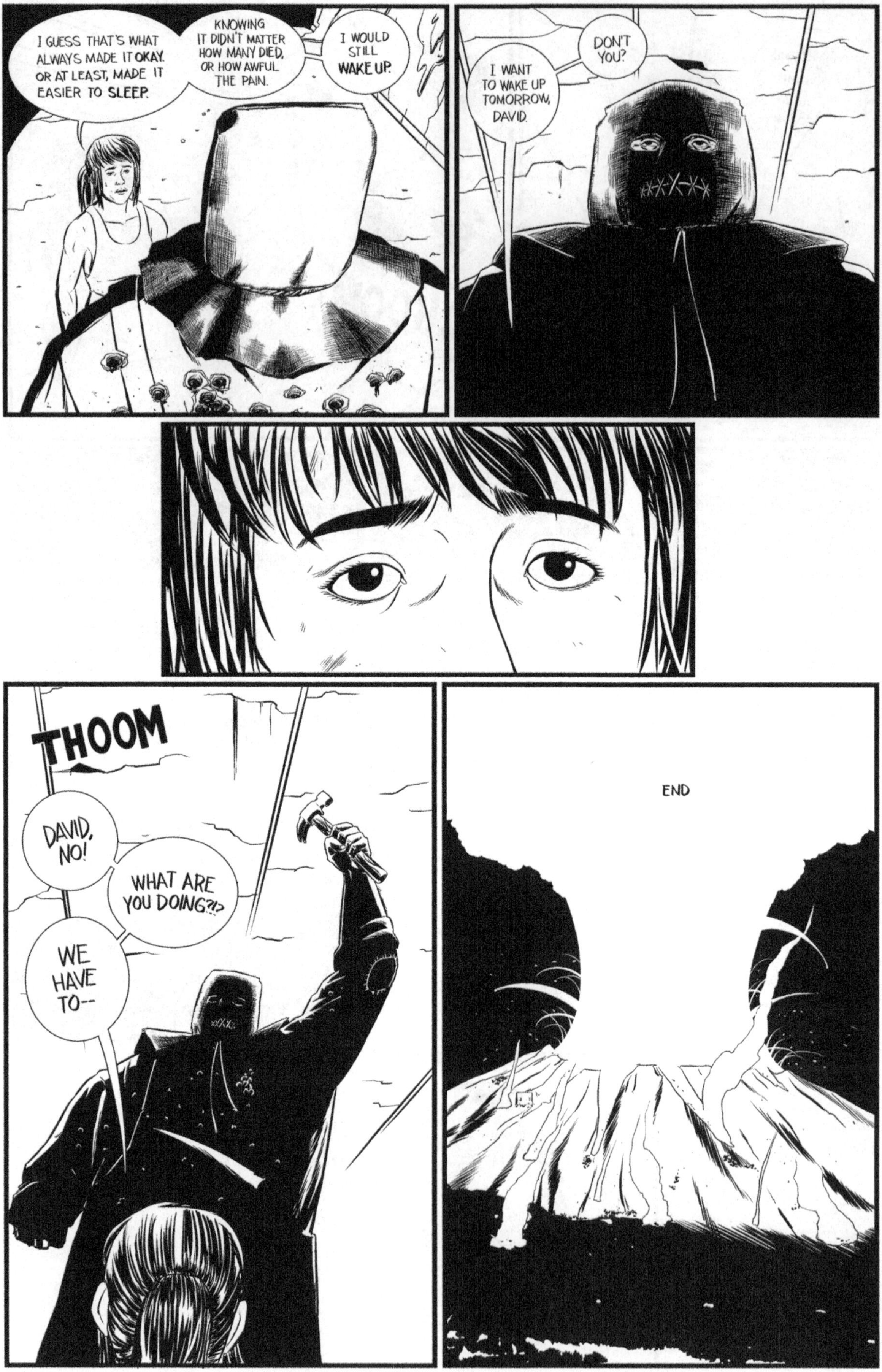
I GUESS THAT'S WHAT ALWAYS MADE IT OKAY. OR AT LEAST, MADE IT EASIER TO SLEEP.
KNOWING IT DIDN'T MATTER HOW MANY DIED, OR HOW AWFUL THE PAIN.
I WOULD STILL WAKE UP.
I WANT TO WAKE UP TOMORROW, DAVID.
DON'T YOU?
THOOM
DAVID, NO!
WHAT ARE YOU DOING?!?
WE HAVE TO--
END

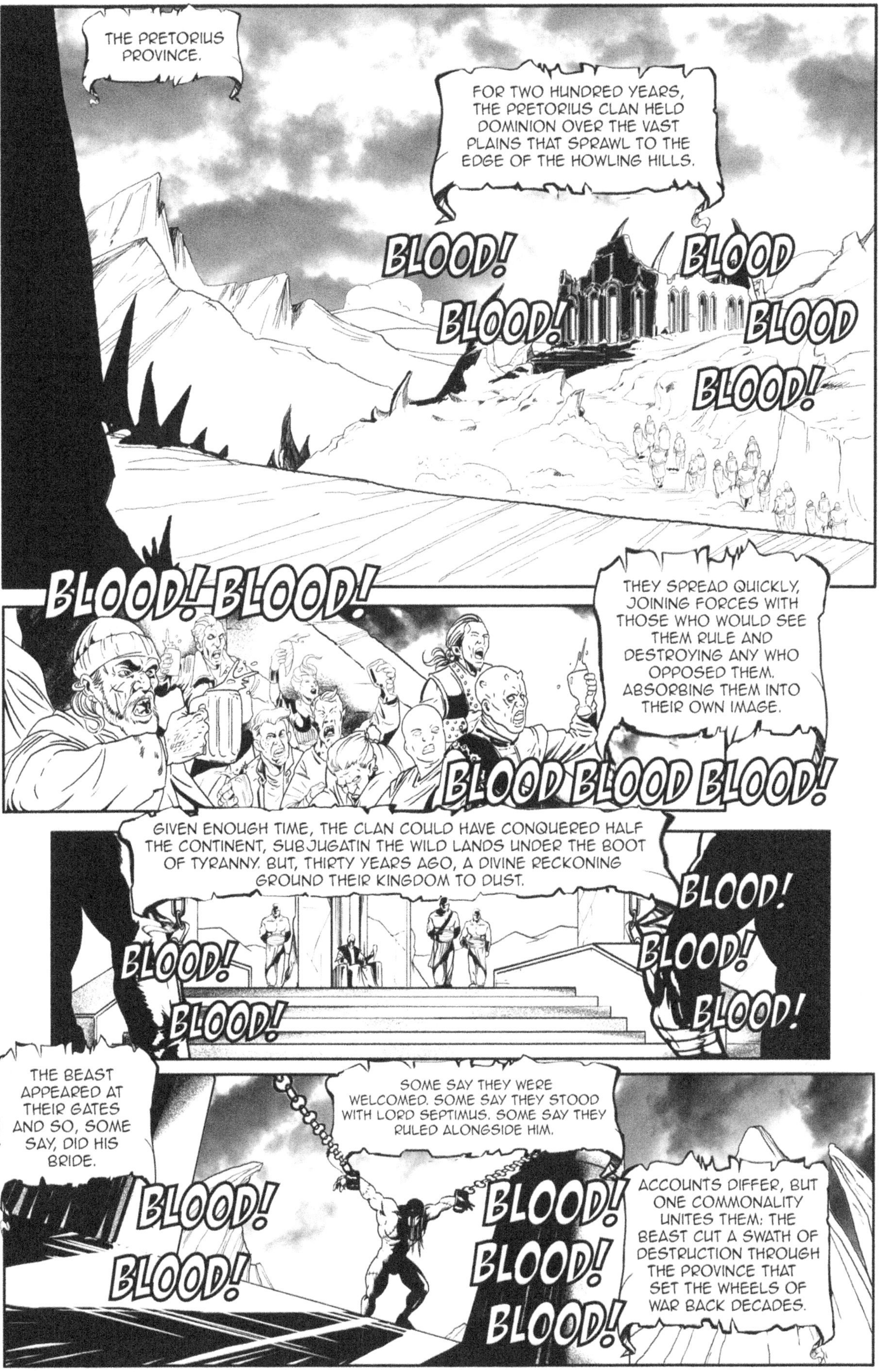
THE PRETORIUS PROVINCE.
FOR TWO HUNDRED YEARS, THE PRETORIUS CLAN HELD DOMINION OVER THE VAST PLAINS THAT SPRAWL TO THE EDGE OF THE HOWLING HILLS.
BLOOD! BLOOD!
BLOOD BLOOD BLOOD!
BLOOD! BLOOD!
THEY SPREAD QUICKLY, JOINING FORCES WITH THOSE WHO WOULD SEE THEM RULE AND DESTROYING ANY WHO OPPOSED THEM. ABSORBING THEM INTO THEIR OWN IMAGE.
BLOOD BLOOD BLOOD!
GIVEN ENOUGH TIME, THE CLAN COULD HAVE CONQUERED HALF THE CONTINENT, SUBJUGATIN THE WILD LANDS UNDER THE BOOT OF TYRANNY. BUT, THIRTY YEARS AGO, A DIVINE RECKONING GROUND THEIR KINGDOM TO DUST.
BLOOD! BLOOD!
BLOOD! BLOOD! BLOOD!
THE BEAST APPEARED AT THEIR GATES AND SO, SOME SAY, DID HIS BRIDE.
SOME SAY THEY WERE WELCOMED. SOME SAY THEY STOOD WITH LORD SEPTIMUS. SOME SAY THEY RULED ALONGSIDE HIM.
BLOOD! BLOOD!
BLOOD! BLOOD! BLOOD!
ACCOUNTS DIFFER, BUT ONE COMMONALITY UNITES THEM: THE BEAST CUT A SWATH OF DESTRUCTION THROUGH THE PROVINCE THAT SET THE WHEELS OF WAR BACK DECADES.

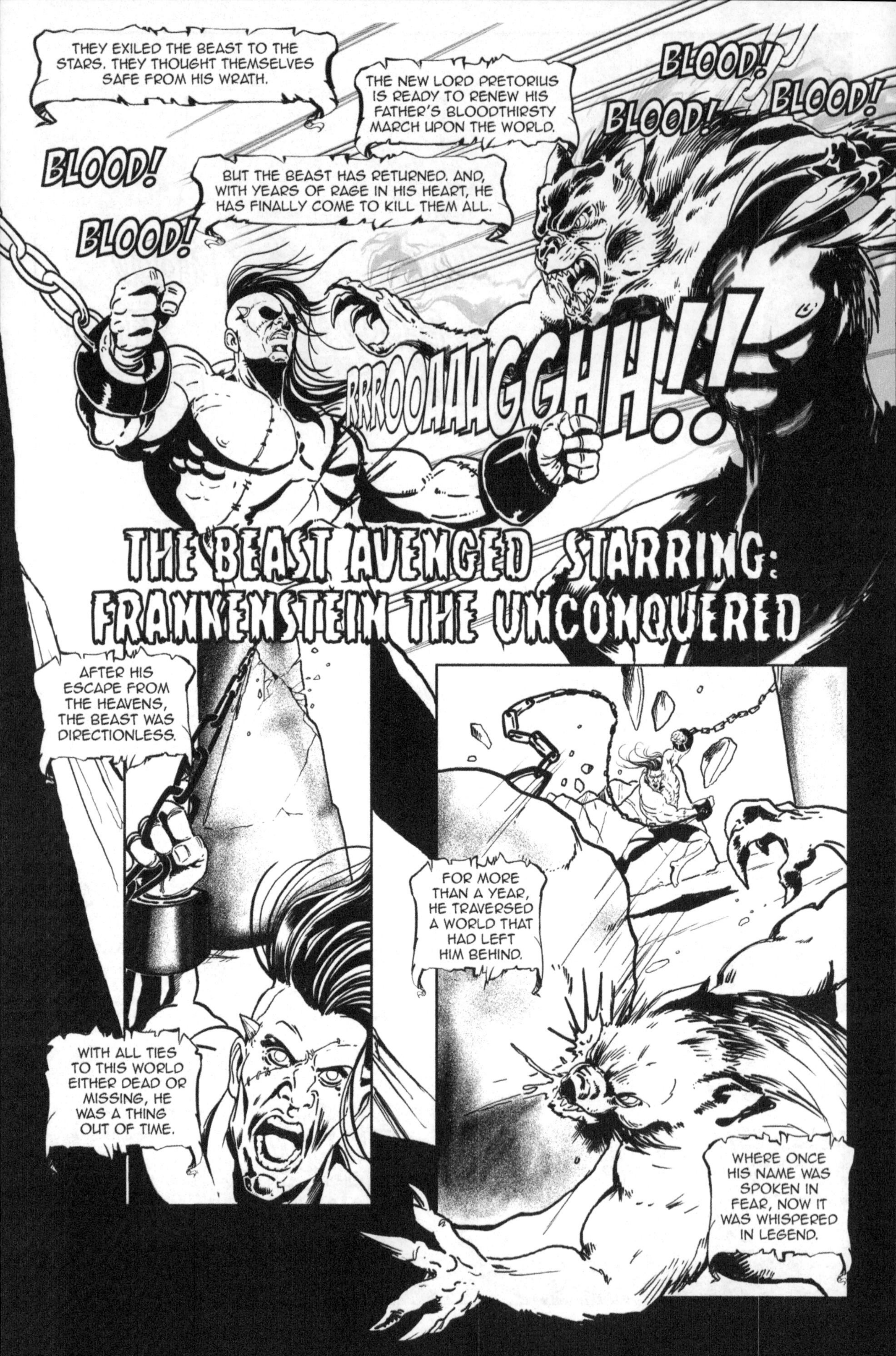
THEY EXILED THE BEAST TO THE STARS. THEY THOUGHT THEMSELVES SAFE FROM HIS WRATH.
THE NEW LORD PRETORIUS IS READY TO RENEW HIS FATHER'S BLOODTHIRSTY MARCH UPON THE WORLD.
BLOOD!
BLOOD!
BLOOD!
BLOOD!
BLOOD!
BUT THE BEAST HAS RETURNED. AND, WITH YEARS OF RAGE IN HIS HEART, HE HAS FINALLY COME TO KILL THEM ALL.
RRROOAAAGGHH!!!
THE BEAST AVENGED STARRING: FRANKENSTEIN THE UNCONQUERED
AFTER HIS ESCAPE FROM THE HEAVENS, THE BEAST WAS DIRECTIONLESS.
WITH ALL TIES TO THIS WORLD EITHER DEAD OR MISSING, HE WAS A THING OUT OF TIME.
FOR MORE THAN A YEAR, HE TRAVERSED A WORLD THAT HAD LEFT HIM BEHIND.
WHERE ONCE HIS NAME WAS SPOKEN IN FEAR, NOW IT WAS WHISPERED IN LEGEND.

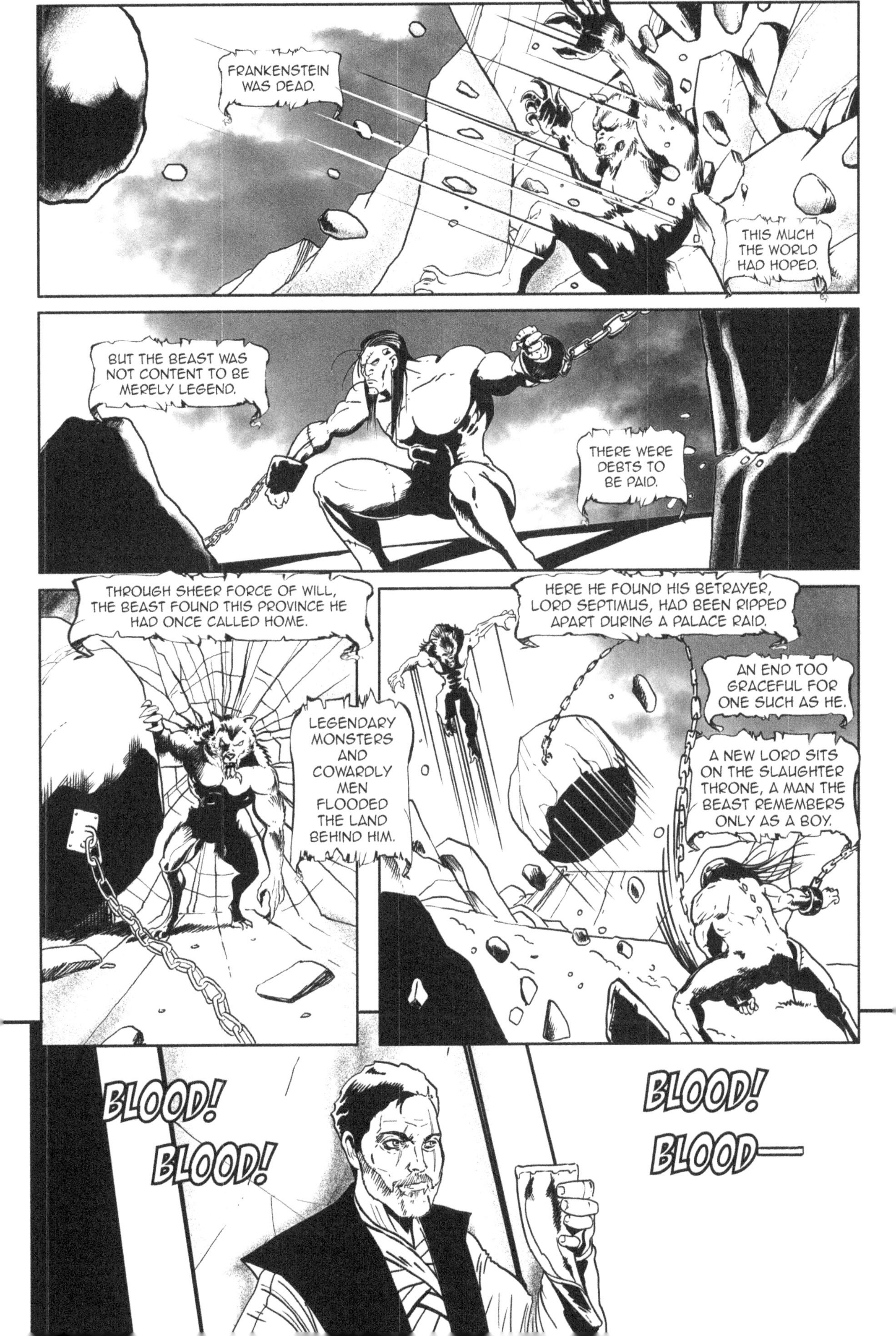
FRANKENSTEIN WAS DEAD.
THIS MUCH THE WORLD HAD HOPED.
BUT THE BEAST WAS NOT CONTENT TO BE MERELY LEGEND.
THERE WERE DEBTS TO BE PAID.
THROUGH SHEER FORCE OF WILL, THE BEAST FOUND THIS PROVINCE HE HAD ONCE CALLED HOME.
LEGENDARY MONSTERS AND COWARDLY MEN FLOODED THE LAND BEHIND HIM.
HERE HE FOUND HIS BETRAYER, LORD SEPTIMUS, HAD BEEN RIPPED APART DURING A PALACE RAID.
AN END TOO GRACEFUL FOR ONE SUCH AS HE.
A NEW LORD SITS ON THE SLAUGHTER THRONE, A MAN THE BEAST REMEMBERS ONLY AS A BOY.
BLOOD!
BLOOD!
BLOOD!
BLOOD—

OOHHHH!!!

LORD SEPTIMUS HAD BEEN A FRIEND. HIS SON WAS... SOMETHING MORE.

HE TRIES NOT TO THINK OF IT.

THE CUPS HOLD A DRINK NONE OUTSIDE THE PROVINCE HAVE EVER TASTED.

TO DRINK IS TO BECOME PRETORIOUS.

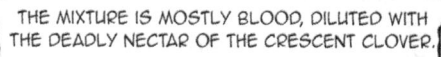

THE MIXTURE IS MOSTLY BLOOD, DILUTED WITH THE DEADLY NECTAR OF THE CRESCENT CLOVER.

A MIND ALTERING CHEMICAL THAT, WHEN MIXED, BECOMES HIGLY ADDICTIVE.

ITS POTENCY FORMS A SPECIAL GRIP UPON THE DRINKER NO AMOUNT OF REHABILITATION CAN CURE.

ENTIRE GENERATIONS HELD IN CHECK BY DEPENDENCY.

BUT THE BEAST HAS TASTED THIS FOUL THING...

...HE FINDS IT LACKING.

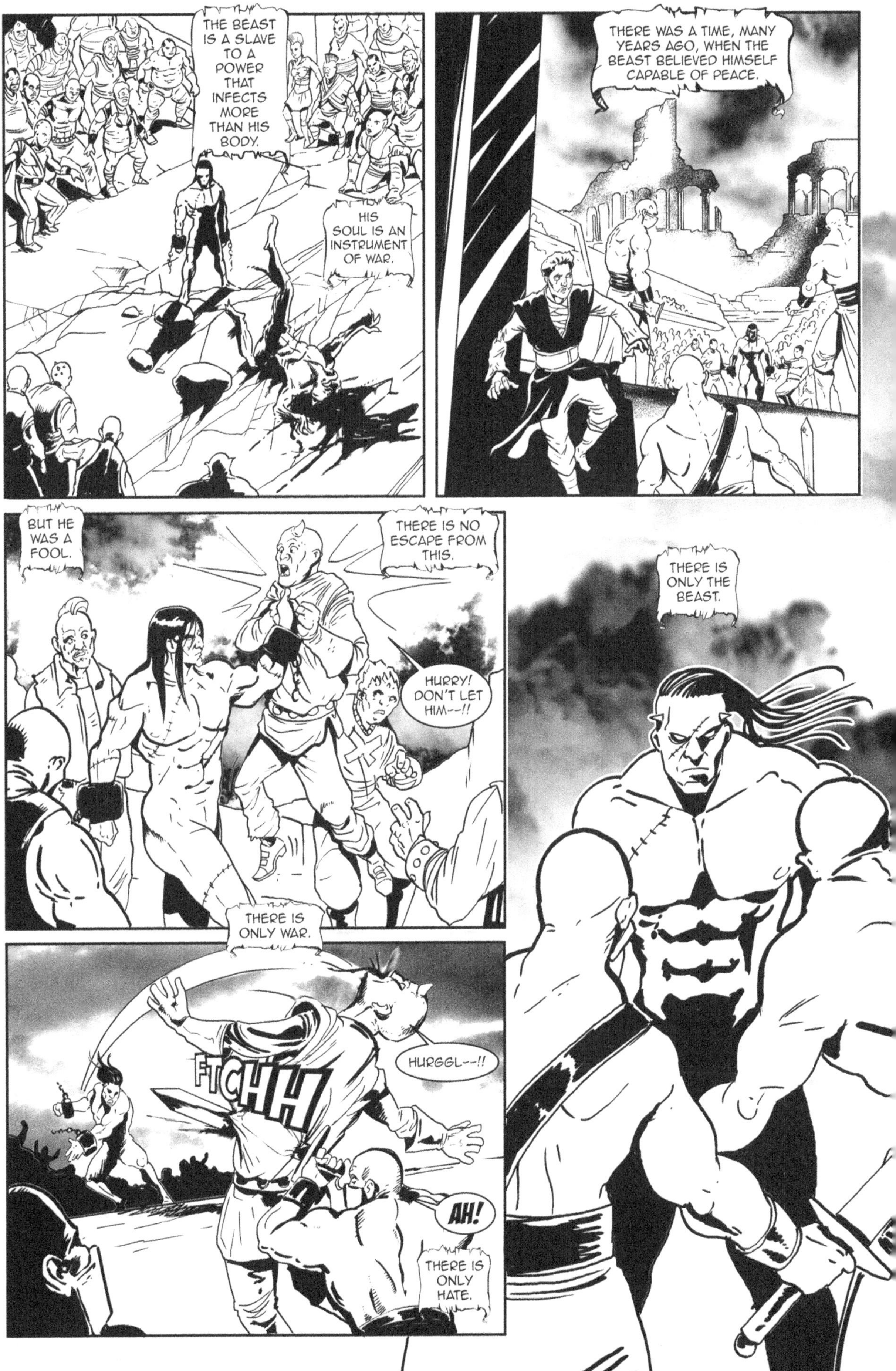
THE BEAST IS A SLAVE TO A POWER THAT INFECTS MORE THAN HIS BODY.
HIS SOUL IS AN INSTRUMENT OF WAR.
THERE WAS A TIME, MANY YEARS AGO, WHEN THE BEAST BELIEVED HIMSELF CAPABLE OF PEACE.
BUT HE WAS A FOOL.
THERE IS NO ESCAPE FROM THIS.
HURRY! DON'T LET HIM--!!
THERE IS ONLY WAR.
FTCHH
HURGGL--!!
AH!
THERE IS ONLY HATE.
THERE IS ONLY THE BEAST.

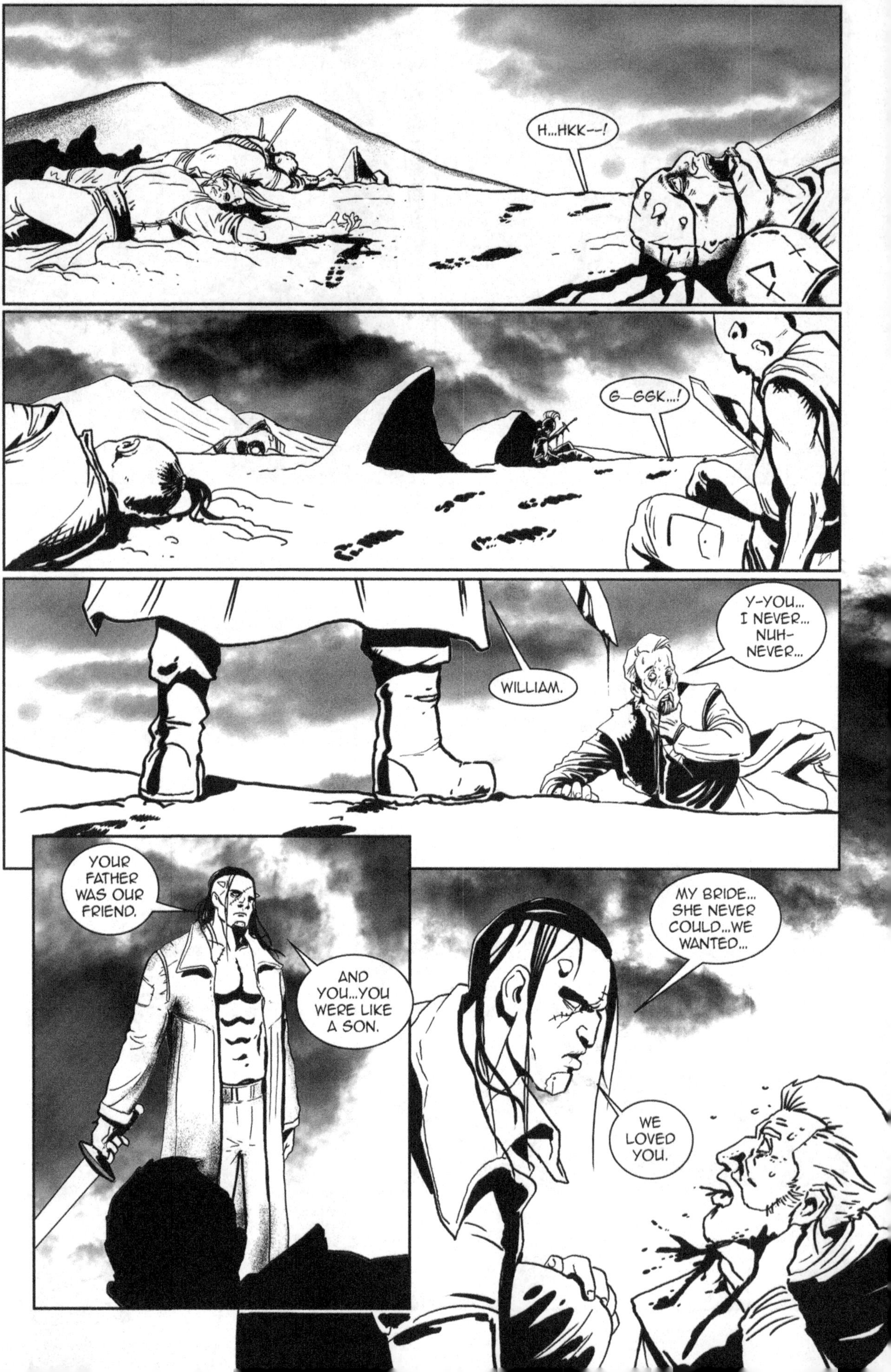
H...HKK--!
G--GGK...!
WILLIAM.
Y-YOU... I NEVER... NUH-NEVER...
YOUR FATHER WAS OUR FRIEND.
AND YOU...YOU WERE LIKE A SON.
MY BRIDE... SHE NEVER COULD...WE WANTED...
WE LOVED YOU.

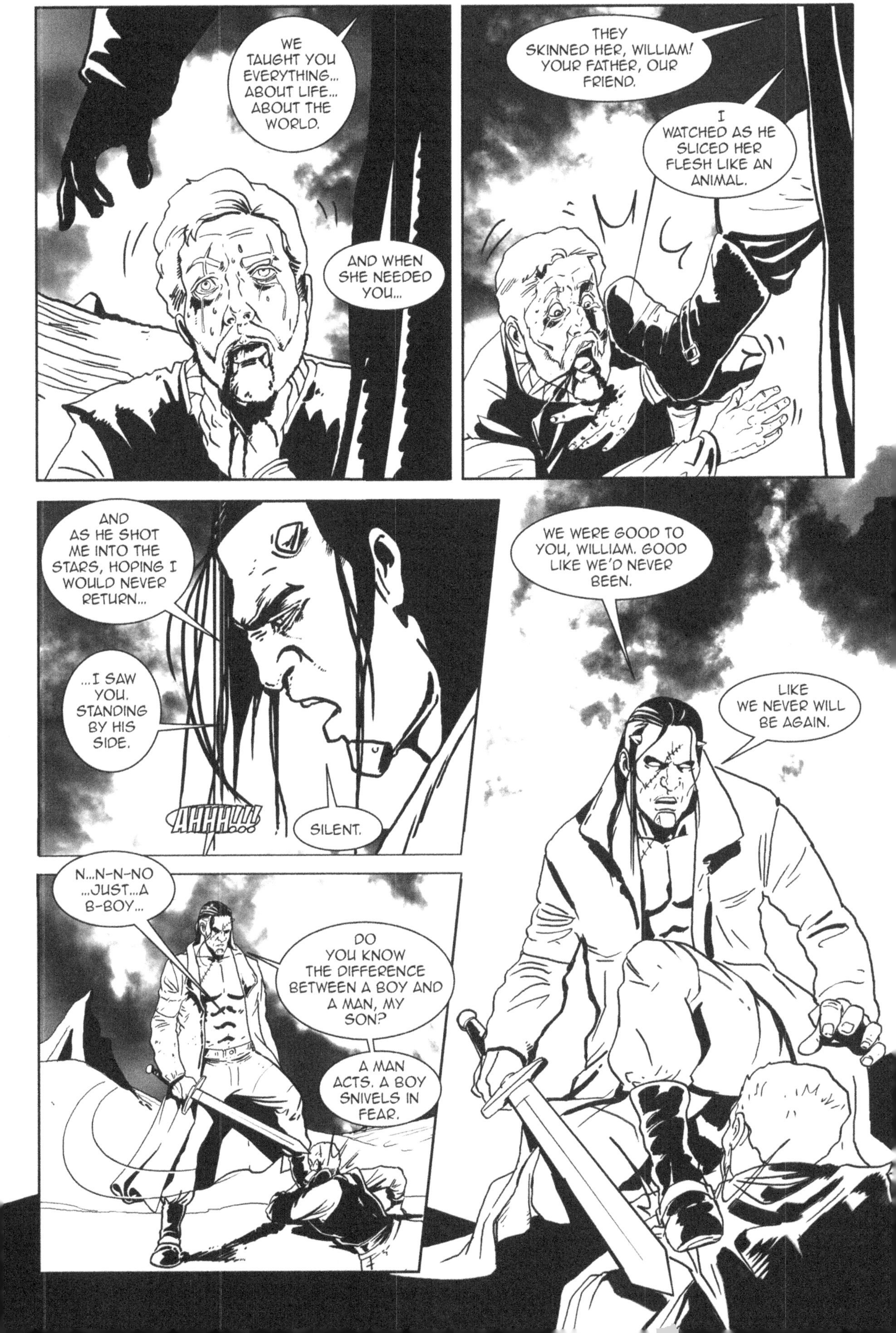
WE TAUGHT YOU EVERYTHING... ABOUT LIFE... ABOUT THE WORLD.
AND WHEN SHE NEEDED YOU...
THEY SKINNED HER, WILLIAM! YOUR FATHER, OUR FRIEND.
I WATCHED AS HE SLICED HER FLESH LIKE AN ANIMAL.
AND AS HE SHOT ME INTO THE STARS, HOPING I WOULD NEVER RETURN...
...I SAW YOU. STANDING BY HIS SIDE.
AHHH!!!...
SILENT.
WE WERE GOOD TO YOU, WILLIAM. GOOD LIKE WE'D NEVER BEEN.
LIKE WE NEVER WILL BE AGAIN.
N...N-N-NO ...JUST...A B-BOY...
DO YOU KNOW THE DIFFERENCE BETWEEN A BOY AND A MAN, MY SON?
A MAN ACTS. A BOY SNIVELS IN FEAR.

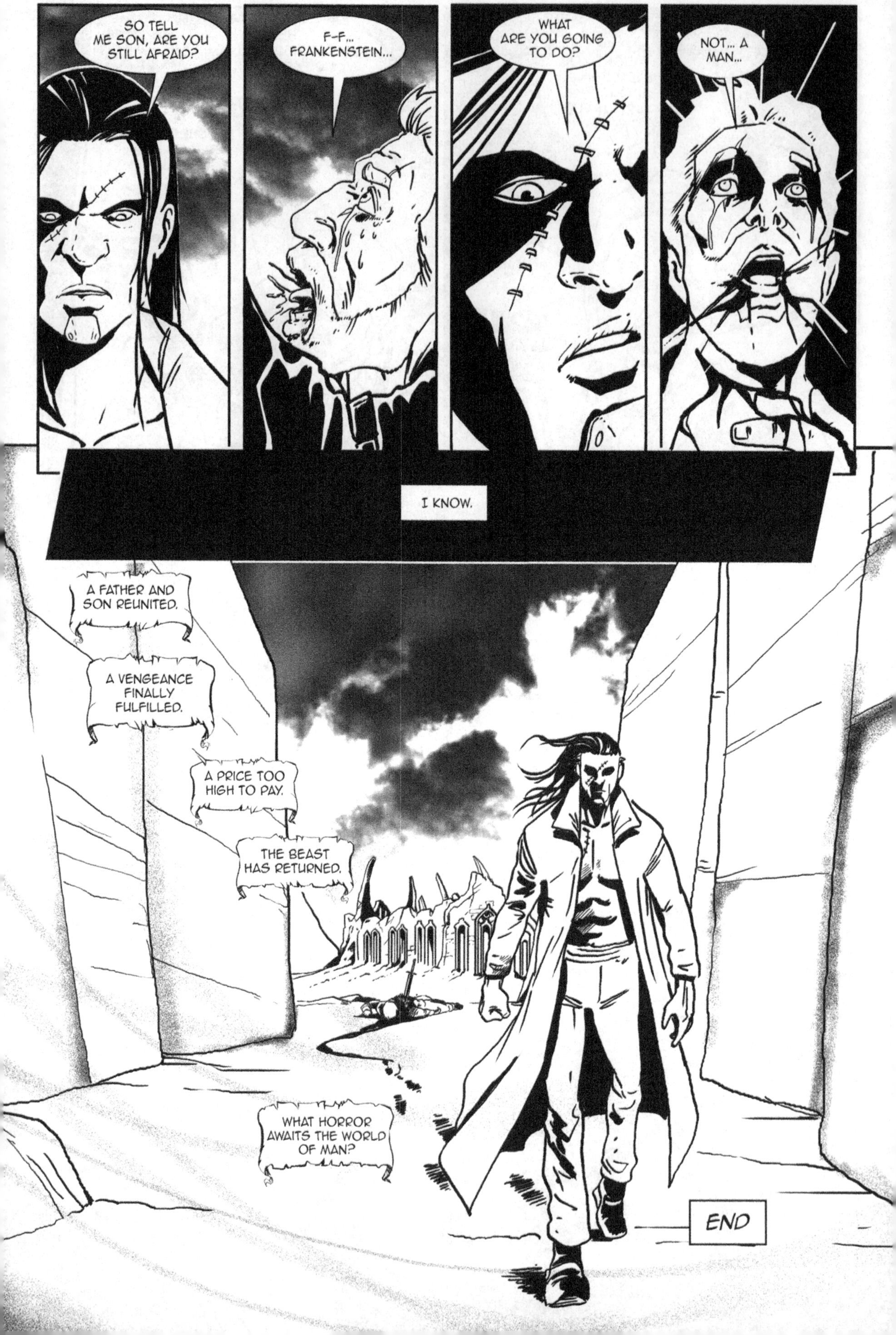
SO TELL ME SON, ARE YOU STILL AFRAID?
F-F... FRANKENSTEIN...
WHAT ARE YOU GOING TO DO?
NOT... A MAN...
I KNOW.
A FATHER AND SON REUNITED.
A VENGEANCE FINALLY FULFILLED.
A PRICE TOO HIGH TO PAY.
THE BEAST HAS RETURNED.
WHAT HORROR AWAITS THE WORLD OF MAN?
END

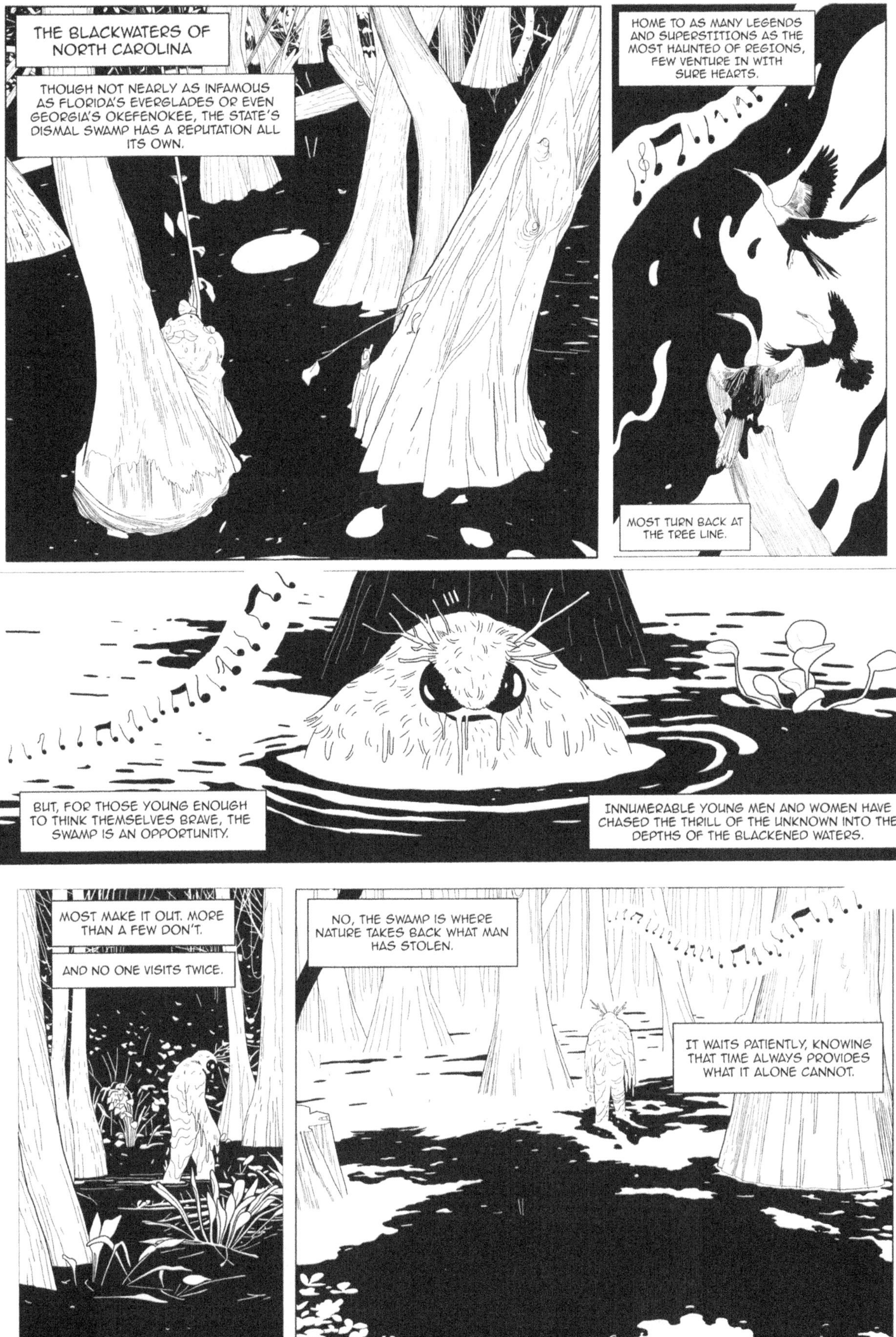
THE BLACKWATERS OF NORTH CAROLINA
THOUGH NOT NEARLY AS INFAMOUS AS FLORIDA'S EVERGLADES OR EVEN GEORGIA'S OKEFENOKEE, THE STATE'S DISMAL SWAMP HAS A REPUTATION ALL ITS OWN.
HOME TO AS MANY LEGENDS AND SUPERSTITIONS AS THE MOST HAUNTED OF REGIONS, FEW VENTURE IN WITH SURE HEARTS.
MOST TURN BACK AT THE TREE LINE.
BUT, FOR THOSE YOUNG ENOUGH TO THINK THEMSELVES BRAVE, THE SWAMP IS AN OPPORTUNITY.
INNUMERABLE YOUNG MEN AND WOMEN HAVE CHASED THE THRILL OF THE UNKNOWN INTO THE DEPTHS OF THE BLACKENED WATERS.
MOST MAKE IT OUT. MORE THAN A FEW DON'T.
AND NO ONE VISITS TWICE.
NO, THE SWAMP IS WHERE NATURE TAKES BACK WHAT MAN HAS STOLEN.
IT WAITS PATIENTLY, KNOWING THAT TIME ALWAYS PROVIDES WHAT IT ALONE CANNOT.

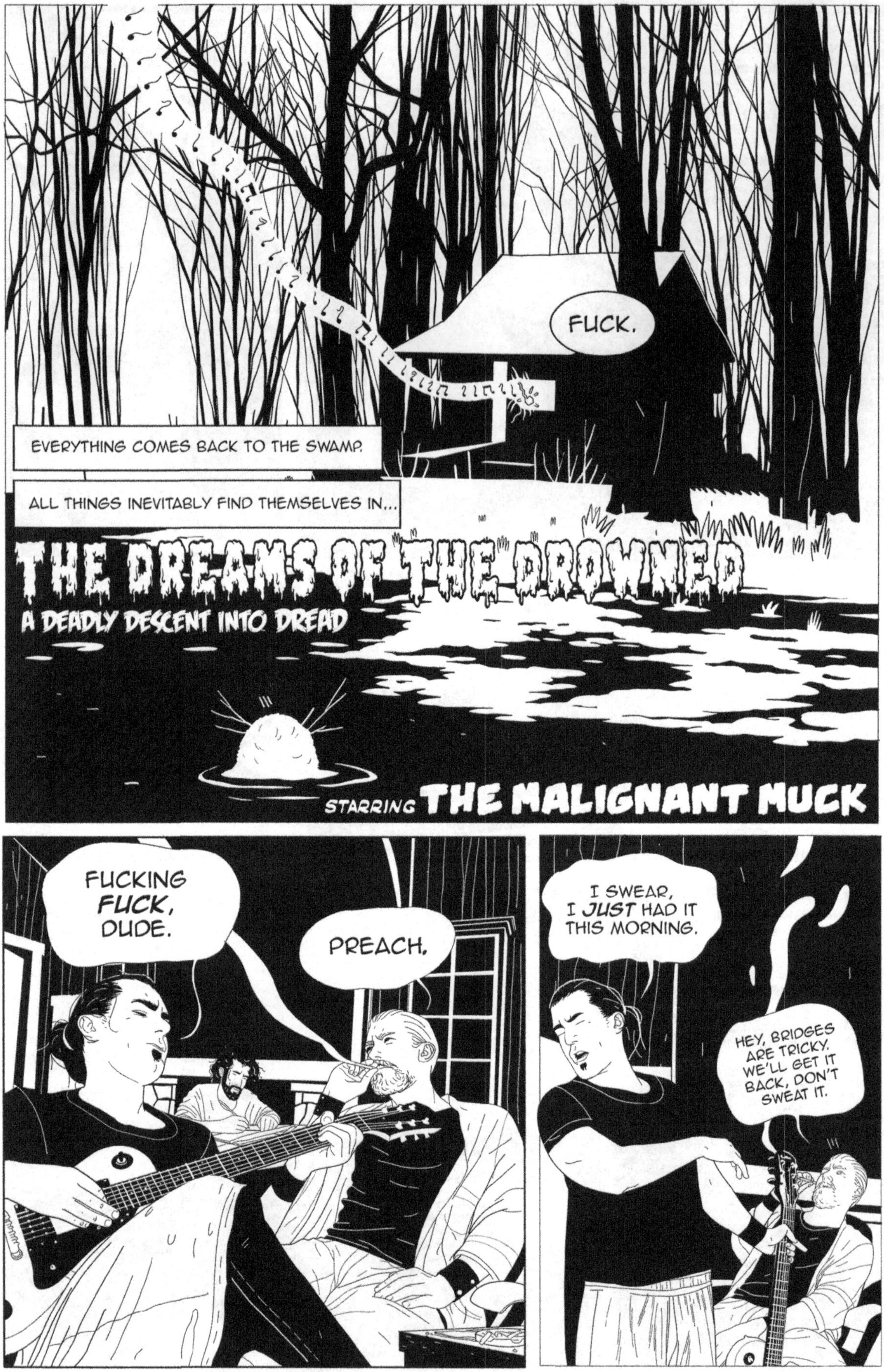
FUCK.
EVERYTHING COMES BACK TO THE SWAMP.
ALL THINGS INEVITABLY FIND THEMSELVES IN...
THE DREAMS OF THE DROWNED
A DEADLY DESCENT INTO DREAD
STARRING THE MALIGNANT MUCK
FUCKING FUCK, DUDE.
PREACH.
I SWEAR, I JUST HAD IT THIS MORNING.
HEY, BRIDGES ARE TRICKY. WE'LL GET IT BACK, DON'T SWEAT IT.

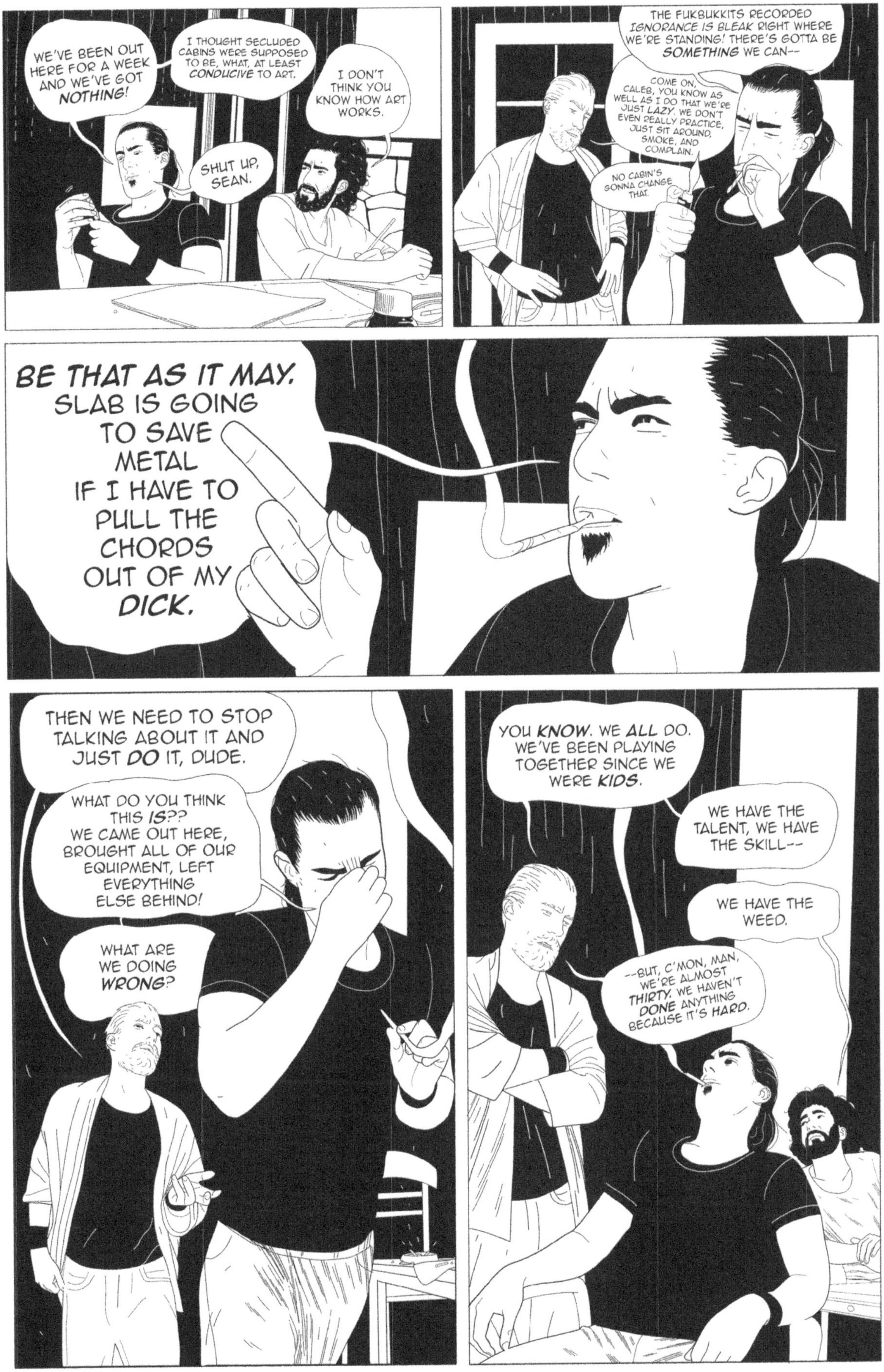
WE'VE BEEN OUT HERE FOR A WEEK AND WE'VE GOT NOTHING!
I THOUGHT SECLUDED CABINS WERE SUPPOSED TO BE, WHAT, AT LEAST CONDUCIVE TO ART.
I DON'T THINK YOU KNOW HOW ART WORKS.
SHUT UP, SEAN.
THE FUKBUKKITS RECORDED IGNORANCE IS BLEAK RIGHT WHERE WE'RE STANDING! THERE'S GOTTA BE SOMETHING WE CAN--
COME ON, CALEB, YOU KNOW AS WELL AS I DO THAT WE'RE JUST LAZY. WE DON'T EVEN REALLY PRACTICE, JUST SIT AROUND, SMOKE, AND COMPLAIN.
NO CABIN'S GONNA CHANGE THAT.
BE THAT AS IT MAY. SLAB IS GOING TO SAVE METAL IF I HAVE TO PULL THE CHORDS OUT OF MY DICK.
THEN WE NEED TO STOP TALKING ABOUT IT AND JUST DO IT, DUDE.
WHAT DO YOU THINK THIS IS?? WE CAME OUT HERE, BROUGHT ALL OF OUR EQUIPMENT, LEFT EVERYTHING ELSE BEHIND!
WHAT ARE WE DOING WRONG?
YOU KNOW. WE ALL DO. WE'VE BEEN PLAYING TOGETHER SINCE WE WERE KIDS.
WE HAVE THE TALENT, WE HAVE THE SKILL--
WE HAVE THE WEED.
--BUT, C'MON, MAN, WE'RE ALMOST THIRTY. WE HAVEN'T DONE ANYTHING BECAUSE IT'S HARD.

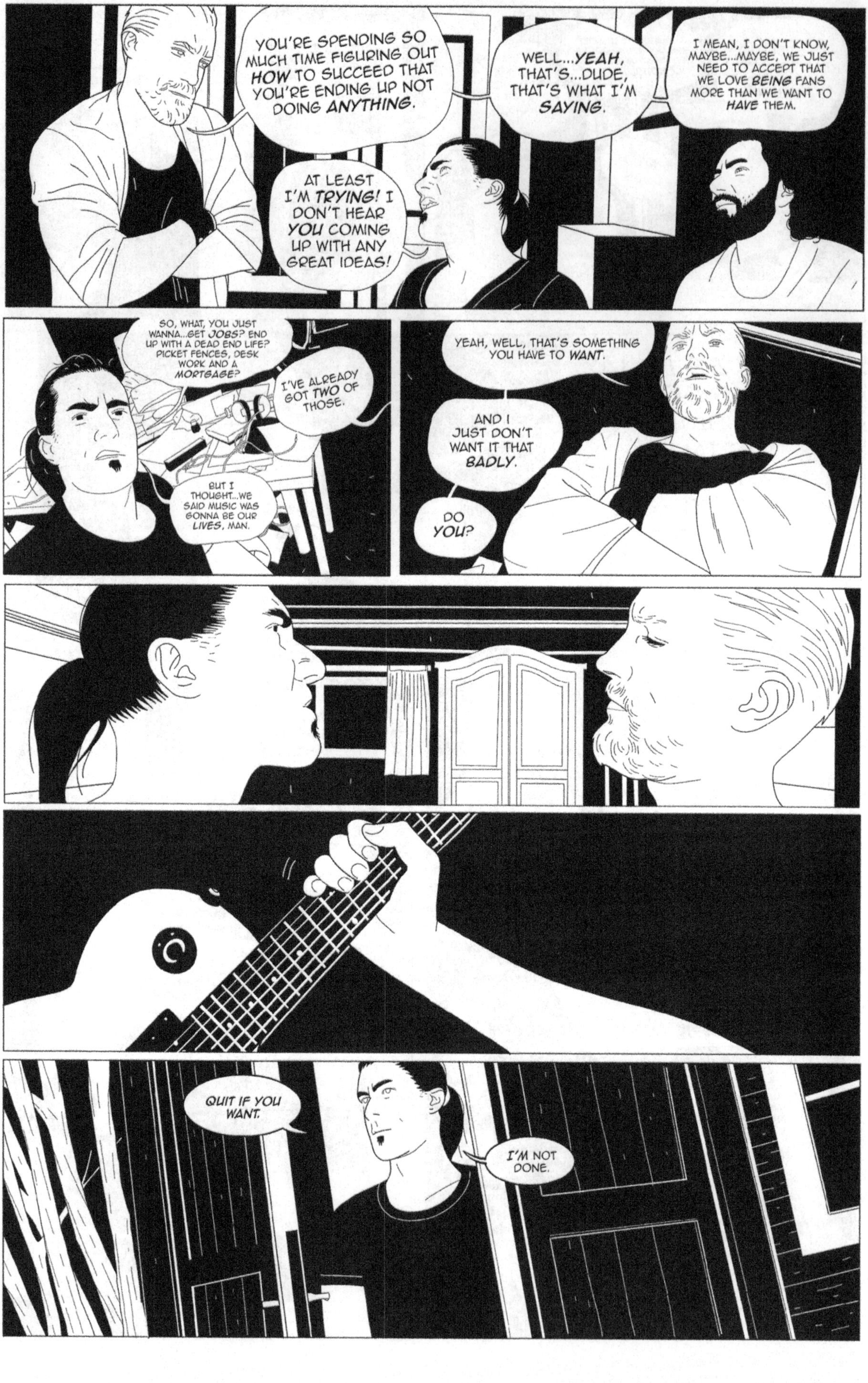
YOU'RE SPENDING SO MUCH TIME FIGURING OUT HOW TO SUCCEED THAT YOU'RE ENDING UP NOT DOING ANYTHING.
AT LEAST I'M TRYING! I DON'T HEAR YOU COMING UP WITH ANY GREAT IDEAS!
WELL...YEAH, THAT'S...DUDE, THAT'S WHAT I'M SAYING.
I MEAN, I DON'T KNOW, MAYBE...MAYBE, WE JUST NEED TO ACCEPT THAT WE LOVE BEING FANS MORE THAN WE WANT TO HAVE THEM.
SO, WHAT, YOU JUST WANNA...GET JOBS? END UP WITH A DEAD END LIFE? PICKET FENCES, DESK WORK AND A MORTGAGE?
I'VE ALREADY GOT TWO OF THOSE.
BUT I THOUGHT...WE SAID MUSIC WAS GONNA BE OUR LIVES, MAN.
YEAH, WELL, THAT'S SOMETHING YOU HAVE TO WANT.
AND I JUST DON'T WANT IT THAT BADLY.
DO YOU?
QUIT IF YOU WANT.
I'M NOT DONE.

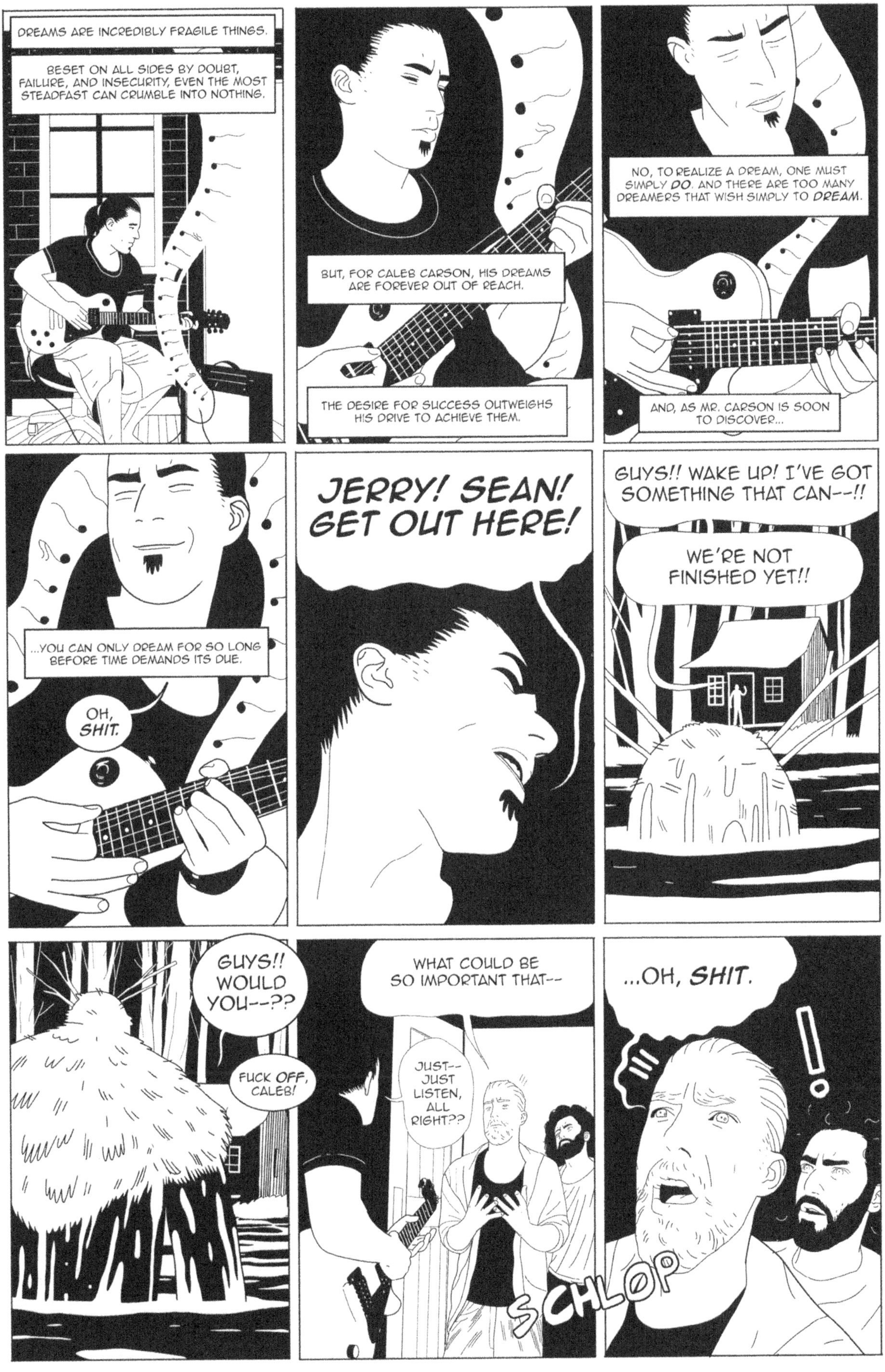
DREAMS ARE INCREDIBLY FRAGILE THINGS.
BESET ON ALL SIDES BY DOUBT, FAILURE, AND INSECURITY, EVEN THE MOST STEADFAST CAN CRUMBLE INTO NOTHING.
BUT, FOR CALEB CARSON, HIS DREAMS ARE FOREVER OUT OF REACH.
THE DESIRE FOR SUCCESS OUTWEIGHS HIS DRIVE TO ACHIEVE THEM.
NO, TO REALIZE A DREAM, ONE MUST SIMPLY *DO*. AND THERE ARE TOO MANY DREAMERS THAT WISH SIMPLY TO ***DREAM***.
AND, AS MR. CARSON IS SOON TO DISCOVER...
...YOU CAN ONLY DREAM FOR SO LONG BEFORE TIME DEMANDS ITS DUE.
OH, ***SHIT.***
JERRY! SEAN! GET OUT HERE!
GUYS!! WAKE UP! I'VE GOT SOMETHING THAT CAN--!!
WE'RE NOT FINISHED YET!!
GUYS!! WOULD YOU--??
FUCK ***OFF***, CALEB!
WHAT COULD BE SO IMPORTANT THAT--
JUST-- JUST LISTEN, ALL RIGHT??
...OH, ***SHIT***.
!!!
!
SCHLOP

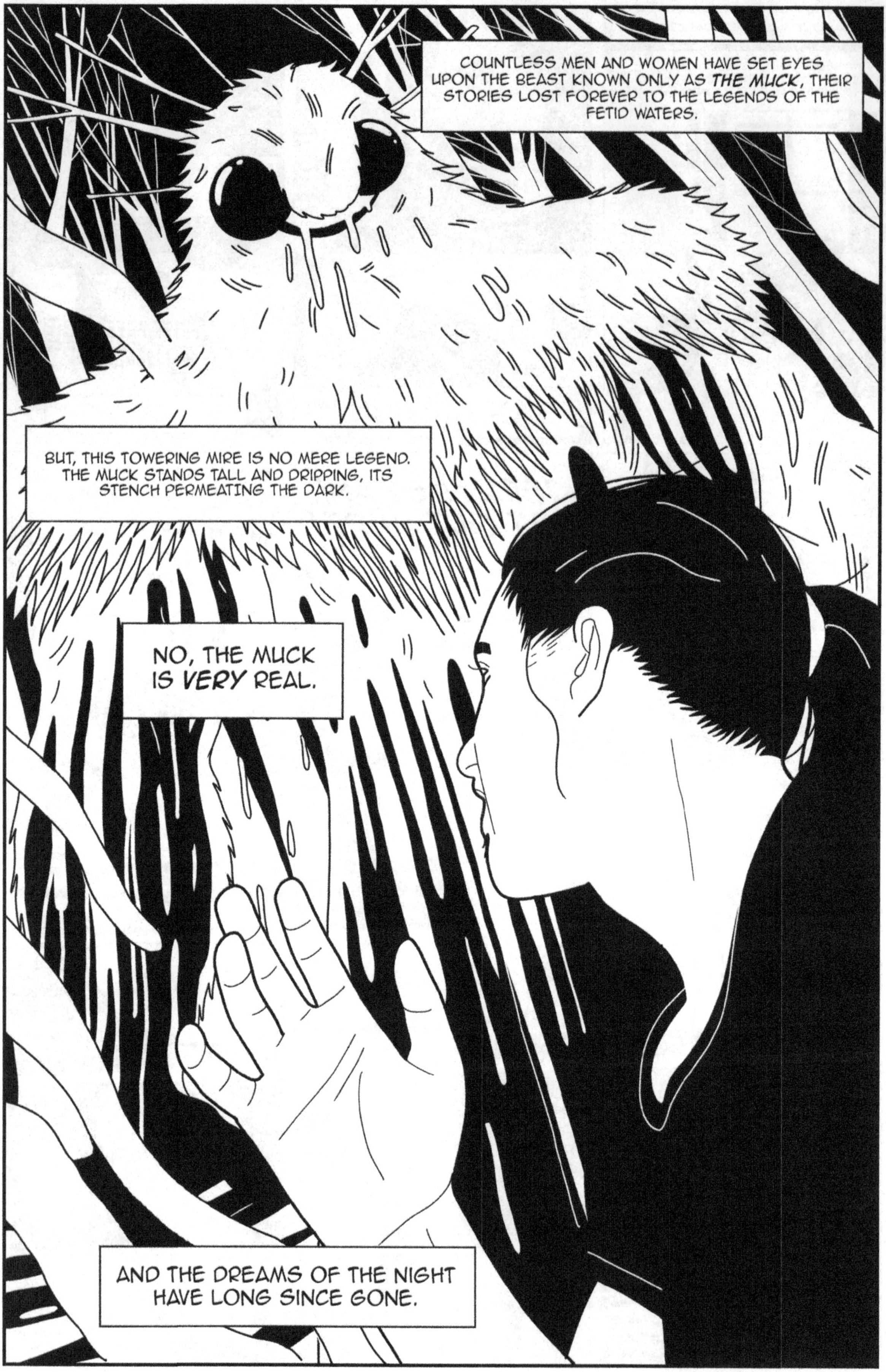
COUNTLESS MEN AND WOMEN HAVE SET EYES UPON THE BEAST KNOWN ONLY AS *THE MUCK*, THEIR STORIES LOST FOREVER TO THE LEGENDS OF THE FETID WATERS.
BUT, THIS TOWERING MIRE IS NO MERE LEGEND. THE MUCK STANDS TALL AND DRIPPING, ITS STENCH PERMEATING THE DARK.
NO, THE MUCK IS *VERY* REAL.
AND THE DREAMS OF THE NIGHT HAVE LONG SINCE GONE.

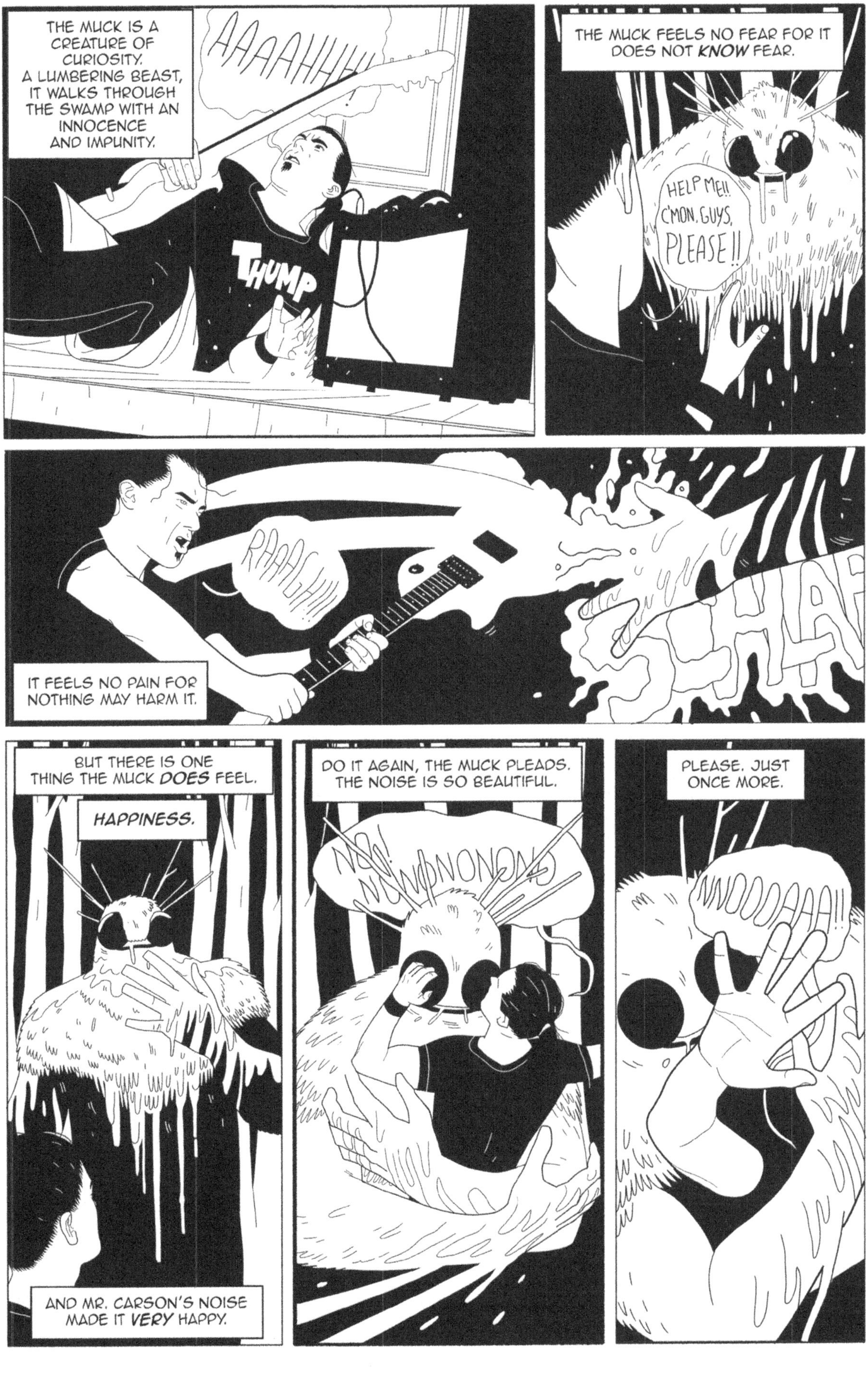
THE MUCK IS A CREATURE OF CURIOSITY. A LUMBERING BEAST, IT WALKS THROUGH THE SWAMP WITH AN INNOCENCE AND IMPUNITY.
AAAAHHHH
THUMP
THE MUCK FEELS NO FEAR FOR IT DOES NOT ***KNOW*** FEAR.
HELP ME!! C'MON, GUYS, PLEASE!!
RAAAGH!!
IT FEELS NO PAIN FOR NOTHING MAY HARM IT.
BUT THERE IS ONE THING THE MUCK ***DOES*** FEEL.
HAPPINESS.
AND MR. CARSON'S NOISE MADE IT ***VERY*** HAPPY.
DO IT AGAIN, THE MUCK PLEADS. THE NOISE IS SO BEAUTIFUL.
NO! NONONONONONO
PLEASE. JUST ONCE MORE.
NNOOOAAA!!

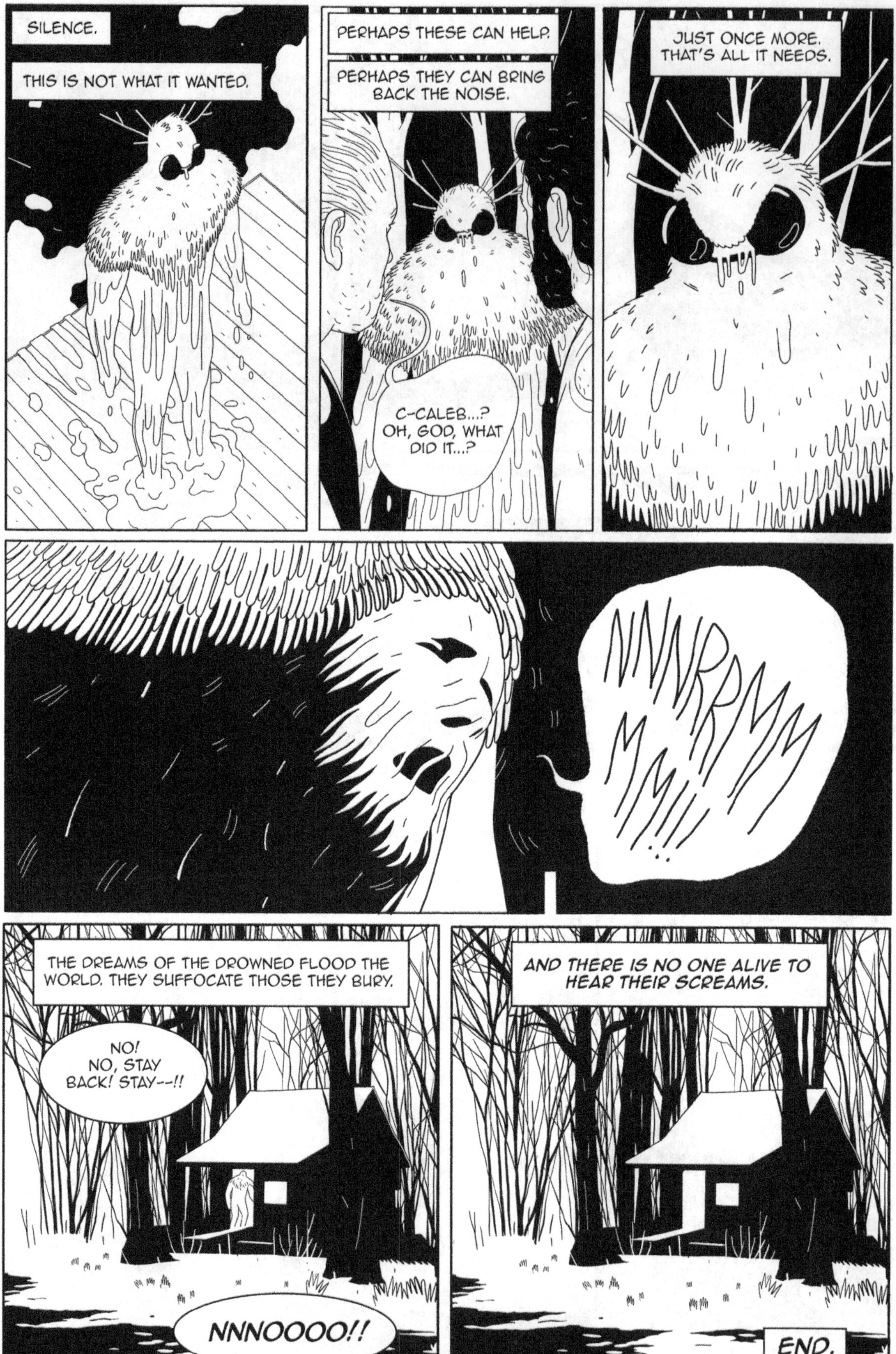
SILENCE.
THIS IS NOT WHAT IT WANTED.
PERHAPS THESE CAN HELP.
PERHAPS THEY CAN BRING BACK THE NOISE.
C-CALEB...? OH, GOD, WHAT DID IT...?
JUST ONCE MORE. THAT'S ALL IT NEEDS.
NNNRRMMMMM...
THE DREAMS OF THE DROWNED FLOOD THE WORLD. THEY SUFFOCATE THOSE THEY BURY.
NO! NO, STAY BACK! STAY--!!
NNNOOOO!!
AND THERE IS NO ONE ALIVE TO HEAR THEIR SCREAMS.
END.

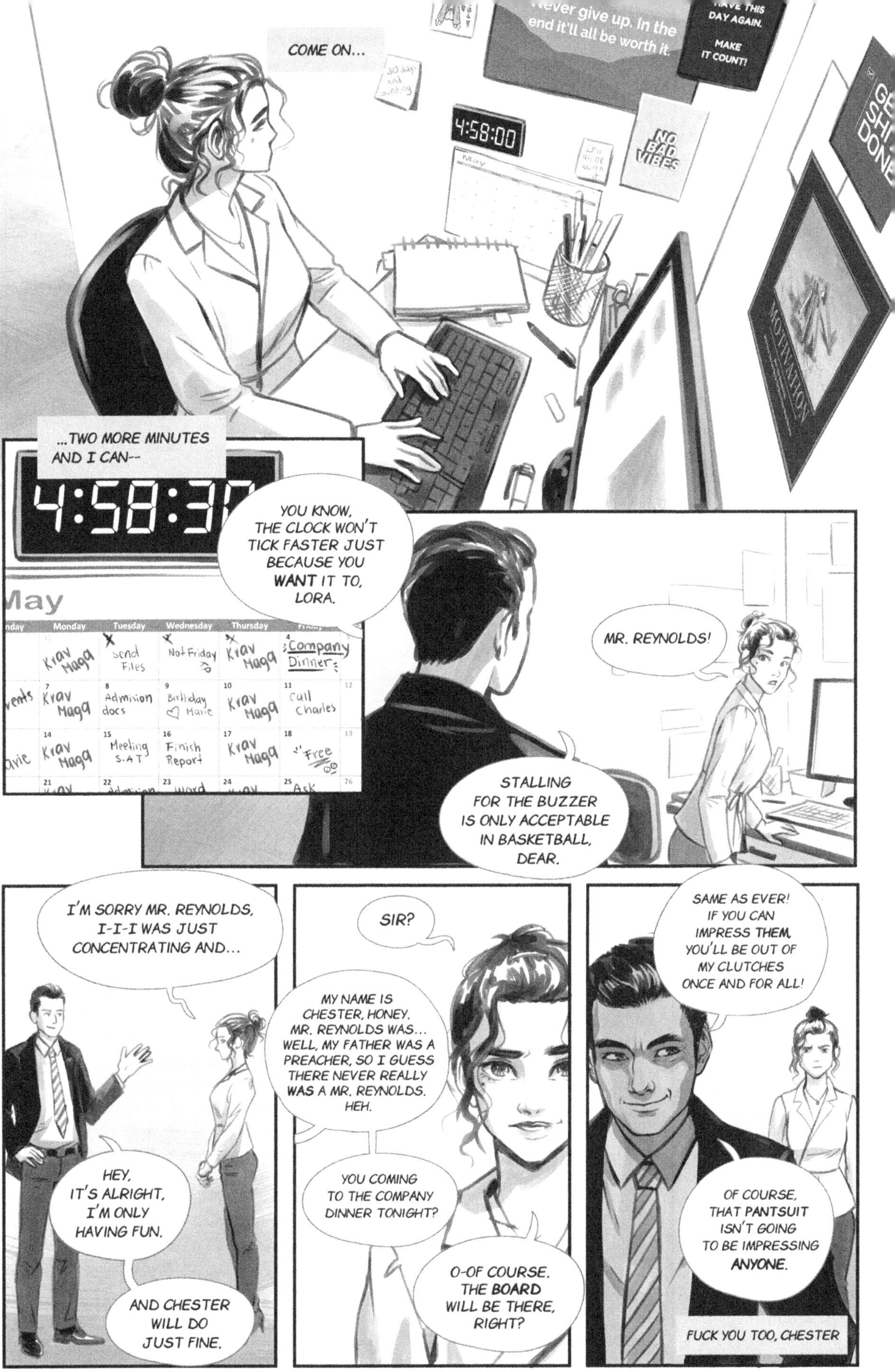
COME ON...
end it'll all be worth it.
DAY AGAIN.
MAKE IT COUNT!
4:58:00
NO BAD VIBES
MOTIVATION
...TWO MORE MINUTES AND I CAN--
May
Monday
Tuesday
Wednesday
Thursday
Krav Maga
Send Files
Not Friday
Krav Maga
Company Dinner
Krav Maga
Admision docs
Birthday Marie
Krav Maga
Call Charles
Krav Maga
Meeting S.A.T
Finish Report
Krav Maga
Free
YOU KNOW, THE CLOCK WON'T TICK FASTER JUST BECAUSE YOU WANT IT TO, LORA.
MR. REYNOLDS!
STALLING FOR THE BUZZER IS ONLY ACCEPTABLE IN BASKETBALL, DEAR.
I'M SORRY MR. REYNOLDS, I-I-I WAS JUST CONCENTRATING AND...
HEY, IT'S ALRIGHT, I'M ONLY HAVING FUN.
AND CHESTER WILL DO JUST FINE.
SIR?
MY NAME IS CHESTER, HONEY. MR. REYNOLDS WAS... WELL, MY FATHER WAS A PREACHER, SO I GUESS THERE NEVER REALLY WAS A MR. REYNOLDS. HEH.
YOU COMING TO THE COMPANY DINNER TONIGHT?
O-OF COURSE. THE BOARD WILL BE THERE, RIGHT?
SAME AS EVER! IF YOU CAN IMPRESS THEM, YOU'LL BE OUT OF MY CLUTCHES ONCE AND FOR ALL!
OF COURSE, THAT PANTSUIT ISN'T GOING TO BE IMPRESSING ANYONE.
FUCK YOU TOO, CHESTER

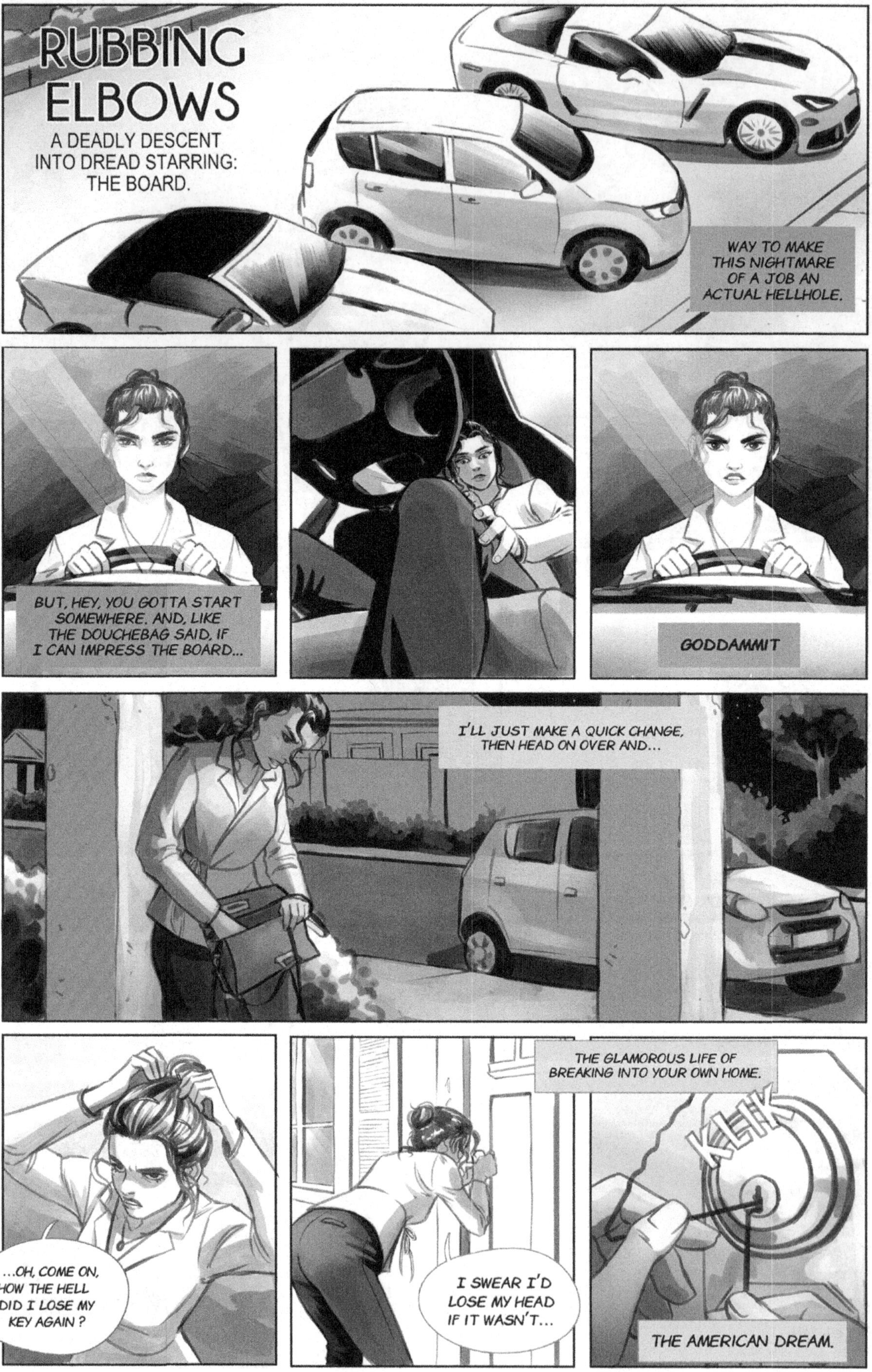
RUBBING ELBOWS
A DEADLY DESCENT INTO DREAD STARRING: THE BOARD.
WAY TO MAKE THIS NIGHTMARE OF A JOB AN ACTUAL HELLHOLE.
BUT, HEY, YOU GOTTA START SOMEWHERE. AND, LIKE THE DOUCHEBAG SAID, IF I CAN IMPRESS THE BOARD...
GODDAMMIT
I'LL JUST MAKE A QUICK CHANGE, THEN HEAD ON OVER AND...
...OH, COME ON, HOW THE HELL DID I LOSE MY KEY AGAIN?
I SWEAR I'D LOSE MY HEAD IF IT WASN'T...
THE GLAMOROUS LIFE OF BREAKING INTO YOUR OWN HOME.
KLIK
THE AMERICAN DREAM.

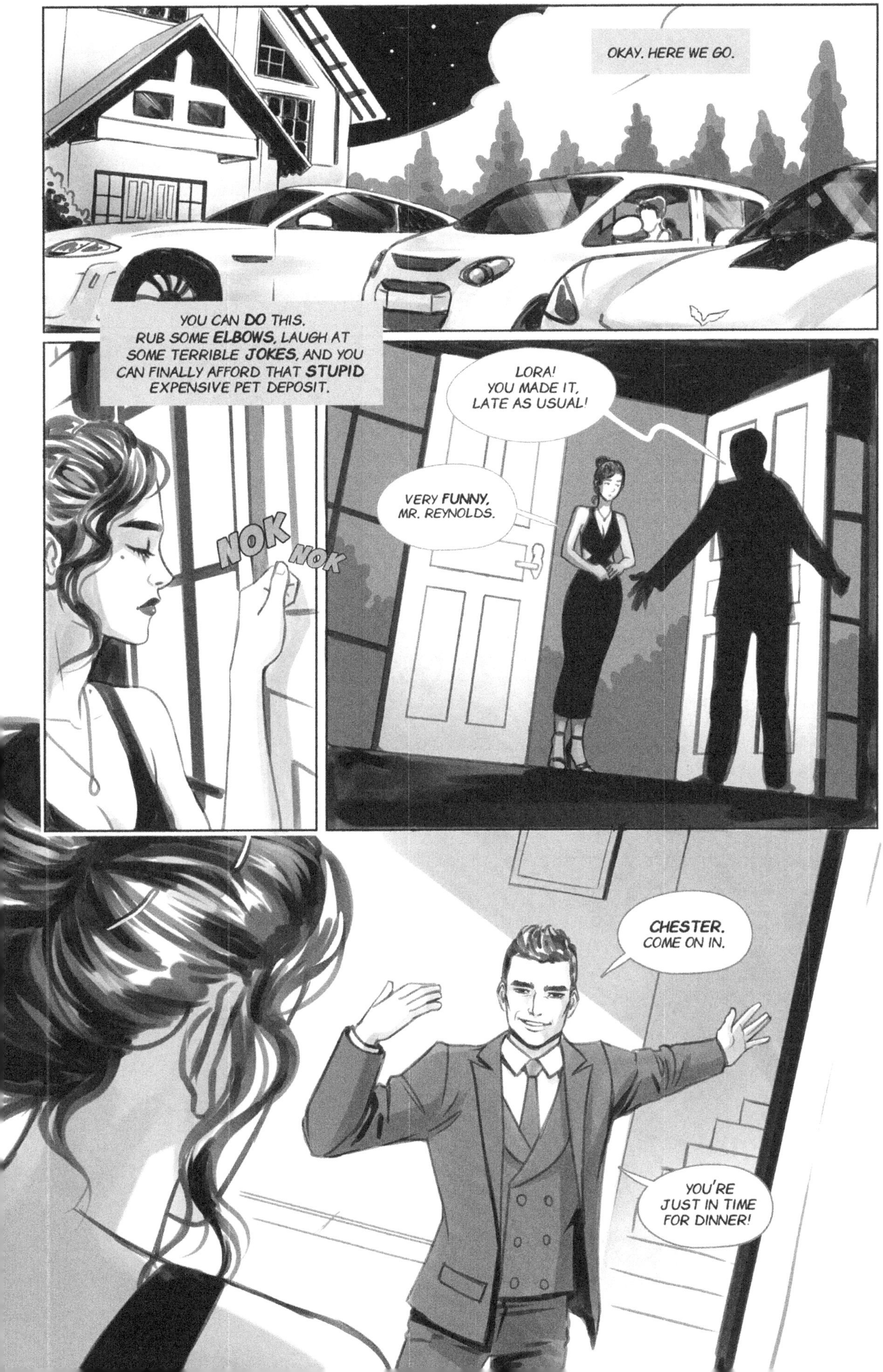

OKAY. HERE WE GO.
YOU CAN DO THIS. RUB SOME ELBOWS, LAUGH AT SOME TERRIBLE JOKES, AND YOU CAN FINALLY AFFORD THAT STUPID EXPENSIVE PET DEPOSIT.
NOK NOK
LORA! YOU MADE IT, LATE AS USUAL!
VERY FUNNY, MR. REYNOLDS.
CHESTER. COME ON IN.
YOU'RE JUST IN TIME FOR DINNER!

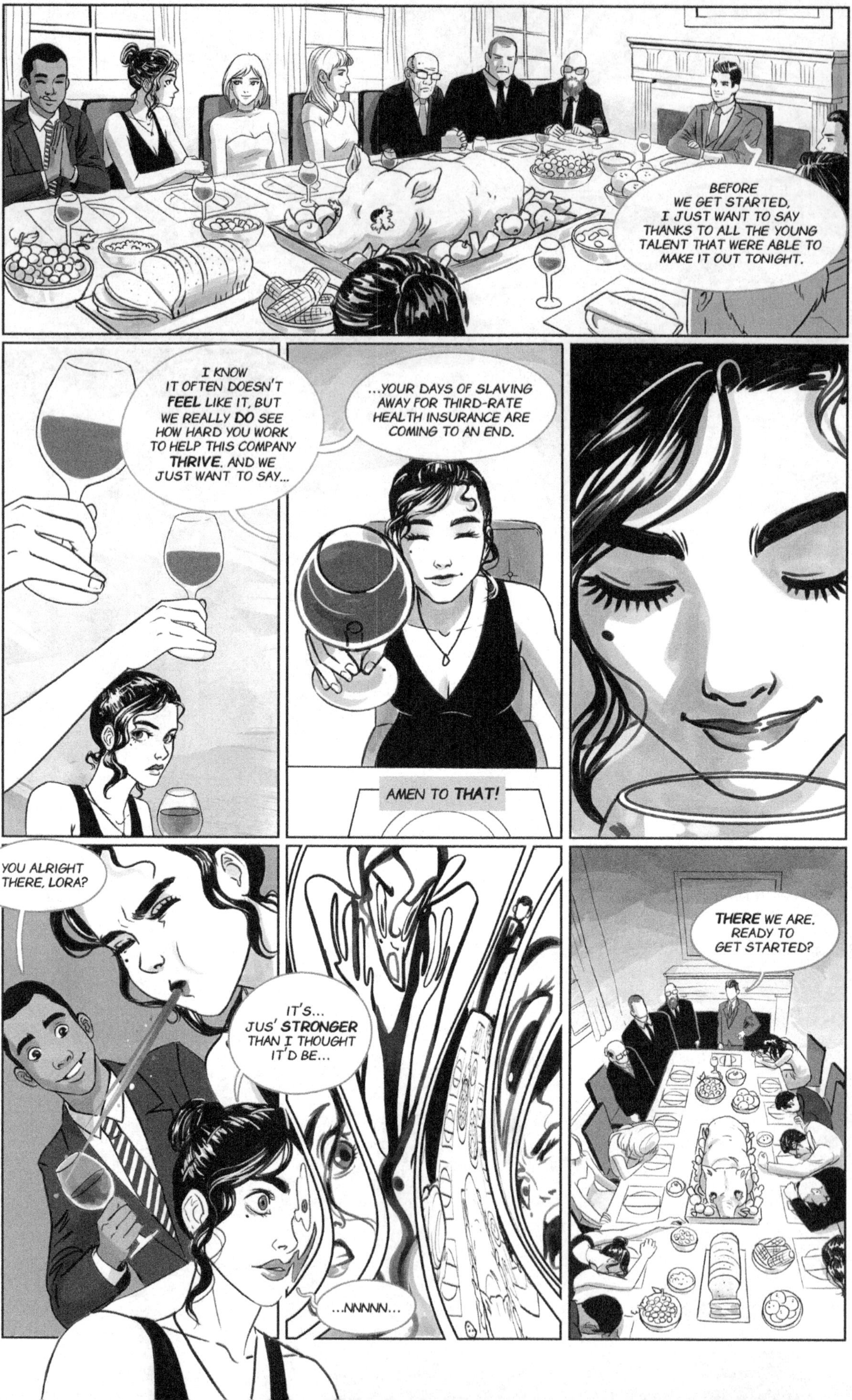
BEFORE WE GET STARTED, I JUST WANT TO SAY THANKS TO ALL THE YOUNG TALENT THAT WERE ABLE TO MAKE IT OUT TONIGHT.
I KNOW IT OFTEN DOESN'T FEEL LIKE IT, BUT WE REALLY DO SEE HOW HARD YOU WORK TO HELP THIS COMPANY THRIVE. AND WE JUST WANT TO SAY...
...YOUR DAYS OF SLAVING AWAY FOR THIRD-RATE HEALTH INSURANCE ARE COMING TO AN END.
AMEN TO THAT!
YOU ALRIGHT THERE, LORA?
IT'S... JUS' STRONGER THAN I THOUGHT IT'D BE...
...NNNNN...
THERE WE ARE. READY TO GET STARTED?

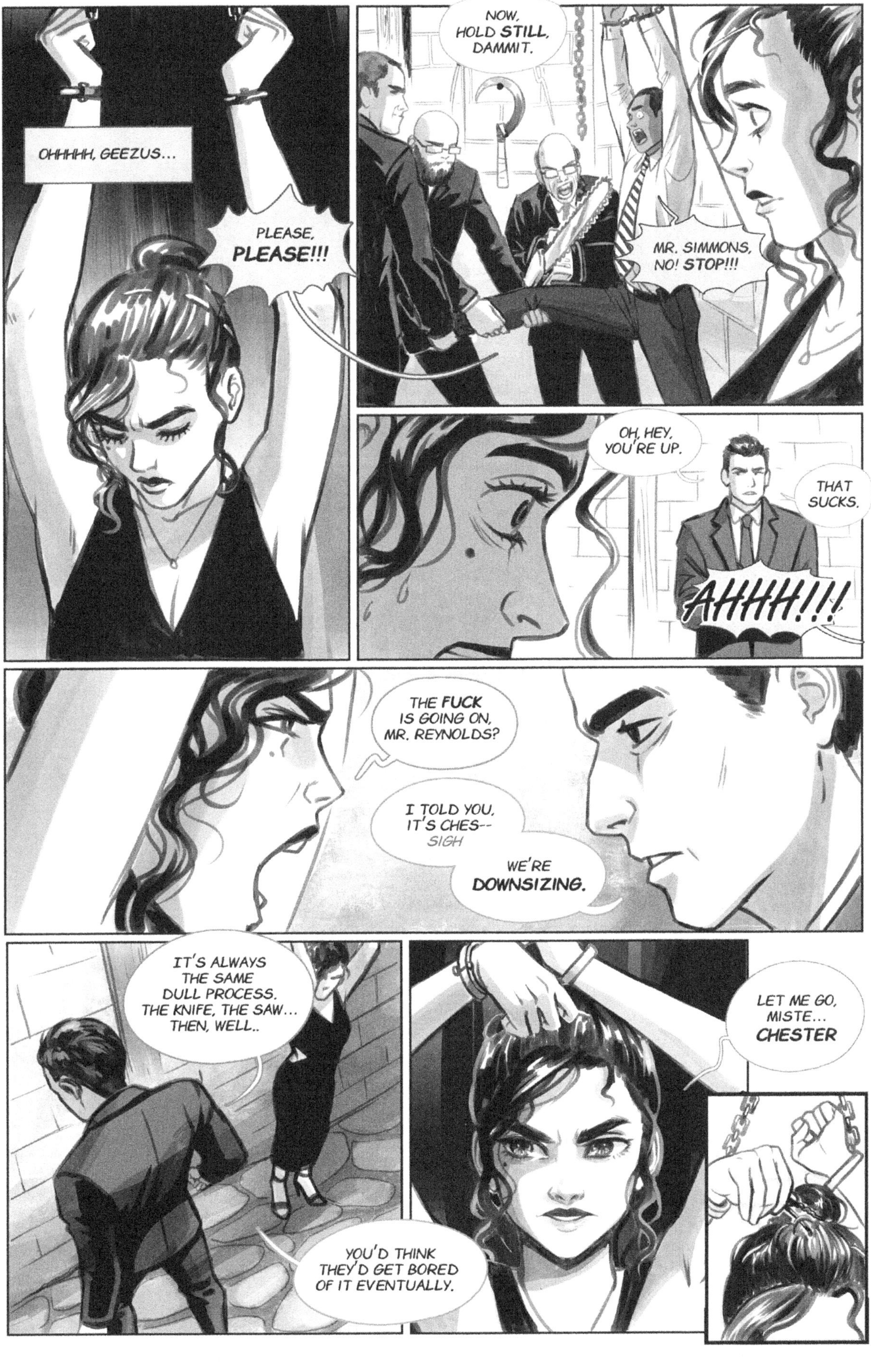
OHHHHH, GEEZUS...
PLEASE, PLEASE!!!
NOW, HOLD STILL, DAMMIT.
MR. SIMMONS, NO! STOP!!!
OH, HEY, YOU'RE UP.
THAT SUCKS.
AHHH!!!
THE FUCK IS GOING ON, MR. REYNOLDS?
I TOLD YOU, IT'S CHES-- SIGH
WE'RE DOWNSIZING.
IT'S ALWAYS THE SAME DULL PROCESS. THE KNIFE, THE SAW... THEN, WELL..
YOU'D THINK THEY'D GET BORED OF IT EVENTUALLY.
LET ME GO, MISTE... CHESTER

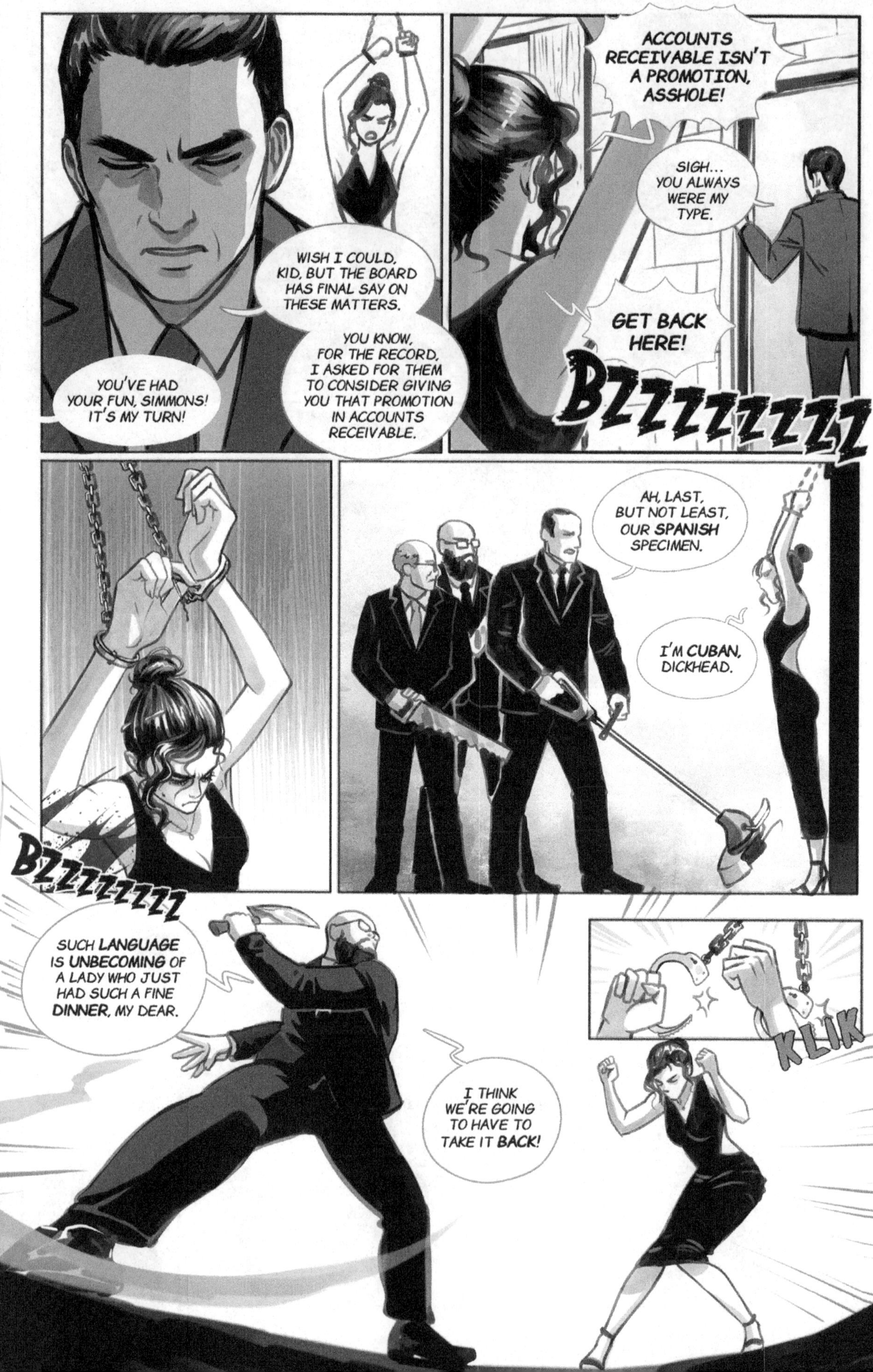

YOU'VE HAD YOUR FUN, SIMMONS! IT'S MY TURN!
WISH I COULD, KID, BUT THE BOARD HAS FINAL SAY ON THESE MATTERS.
YOU KNOW, FOR THE RECORD, I ASKED FOR THEM TO CONSIDER GIVING YOU THAT PROMOTION IN ACCOUNTS RECEIVABLE.
ACCOUNTS RECEIVABLE ISN'T A PROMOTION, ASSHOLE!
SIGH... YOU ALWAYS WERE MY TYPE.
GET BACK HERE!
BZZZZZZZZZ
BZZZZZZZZZ
AH, LAST, BUT NOT LEAST, OUR SPANISH SPECIMEN.
I'M CUBAN, DICKHEAD.
SUCH LANGUAGE IS UNBECOMING OF A LADY WHO JUST HAD SUCH A FINE DINNER, MY DEAR.
KLIK
I THINK WE'RE GOING TO HAVE TO TAKE IT BACK!

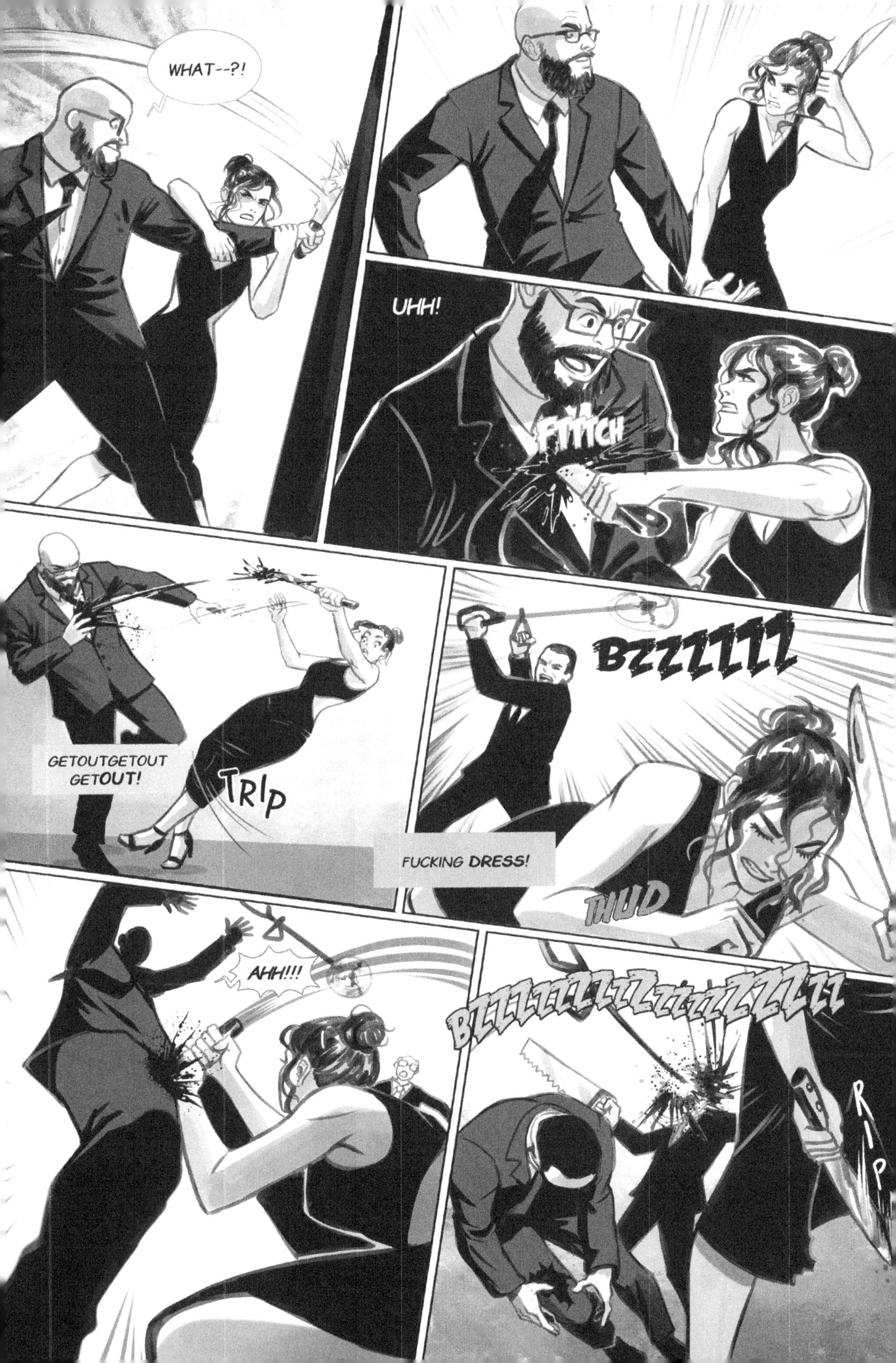
WHAT--?!
UHH!
FTTTCH
GETOUTGETOUT GETOUT!
TRIP
BZZZZZZZ
FUCKING DRESS!
THUD
AHH!!!
BZZZZZZZZZZZZZZZZZZZ
RIP

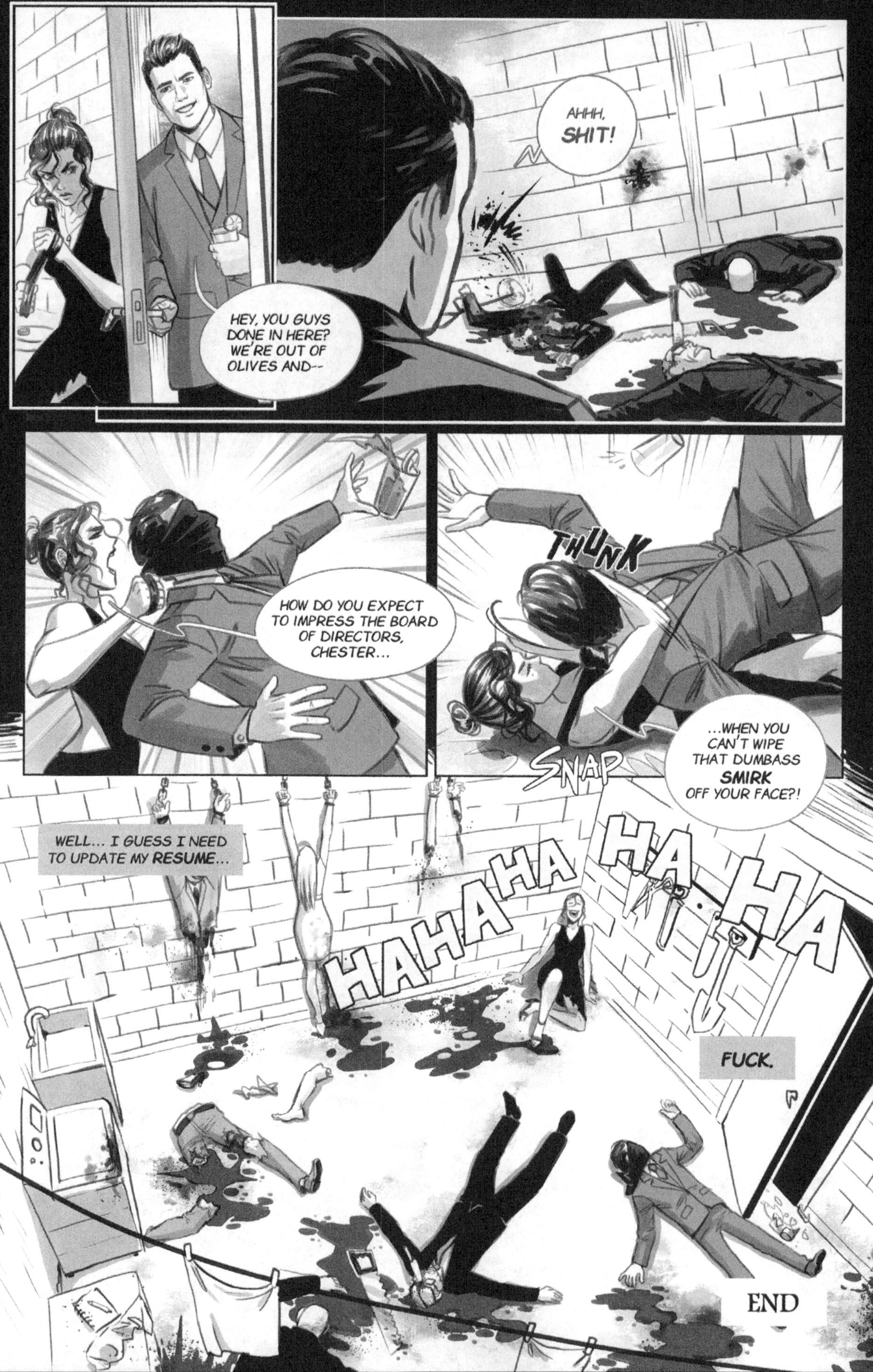
HEY, YOU GUYS DONE IN HERE? WE'RE OUT OF OLIVES AND--
AHHH, SHIT!
HOW DO YOU EXPECT TO IMPRESS THE BOARD OF DIRECTORS, CHESTER...
THUNK
SNAP
...WHEN YOU CAN'T WIPE THAT DUMBASS SMIRK OFF YOUR FACE?!
WELL... I GUESS I NEED TO UPDATE MY RESUME...
HAHAHAHA HA HA HA
FUCK.
END

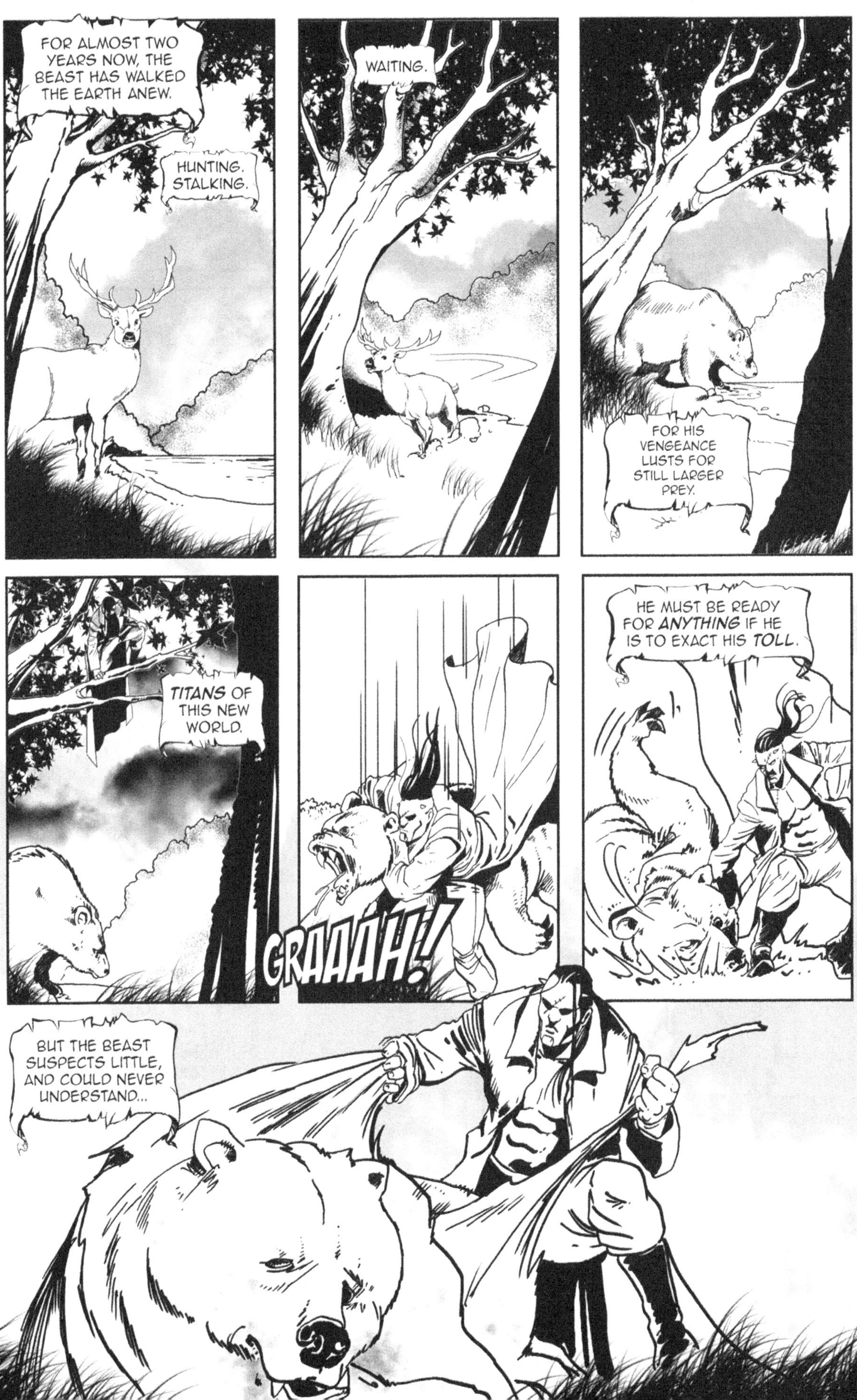

FOR ALMOST TWO YEARS NOW, THE BEAST HAS WALKED THE EARTH ANEW.
HUNTING. STALKING.
WAITING.
FOR HIS VENGEANCE LUSTS FOR STILL LARGER PREY.
TITANS OF THIS NEW WORLD.
GRAAAH!
HE MUST BE READY FOR ANYTHING IF HE IS TO EXACT HIS TOLL.
BUT THE BEAST SUSPECTS LITTLE, AND COULD NEVER UNDERSTAND...

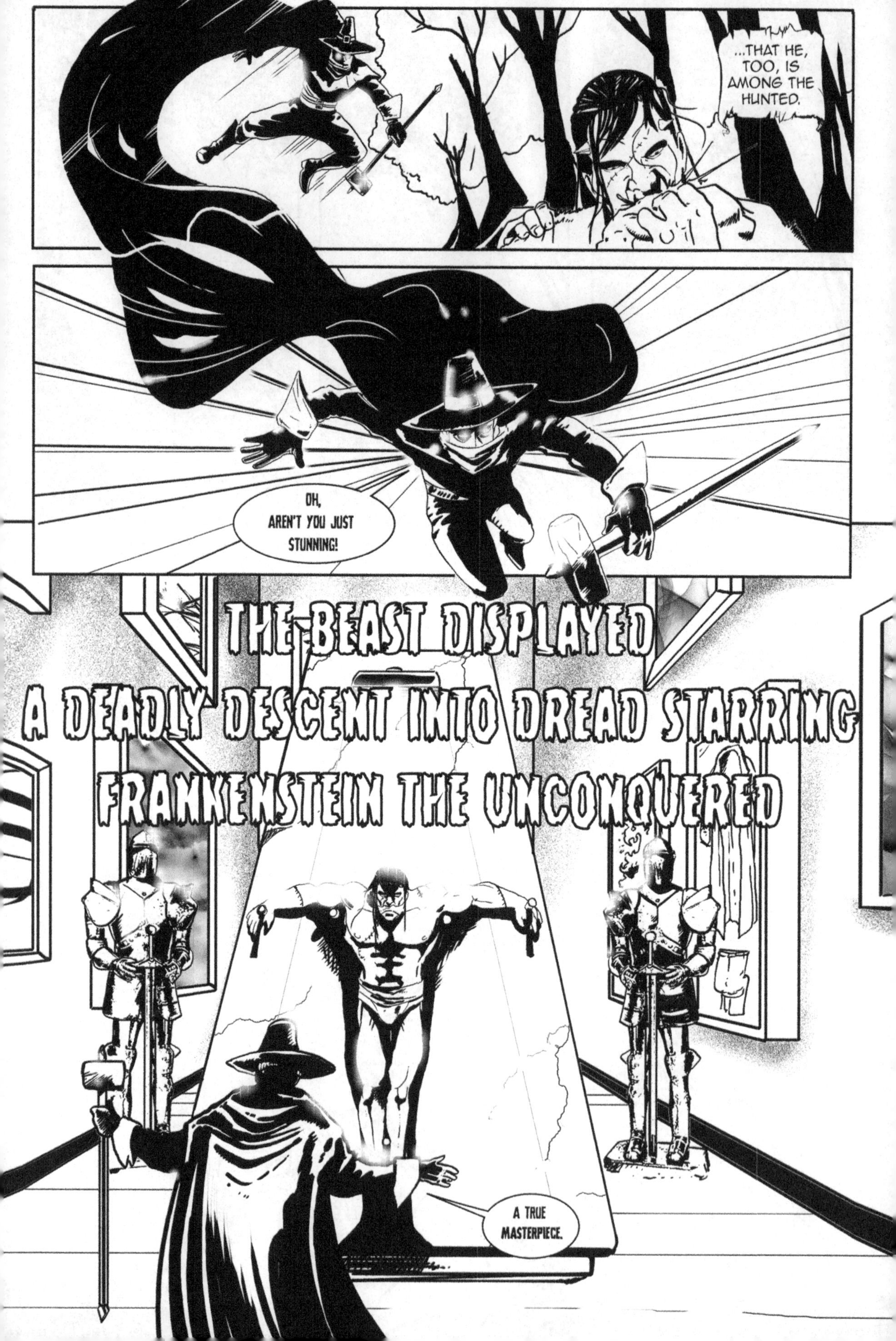

...THAT HE, TOO, IS AMONG THE HUNTED.
OH, AREN'T YOU JUST STUNNING!
THE BEAST DISPLAYED
A DEADLY DESCENT INTO DREAD STARRING
FRANKENSTEIN THE UNCONQUERED
A TRUE MASTERPIECE.

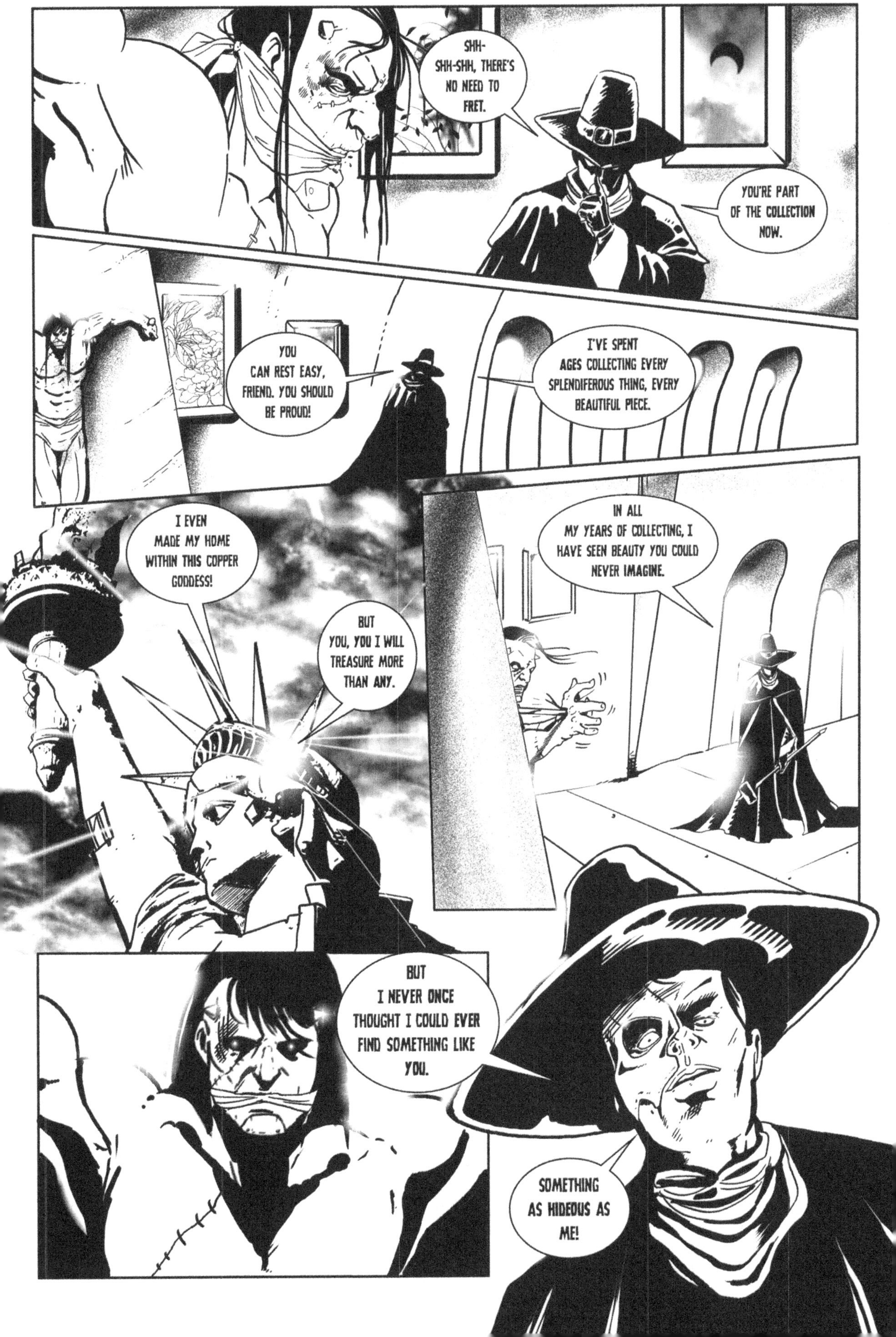
SHH-SHH-SHH, THERE'S NO NEED TO FRET.
YOU'RE PART OF THE COLLECTION NOW.
YOU CAN REST EASY, FRIEND. YOU SHOULD BE PROUD!
I'VE SPENT AGES COLLECTING EVERY SPLENDIFEROUS THING, EVERY BEAUTIFUL PIECE.
I EVEN MADE MY HOME WITHIN THIS COPPER GODDESS!
BUT YOU, YOU I WILL TREASURE MORE THAN ANY.
IN ALL MY YEARS OF COLLECTING, I HAVE SEEN BEAUTY YOU COULD NEVER IMAGINE.
BUT I NEVER ONCE THOUGHT I COULD EVER FIND SOMETHING LIKE YOU.
SOMETHING AS HIDEOUS AS ME!

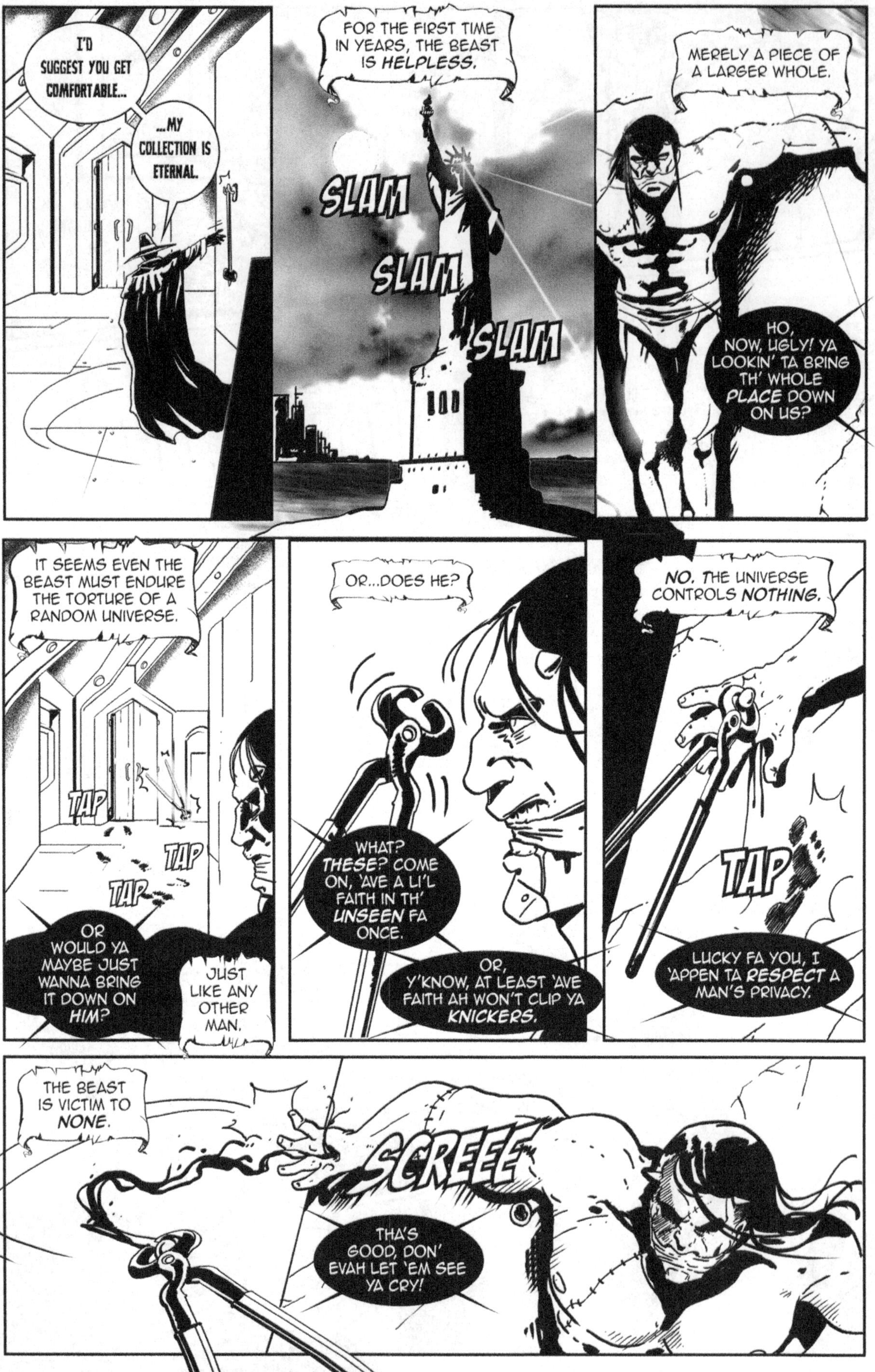
I'D SUGGEST YOU GET COMFORTABLE...
...MY COLLECTION IS ETERNAL.
FOR THE FIRST TIME IN YEARS, THE BEAST IS HELPLESS.
SLAM
SLAM
SLAM
MERELY A PIECE OF A LARGER WHOLE.
HO, NOW, UGLY! YA LOOKIN' TA BRING TH' WHOLE PLACE DOWN ON US?
IT SEEMS EVEN THE BEAST MUST ENDURE THE TORTURE OF A RANDOM UNIVERSE.
TAP
TAP
TAP
OR WOULD YA MAYBE JUST WANNA BRING IT DOWN ON HIM?
JUST LIKE ANY OTHER MAN.
OR...DOES HE?
WHAT? THESE? COME ON, 'AVE A LI'L FAITH IN TH' UNSEEN FA ONCE.
OR, Y'KNOW, AT LEAST 'AVE FAITH AH WON'T CLIP YA KNICKERS.
NO. THE UNIVERSE CONTROLS NOTHING.
TAP
LUCKY FA YOU, I 'APPEN TA RESPECT A MAN'S PRIVACY.
THE BEAST IS VICTIM TO NONE.
SCREEE
THA'S GOOD, DON' EVAH LET 'EM SEE YA CRY!

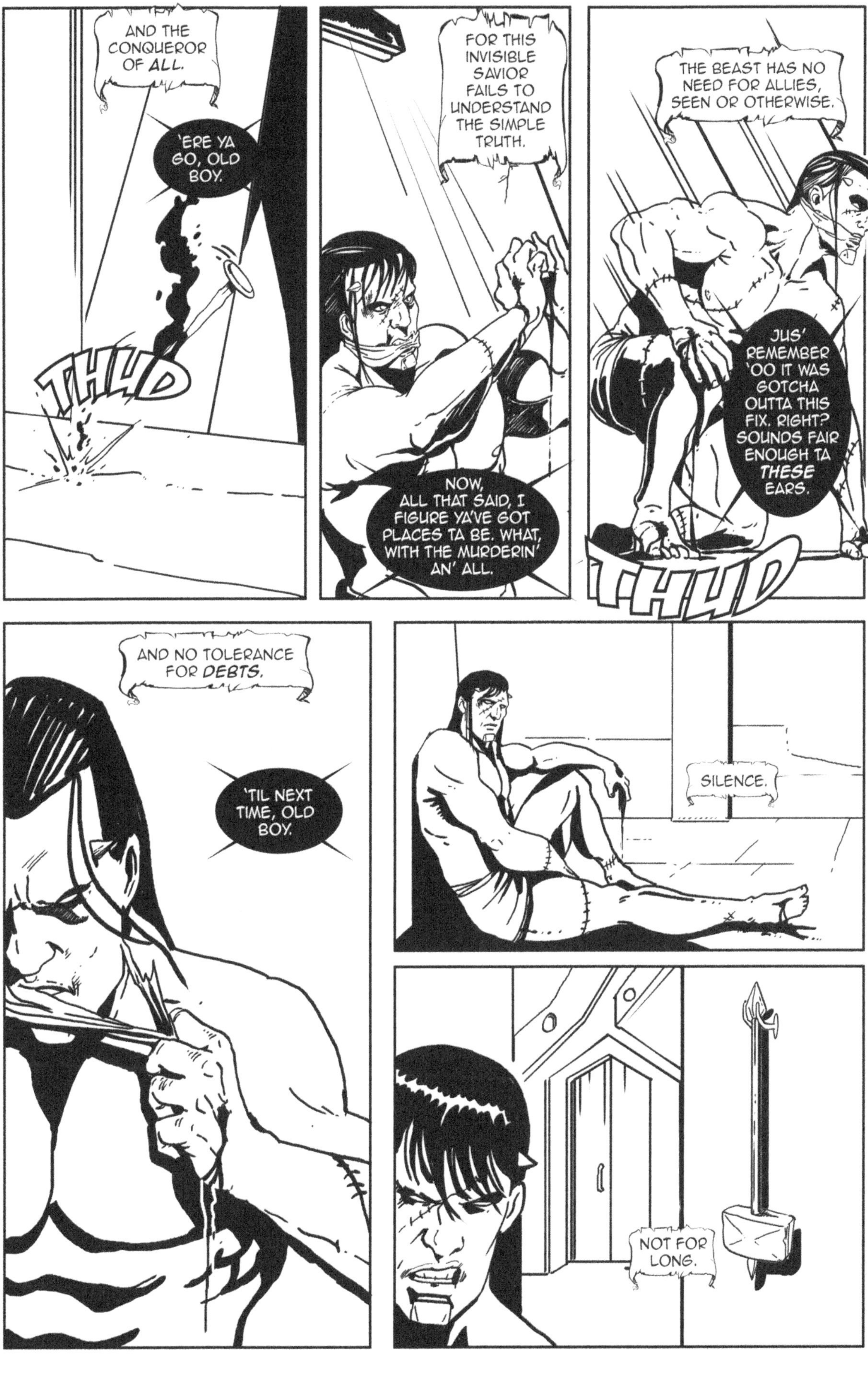
AND THE CONQUEROR OF ALL.
'ERE YA GO, OLD BOY.
THUD
FOR THIS INVISIBLE SAVIOR FAILS TO UNDERSTAND THE SIMPLE TRUTH.
NOW, ALL THAT SAID, I FIGURE YA'VE GOT PLACES TA BE. WHAT, WITH THE MURDERIN' AN' ALL.
THE BEAST HAS NO NEED FOR ALLIES, SEEN OR OTHERWISE.
JUS' REMEMBER 'OO IT WAS GOTCHA OUTTA THIS FIX. RIGHT? SOUNDS FAIR ENOUGH TA THESE EARS.
THUD
AND NO TOLERANCE FOR DEBTS.
'TIL NEXT TIME, OLD BOY.
SILENCE.
NOT FOR LONG.

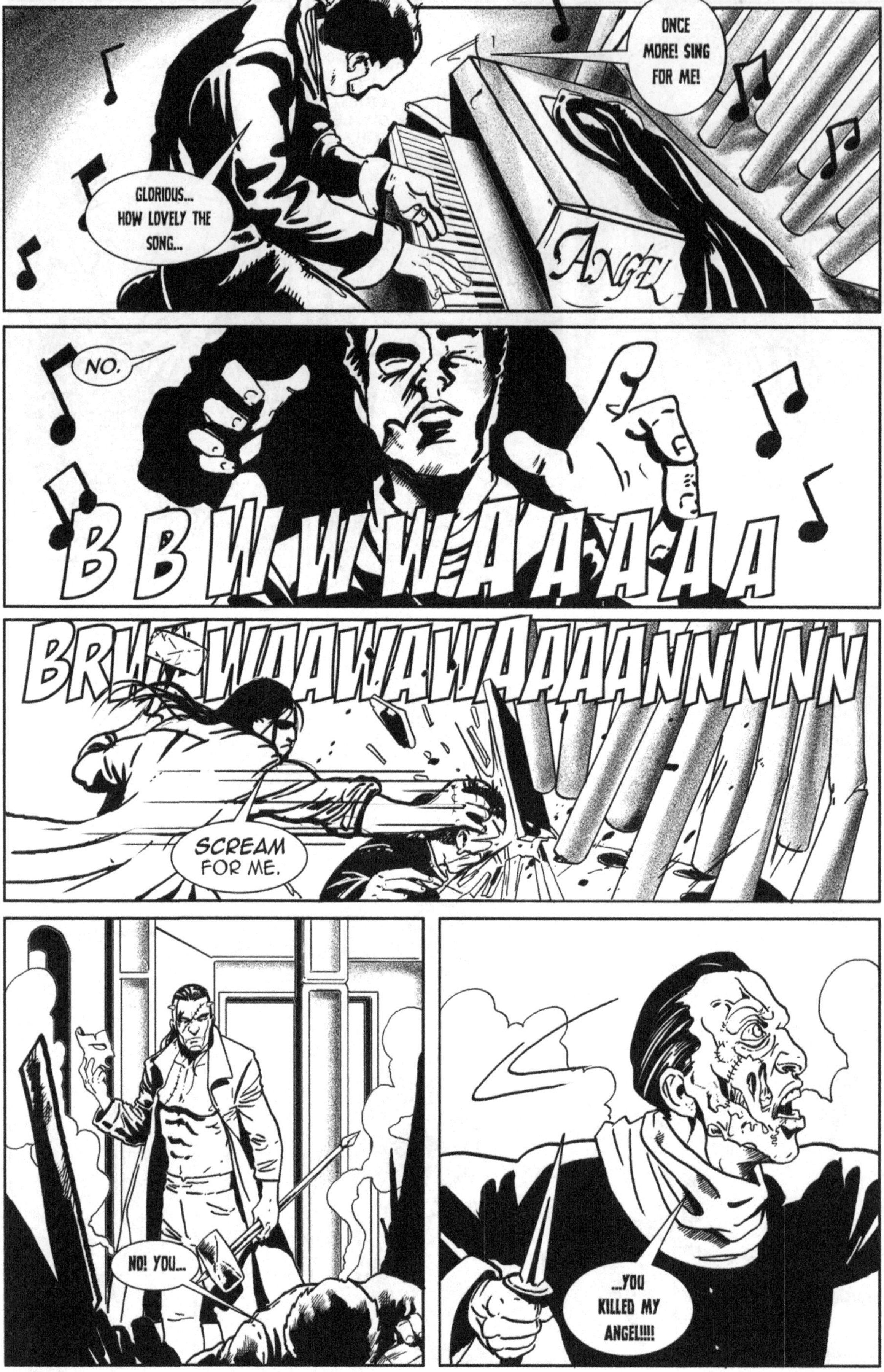
ONCE MORE! SING FOR ME!
GLORIOUS... HOW LOVELY THE SONG...
ANGEL
NO.
BBWWWAAAAA
BRWWOAWAWAAAANNNNN
SCREAM FOR ME.
NO! YOU...
...YOU KILLED MY ANGEL!!!!

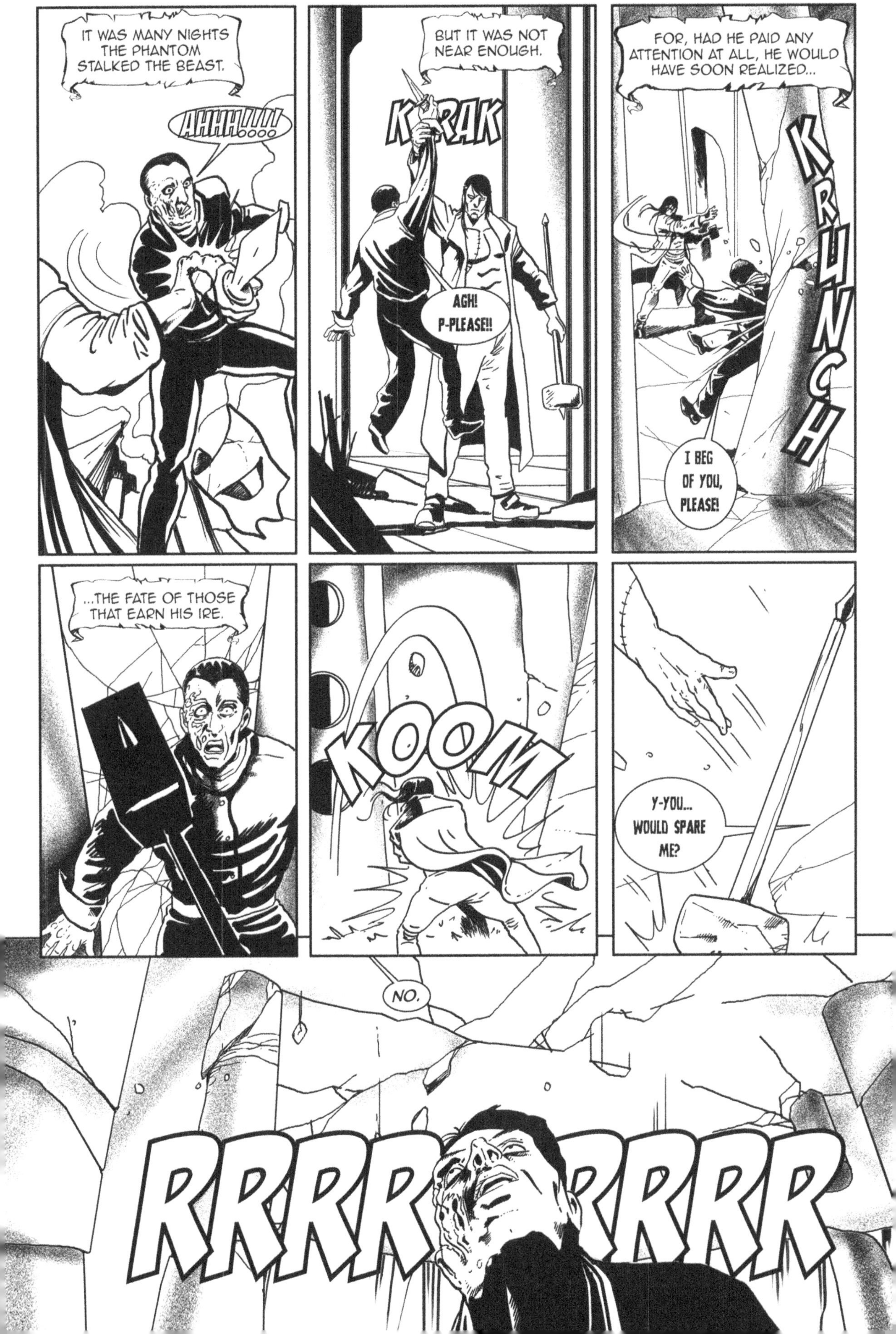
IT WAS MANY NIGHTS THE PHANTOM STALKED THE BEAST.
AHHH!!!!oooo
BUT IT WAS NOT NEAR ENOUGH.
KRAK
AGH! P-PLEASE!!
FOR, HAD HE PAID ANY ATTENTION AT ALL, HE WOULD HAVE SOON REALIZED...
KRUNCH
I BEG OF YOU, PLEASE!
...THE FATE OF THOSE THAT EARN HIS IRE.
KOOM
Y-YOU... WOULD SPARE ME?
NO.
RRRRRRRRR

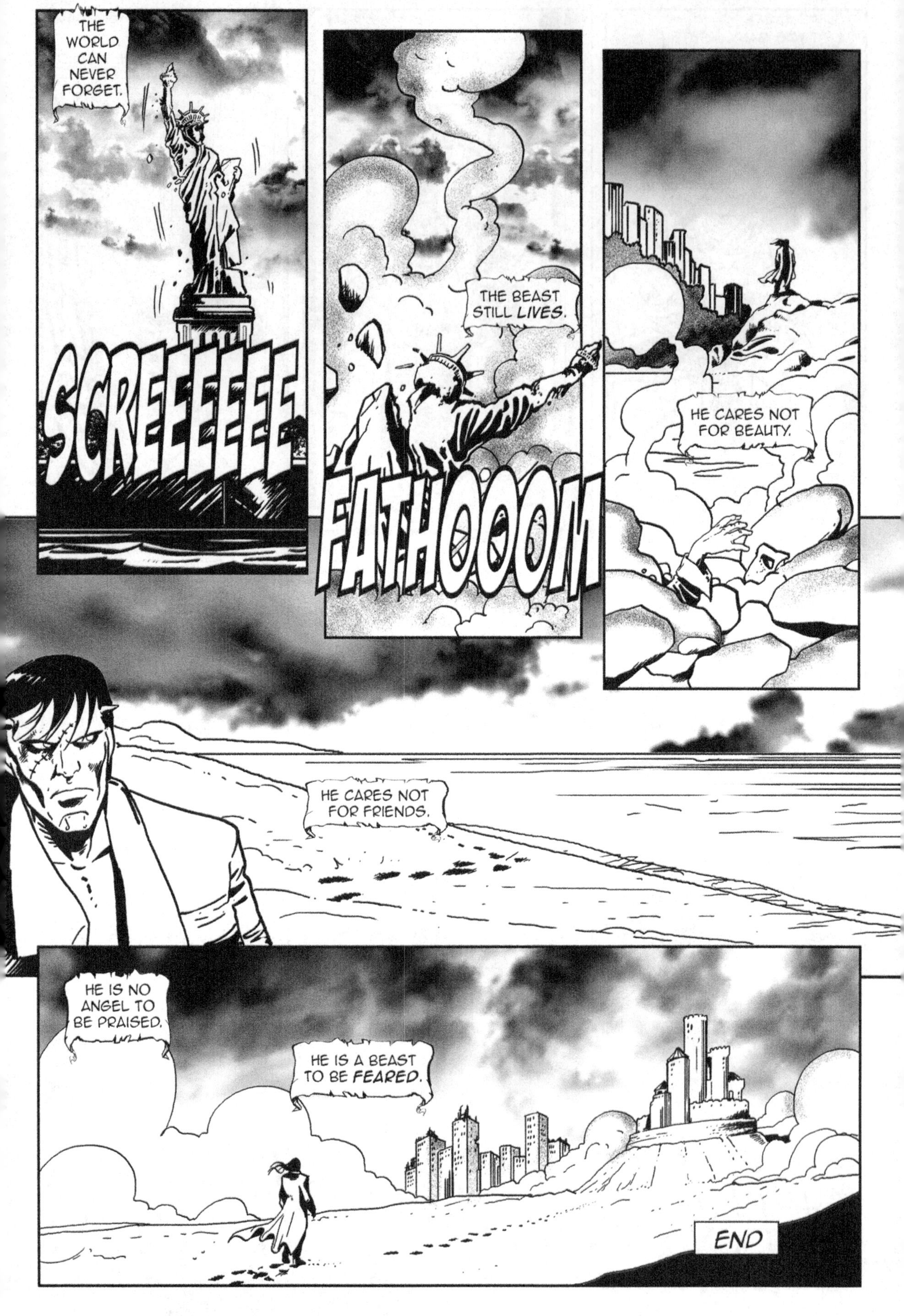
THE WORLD CAN NEVER FORGET.
SCREEEEEE
THE BEAST STILL *LIVES*.
FATHOOOM
HE CARES NOT FOR BEAUTY.
HE CARES NOT FOR FRIENDS.
HE IS NO ANGEL TO BE PRAISED.
HE IS A BEAST TO BE *FEARED*.
END

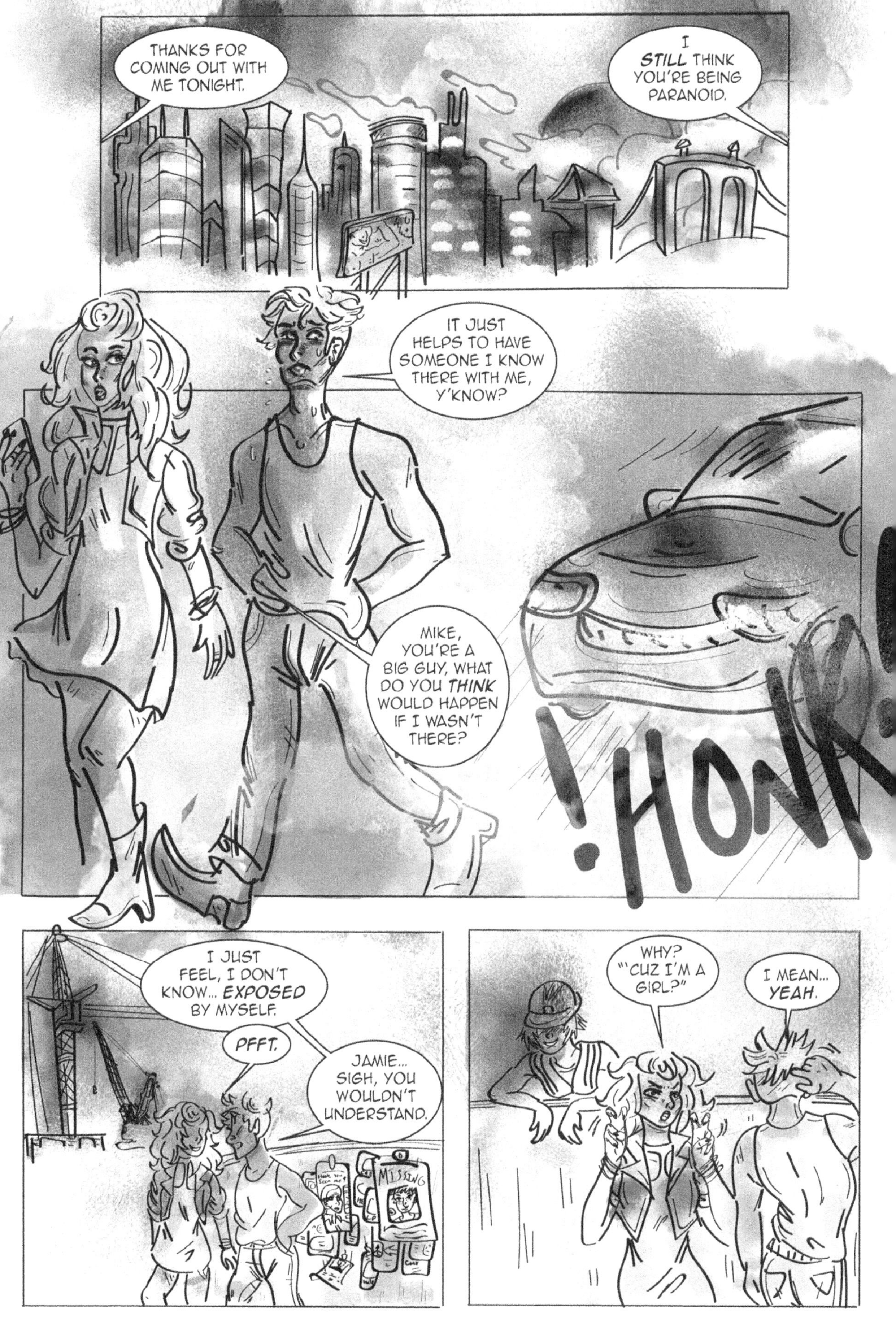
THANKS FOR COMING OUT WITH ME TONIGHT.
I STILL THINK YOU'RE BEING PARANOID.
IT JUST HELPS TO HAVE SOMEONE I KNOW THERE WITH ME, Y'KNOW?
MIKE, YOU'RE A BIG GUY, WHAT DO YOU THINK WOULD HAPPEN IF I WASN'T THERE?
!HONK!
I JUST FEEL, I DON'T KNOW... EXPOSED BY MYSELF.
PFFT.
JAMIE... SIGH, YOU WOULDN'T UNDERSTAND.
MISSING
WHY? "'CUZ I'M A GIRL?"
I MEAN... YEAH.

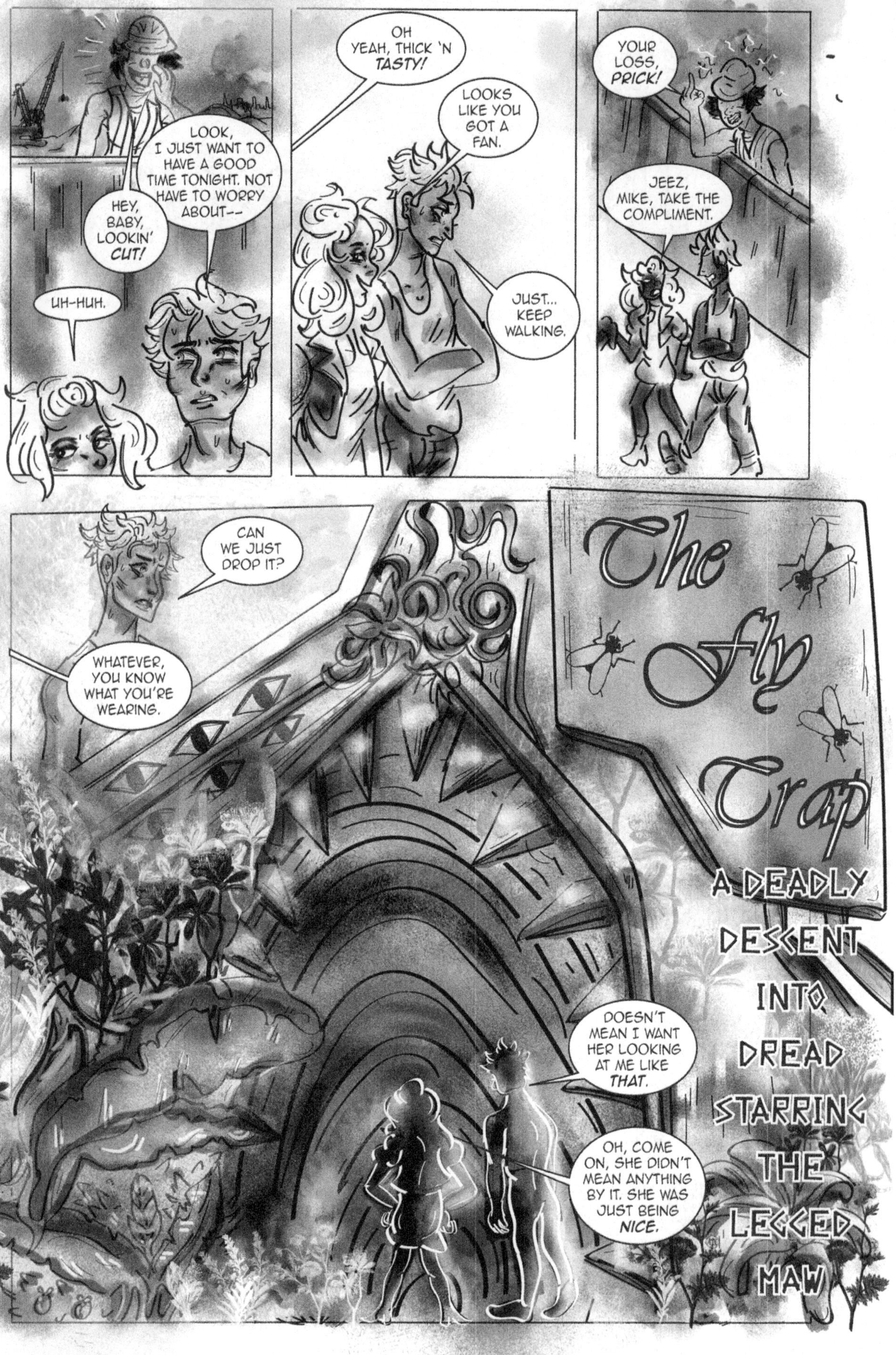
HEY, BABY, LOOKIN' CUT!
LOOK, I JUST WANT TO HAVE A GOOD TIME TONIGHT. NOT HAVE TO WORRY ABOUT--
UH-HUH.
OH YEAH, THICK 'N TASTY!
LOOKS LIKE YOU GOT A FAN.
JUST... KEEP WALKING.
YOUR LOSS, PRICK!
JEEZ, MIKE, TAKE THE COMPLIMENT.
CAN WE JUST DROP IT?
WHATEVER, YOU KNOW WHAT YOU'RE WEARING.
The Fly Trap
DOESN'T MEAN I WANT HER LOOKING AT ME LIKE THAT.
OH, COME ON, SHE DIDN'T MEAN ANYTHING BY IT. SHE WAS JUST BEING NICE.
A DEADLY DESCENT INTO DREAD STARRING THE LEGGED MAW

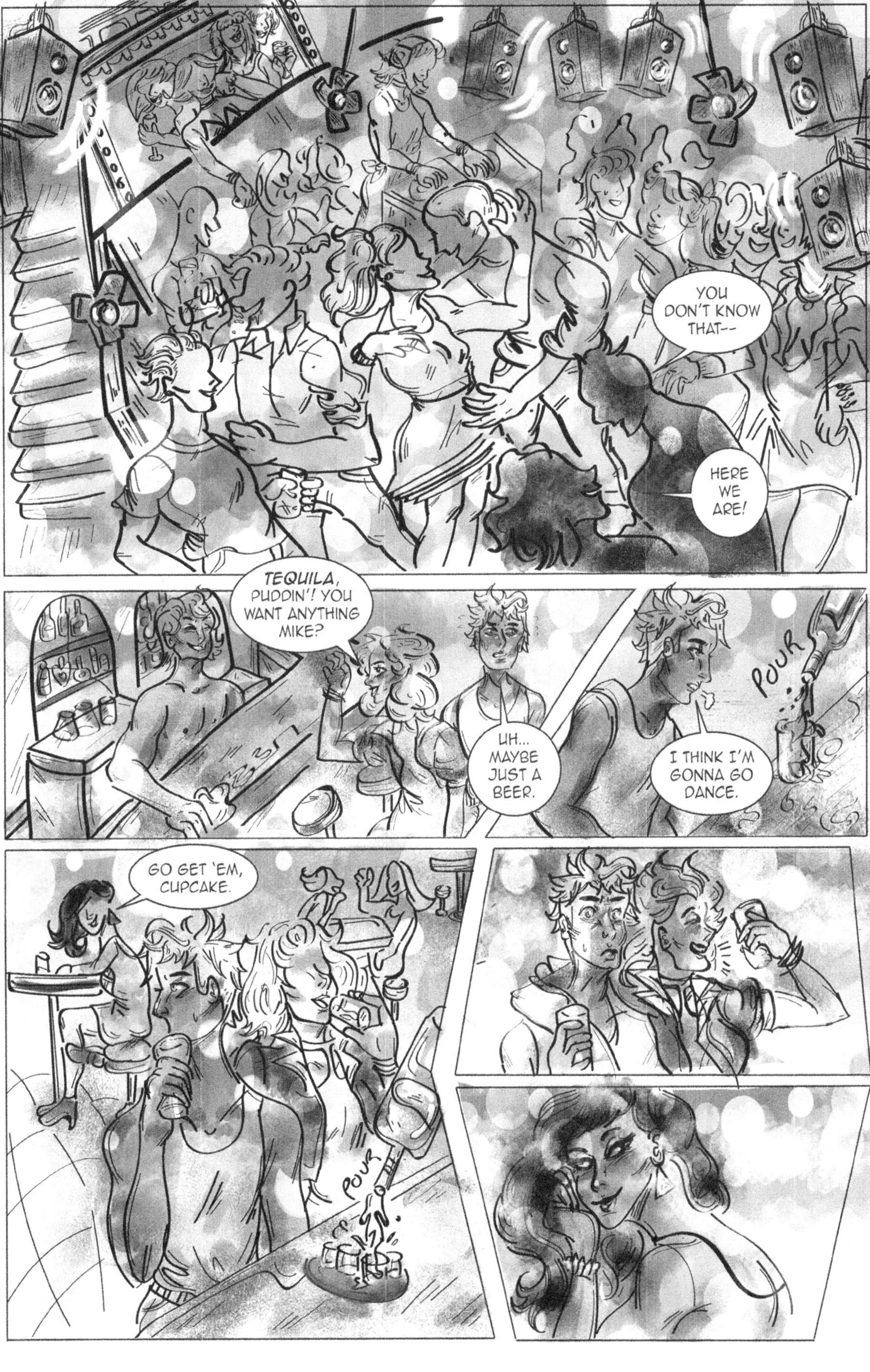
YOU DON'T KNOW THAT--
HERE WE ARE!
TEQUILA, PUDDIN'! YOU WANT ANYTHING MIKE?
UH... MAYBE JUST A BEER.
I THINK I'M GONNA GO DANCE.
POUR
GO GET 'EM, CUPCAKE.
POUR

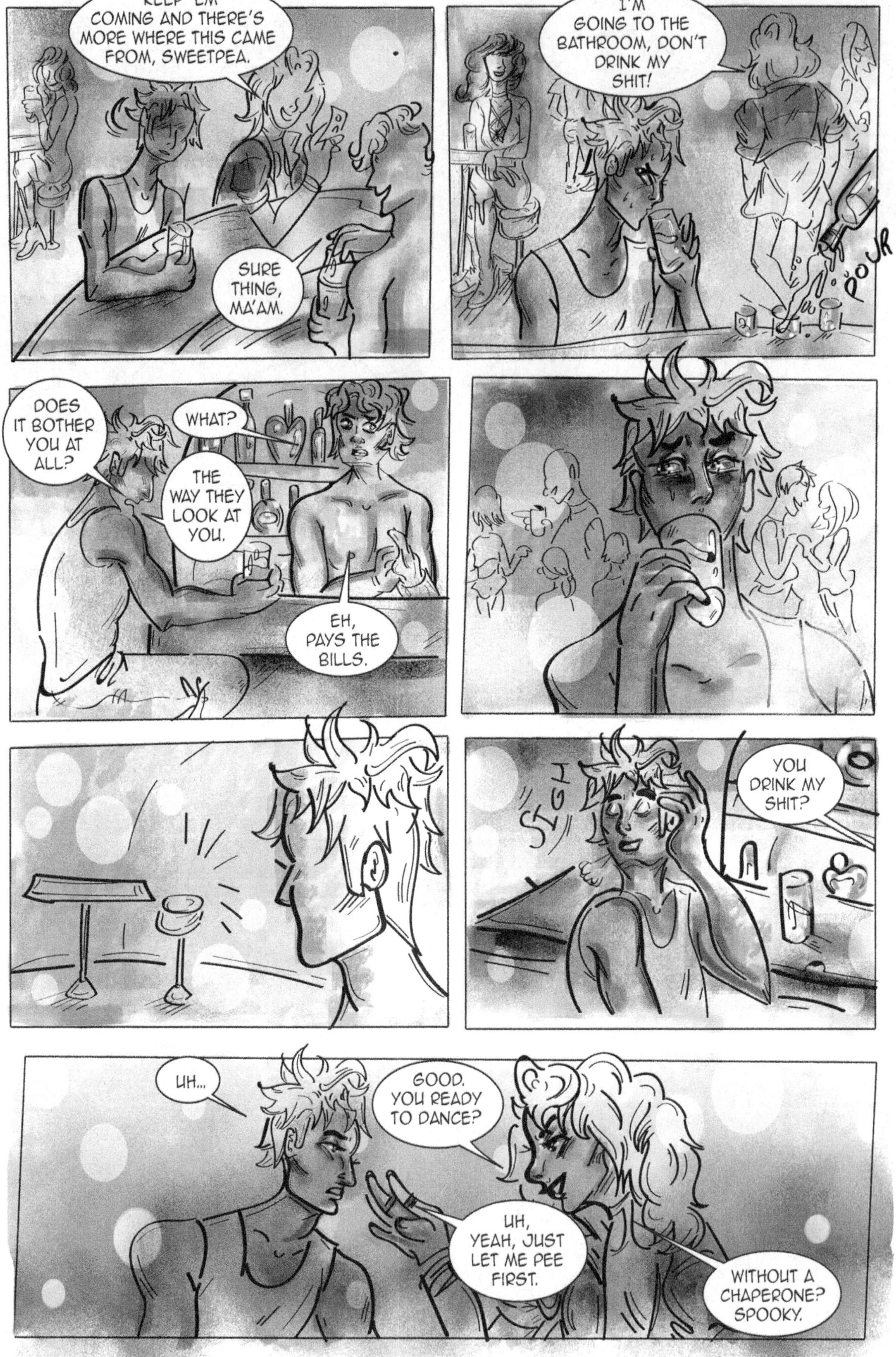
KEEP 'EM COMING AND THERE'S MORE WHERE THIS CAME FROM, SWEETPEA.
SURE THING, MA'AM.
I'M GOING TO THE BATHROOM, DON'T DRINK MY SHIT!
POUR
DOES IT BOTHER YOU AT ALL?
WHAT?
THE WAY THEY LOOK AT YOU.
EH, PAYS THE BILLS.
SIGH
YOU DRINK MY SHIT?
UH...
GOOD. YOU READY TO DANCE?
UH, YEAH, JUST LET ME PEE FIRST.
WITHOUT A CHAPERONE? SPOOKY.

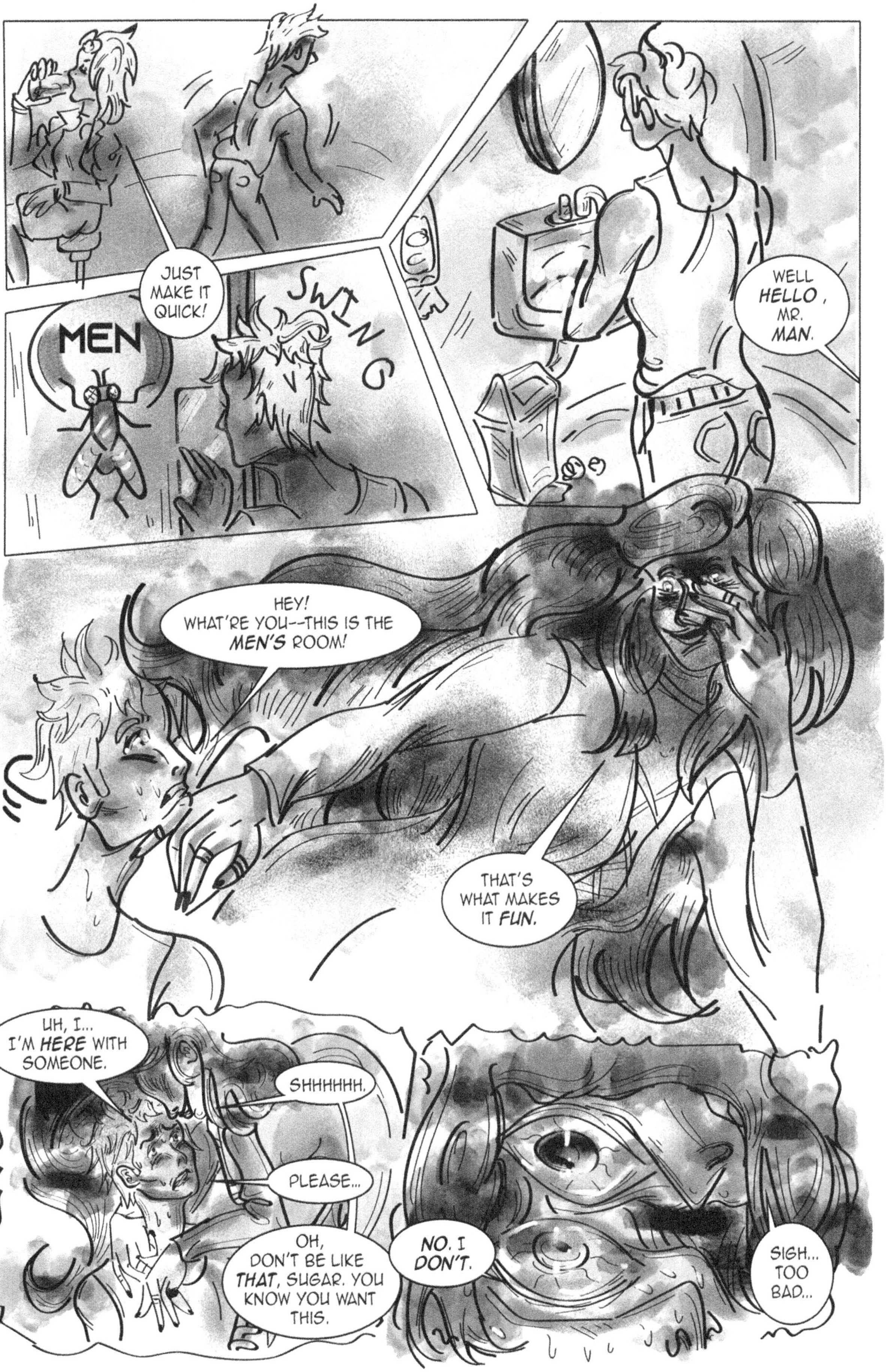
JUST MAKE IT QUICK!
MEN
SWING
WELL HELLO, MR. MAN.
HEY! WHAT'RE YOU--THIS IS THE MEN'S ROOM!
THAT'S WHAT MAKES IT FUN.
UH, I... I'M HERE WITH SOMEONE.
SHHHHHH.
PLEASE...
OH, DON'T BE LIKE THAT, SUGAR. YOU KNOW YOU WANT THIS.
NO. I DON'T.
SIGH... TOO BAD...

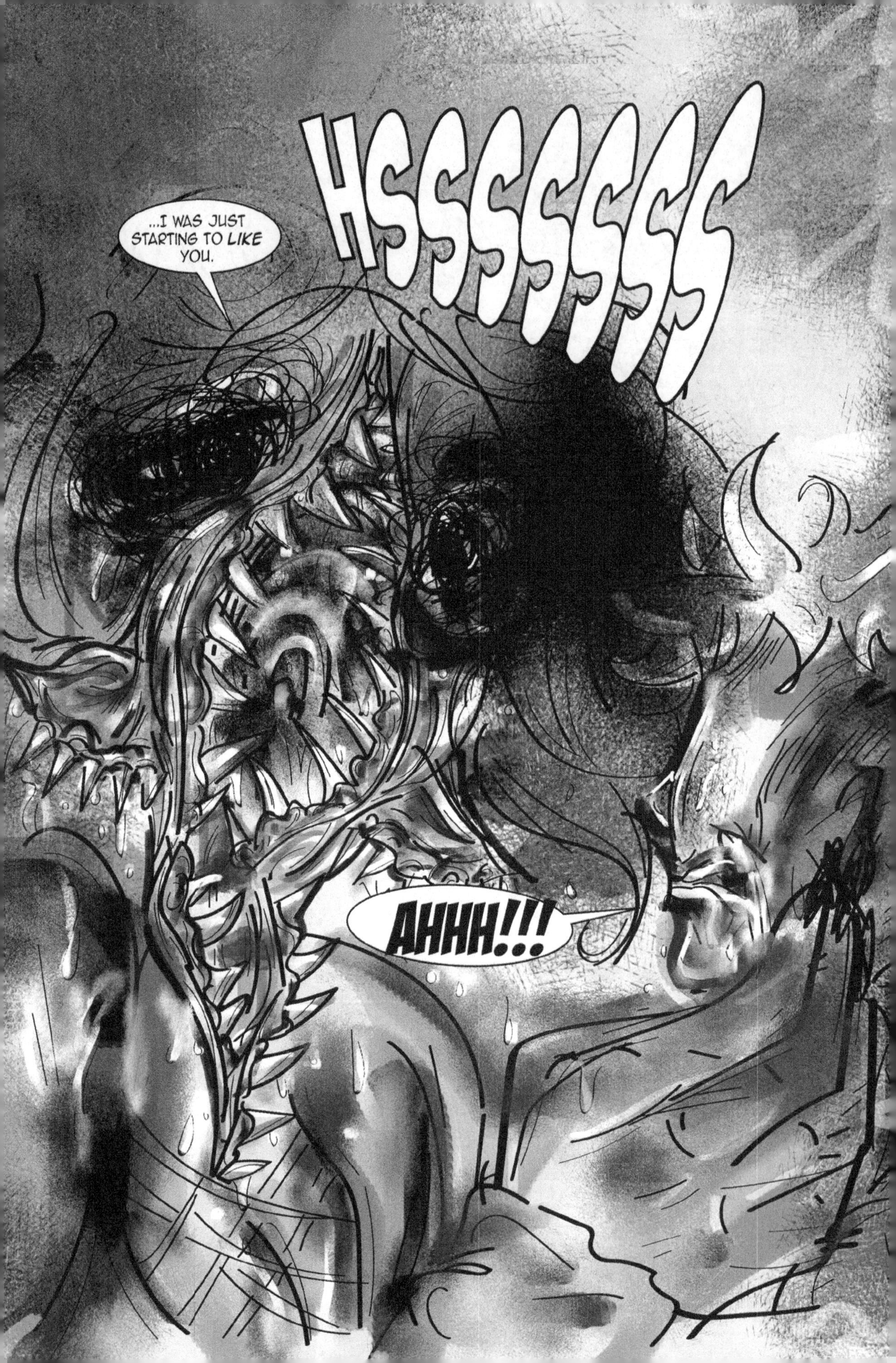
HSSSSSSSS
...I WAS JUST STARTING TO LIKE YOU.
AHHH!!!

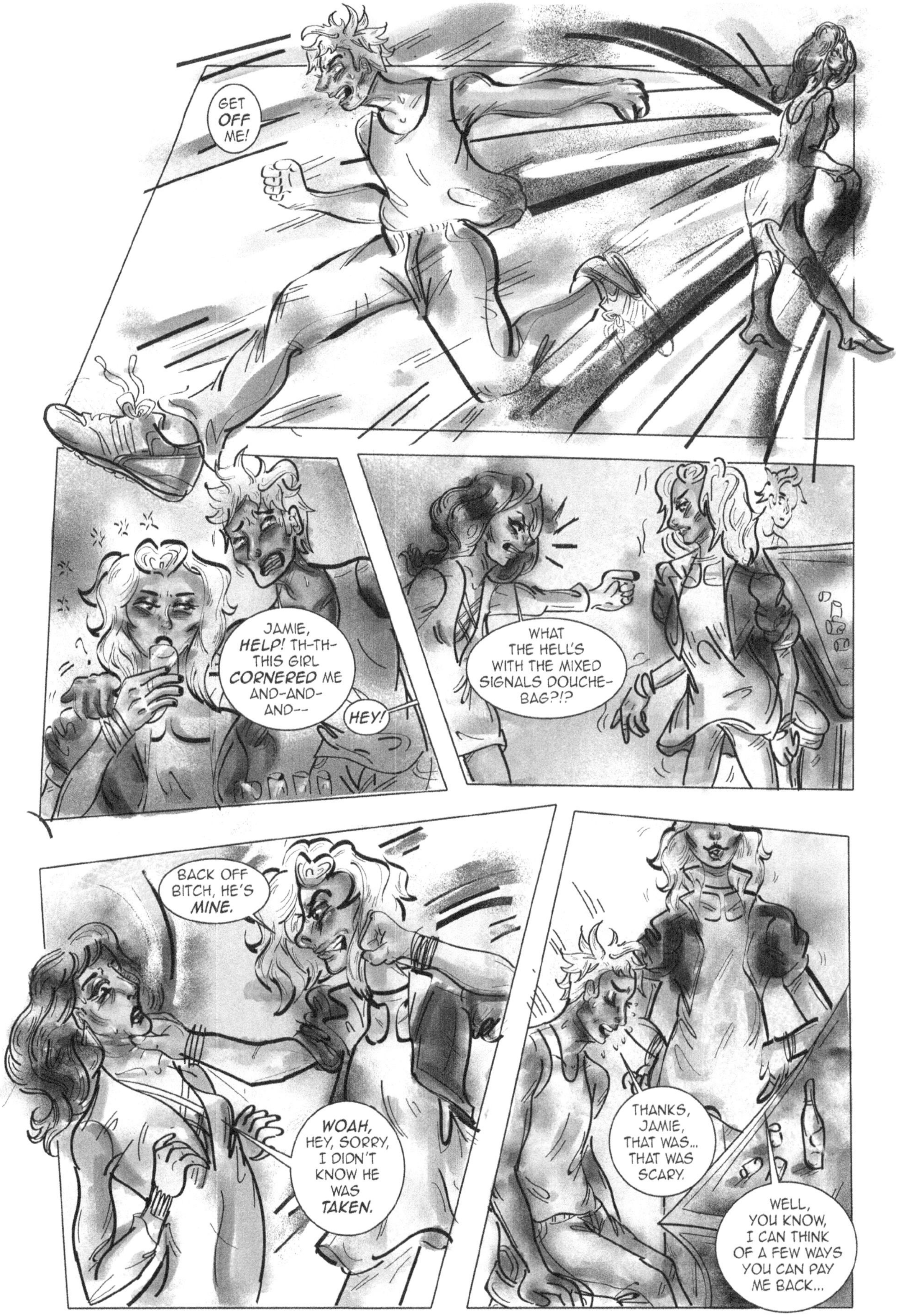
GET OFF ME!
JAMIE, HELP! TH-TH-THIS GIRL CORNERED ME AND-AND-AND--
HEY!
WHAT THE HELL'S WITH THE MIXED SIGNALS DOUCHE-BAG?!?
BACK OFF BITCH, HE'S MINE.
WOAH, HEY, SORRY, I DIDN'T KNOW HE WAS TAKEN.
THANKS, JAMIE, THAT WAS... THAT WAS SCARY.
WELL, YOU KNOW, I CAN THINK OF A FEW WAYS YOU CAN PAY ME BACK...

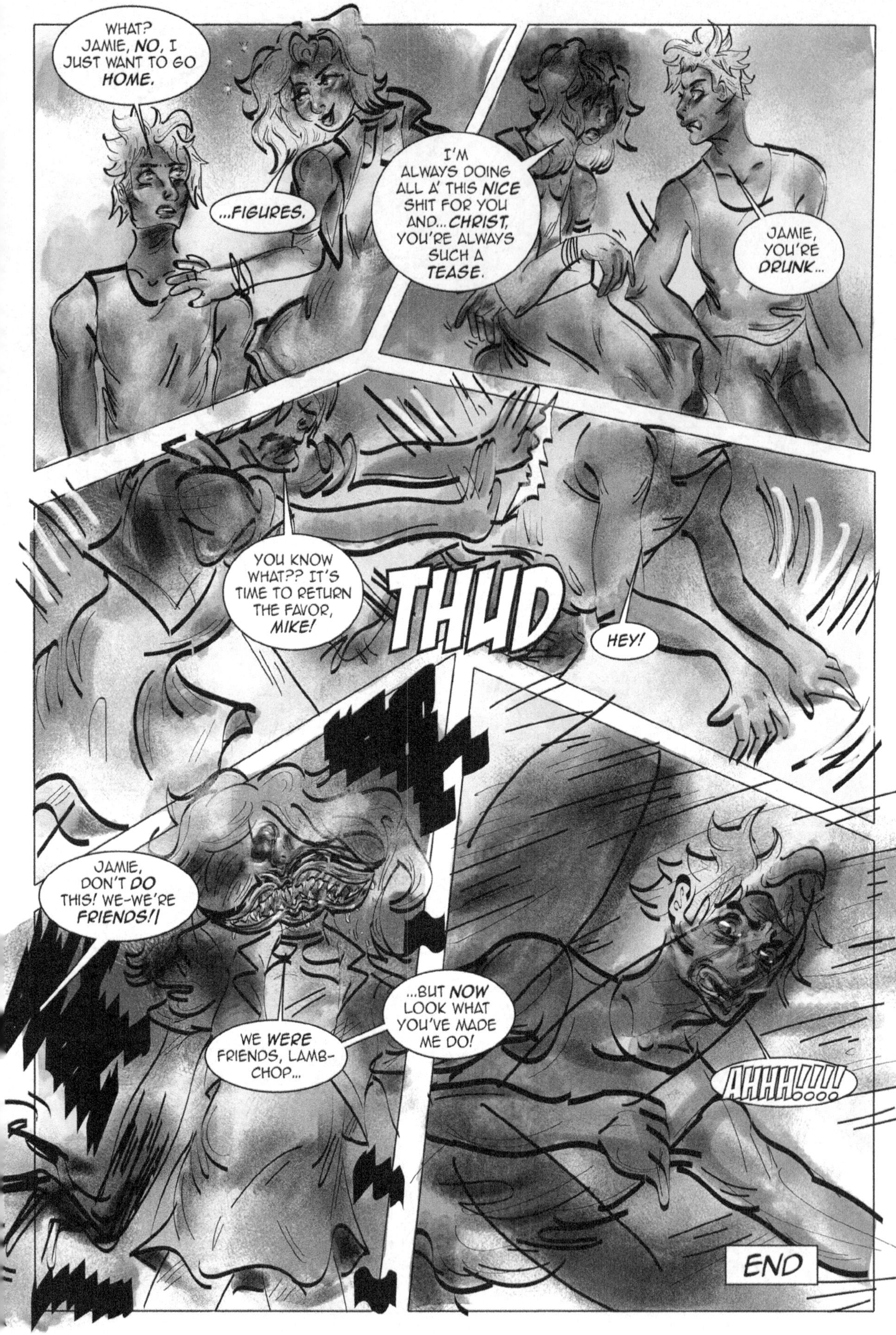
WHAT? JAMIE, NO, I JUST WANT TO GO HOME.
...FIGURES.
I'M ALWAYS DOING ALL A' THIS NICE SHIT FOR YOU AND...CHRIST, YOU'RE ALWAYS SUCH A TEASE.
JAMIE, YOU'RE DRUNK...
YOU KNOW WHAT?? IT'S TIME TO RETURN THE FAVOR, MIKE!
THUD
HEY!
JAMIE, DON'T DO THIS! WE-WE'RE FRIENDS!
WE WERE FRIENDS, LAMB-CHOP...
...BUT NOW LOOK WHAT YOU'VE MADE ME DO!
AHHH!!!!!oooo
END

DEEP IN THE JUNGLES OF BRAZIL

BZZZZZZZZZZZ

THE WHEN MATTERS NOT. FOR ALL INTENTS AND PURPOSES, THIS COULD BE THE FIRST TIME THE GREAT MAHOGANY WAS STRUCK.

OR, PERHAPS NOT.

BZZZZZZRT

THE CREATURE REMAINED PATIENT, HOPEFUL THAT THE SACRILEGE WOULD END BEFORE...

...WELL, BEFORE THINGS GOT WORSE.

HUH?

RUSTLE RUSTLE

BUT NOW THERE CAN BE NO DOUBT.

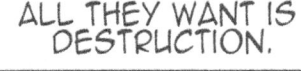

DID YOU GUYS HEAR THAT?

ALL THEY WANT IS DESTRUCTION.

AND THE CREATURE MUST PROTECT ITS CHARGE.

WHAT'S OVER THERE, TOM?

MY GOD, IT'S...

A LINE HAS BEEN CROSSED, AND THE CREATURE MUST CROSS ONE IN KIND.

...IT'S BEAUTIFUL!

THE DESTRUCTION IT HAS WITNESSED MUST BE REDRESSED. SUCH IS THE CREATURE'S....

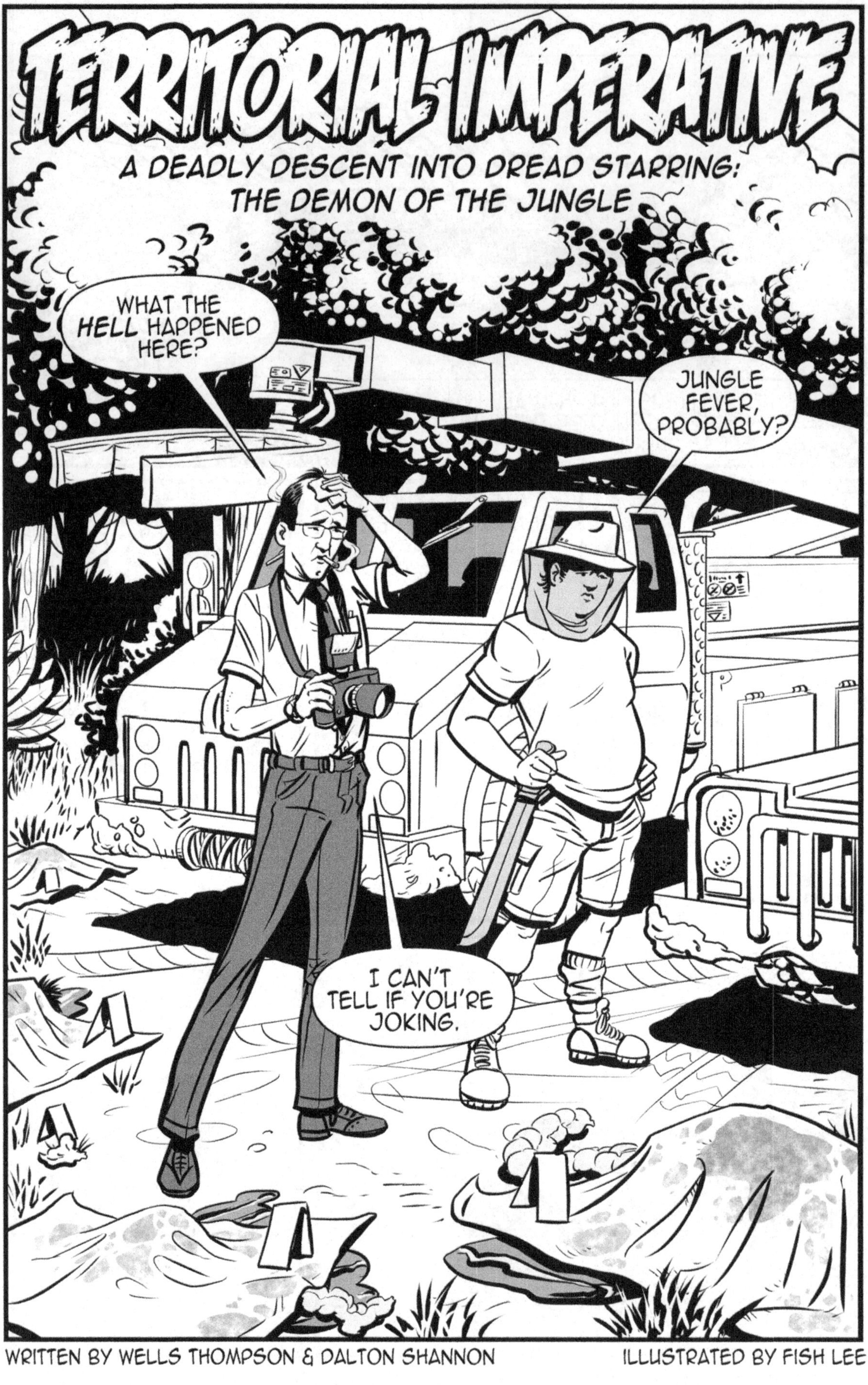
TERRITORIAL IMPERATIVE
A DEADLY DESCENT INTO DREAD STARRING:
THE DEMON OF THE JUNGLE
WHAT THE HELL HAPPENED HERE?
JUNGLE FEVER, PROBABLY?
I CAN'T TELL IF YOU'RE JOKING.

WRITTEN BY WELLS THOMPSON & DALTON SHANNON

ILLUSTRATED BY FISH LEE

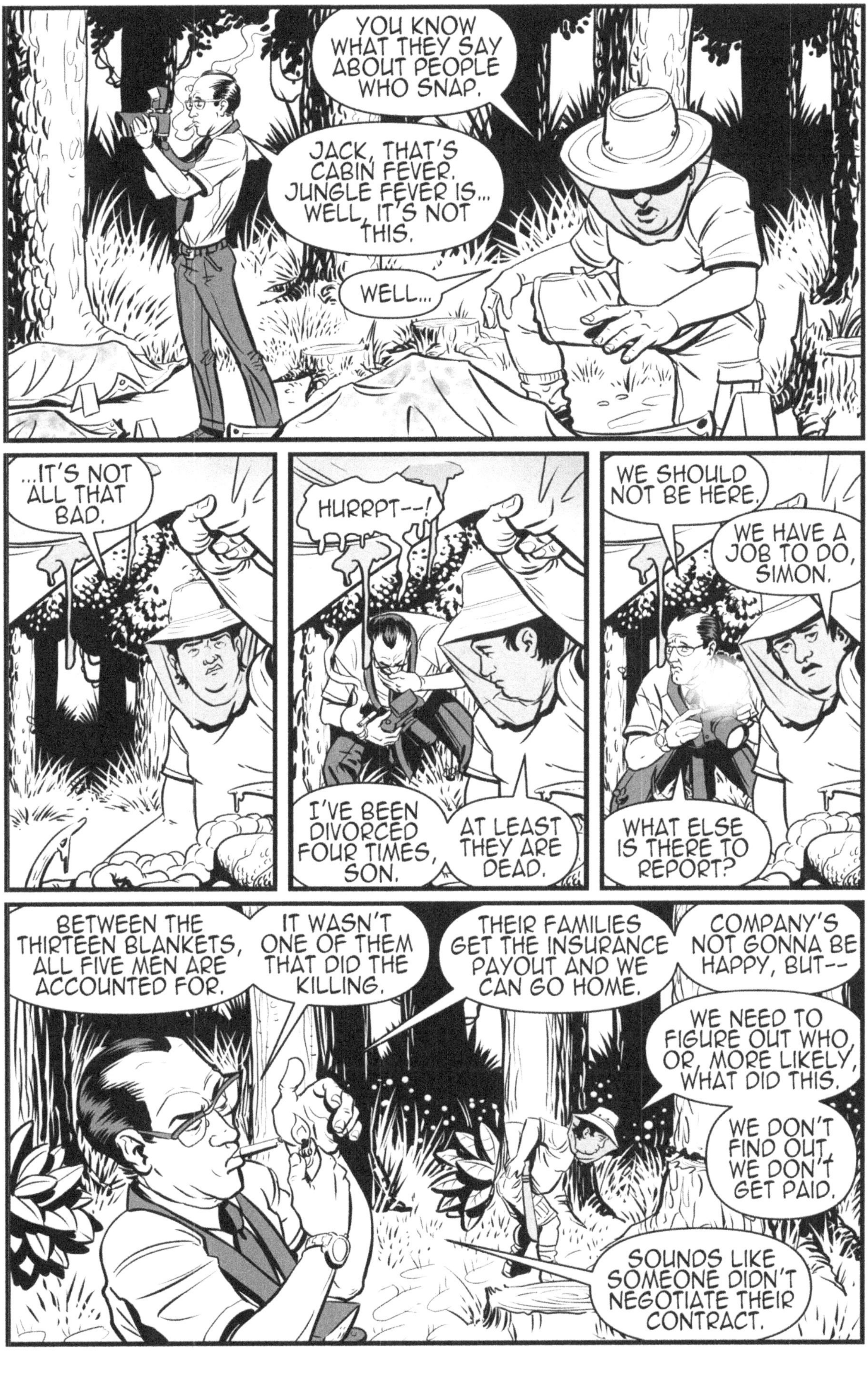
YOU KNOW WHAT THEY SAY ABOUT PEOPLE WHO SNAP.
JACK, THAT'S CABIN FEVER. JUNGLE FEVER IS... WELL, IT'S NOT THIS.
WELL...
...IT'S NOT ALL THAT BAD.
HURRPT--!
I'VE BEEN DIVORCED FOUR TIMES, SON.
AT LEAST THEY ARE DEAD.
WE SHOULD NOT BE HERE.
WE HAVE A JOB TO DO, SIMON.
WHAT ELSE IS THERE TO REPORT?
BETWEEN THE THIRTEEN BLANKETS, ALL FIVE MEN ARE ACCOUNTED FOR.
IT WASN'T ONE OF THEM THAT DID THE KILLING.
THEIR FAMILIES GET THE INSURANCE PAYOUT AND WE CAN GO HOME.
COMPANY'S NOT GONNA BE HAPPY, BUT--
WE NEED TO FIGURE OUT WHO, OR, MORE LIKELY, WHAT DID THIS.
WE DON'T FIND OUT, WE DON'T GET PAID.
SOUNDS LIKE SOMEONE DIDN'T NEGOTIATE THEIR CONTRACT.

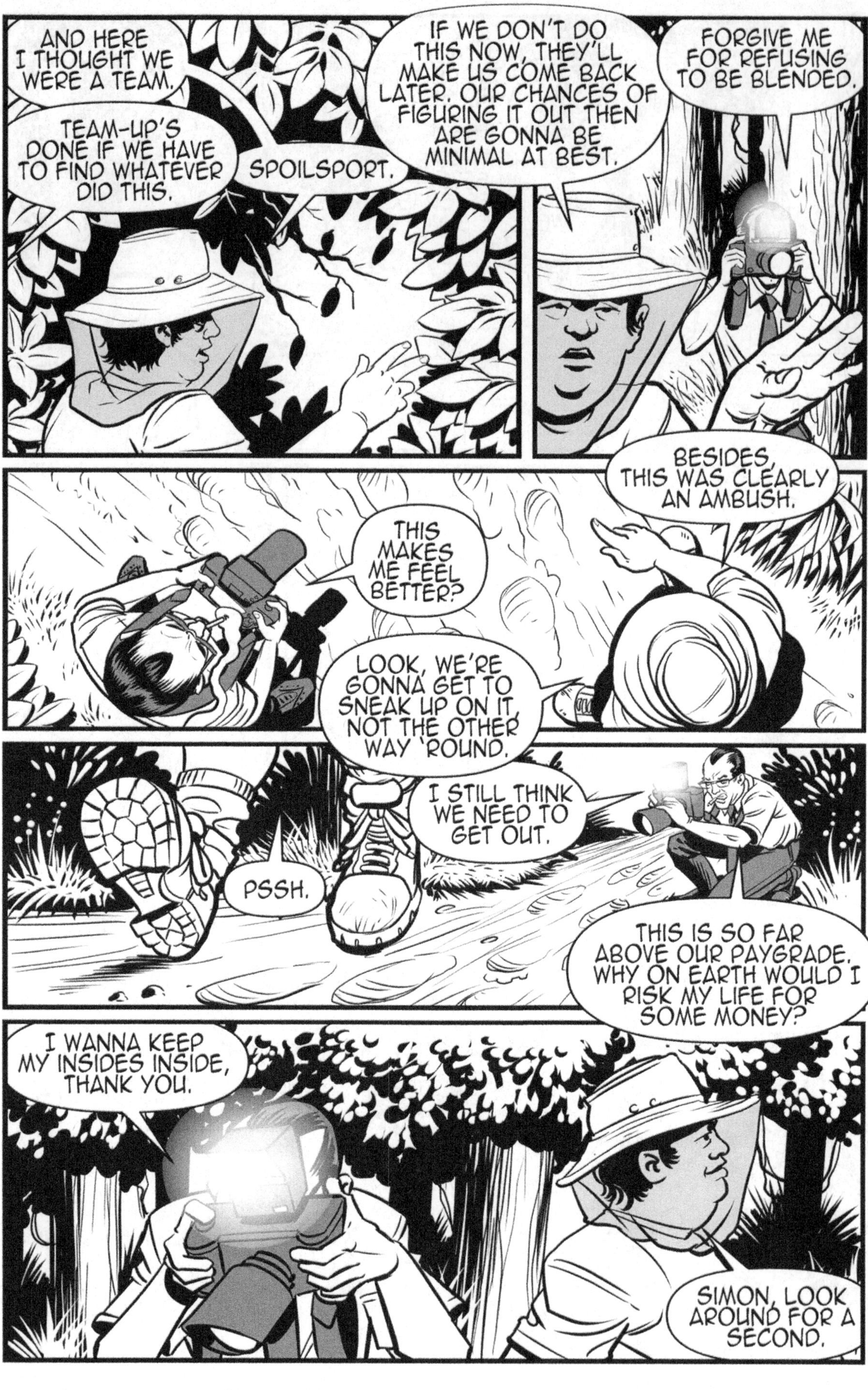
AND HERE I THOUGHT WE WERE A TEAM.
TEAM-UP'S DONE IF WE HAVE TO FIND WHATEVER DID THIS.
SPOILSPORT.
IF WE DON'T DO THIS NOW, THEY'LL MAKE US COME BACK LATER. OUR CHANCES OF FIGURING IT OUT THEN ARE GONNA BE MINIMAL AT BEST.
FORGIVE ME FOR REFUSING TO BE BLENDED.
BESIDES, THIS WAS CLEARLY AN AMBUSH.
THIS MAKES ME FEEL BETTER?
LOOK, WE'RE GONNA GET TO SNEAK UP ON IT, NOT THE OTHER WAY 'ROUND.
PSSH.
I STILL THINK WE NEED TO GET OUT.
THIS IS SO FAR ABOVE OUR PAYGRADE. WHY ON EARTH WOULD I RISK MY LIFE FOR SOME MONEY?
I WANNA KEEP MY INSIDES INSIDE, THANK YOU.
SIMON, LOOK AROUND FOR A SECOND.

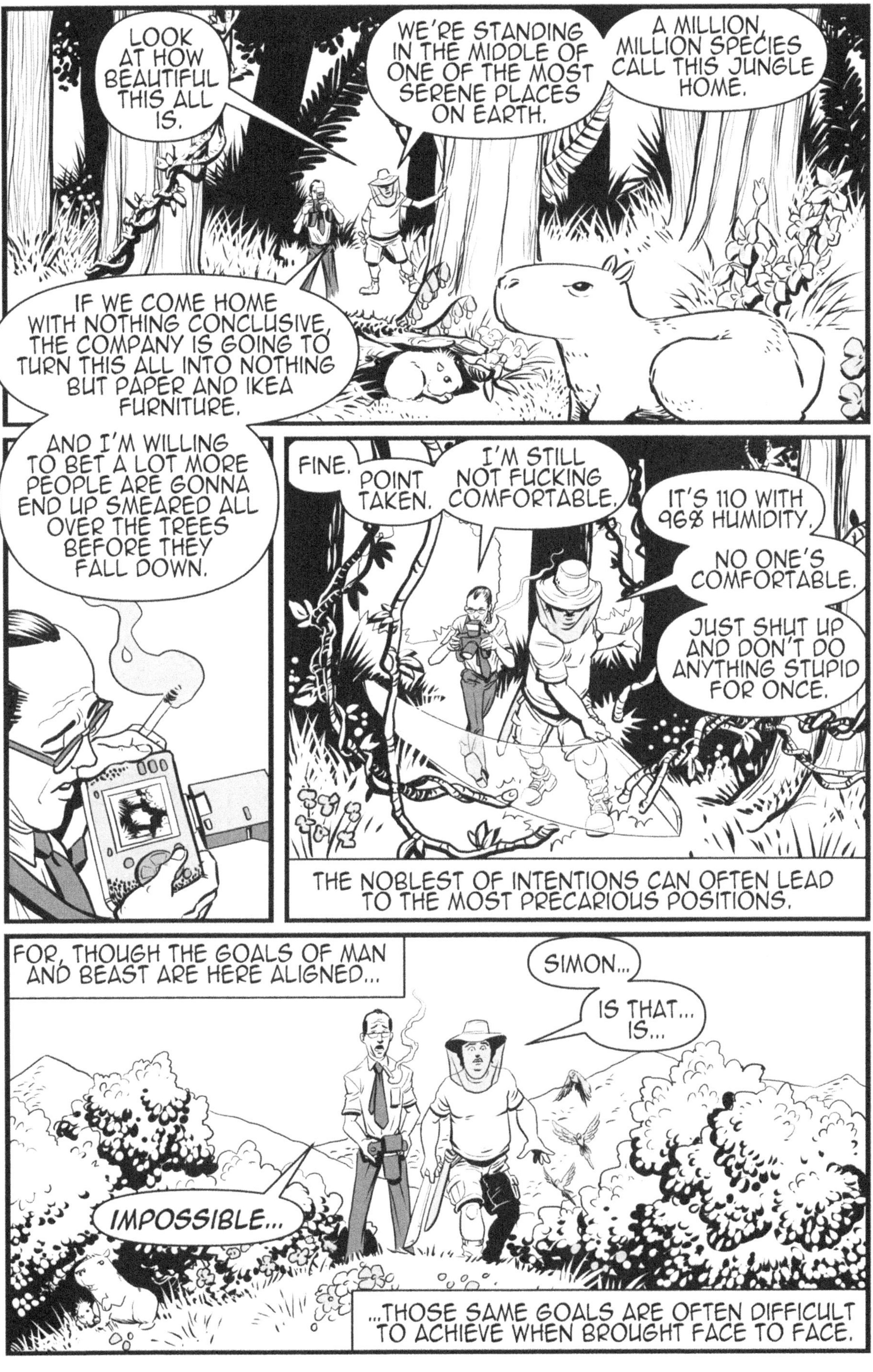
LOOK AT HOW BEAUTIFUL THIS ALL IS.
WE'RE STANDING IN THE MIDDLE OF ONE OF THE MOST SERENE PLACES ON EARTH.
A MILLION, MILLION SPECIES CALL THIS JUNGLE HOME.
IF WE COME HOME WITH NOTHING CONCLUSIVE, THE COMPANY IS GOING TO TURN THIS ALL INTO NOTHING BUT PAPER AND IKEA FURNITURE.
AND I'M WILLING TO BET A LOT MORE PEOPLE ARE GONNA END UP SMEARED ALL OVER THE TREES BEFORE THEY FALL DOWN.
FINE.
POINT TAKEN.
I'M STILL NOT FUCKING COMFORTABLE.
IT'S 110 WITH 96% HUMIDITY.
NO ONE'S COMFORTABLE.
JUST SHUT UP AND DON'T DO ANYTHING STUPID FOR ONCE.
THE NOBLEST OF INTENTIONS CAN OFTEN LEAD TO THE MOST PRECARIOUS POSITIONS.
FOR, THOUGH THE GOALS OF MAN AND BEAST ARE HERE ALIGNED...
SIMON...
IS THAT... IS...
IMPOSSIBLE...
...THOSE SAME GOALS ARE OFTEN DIFFICULT TO ACHIEVE WHEN BROUGHT FACE TO FACE.

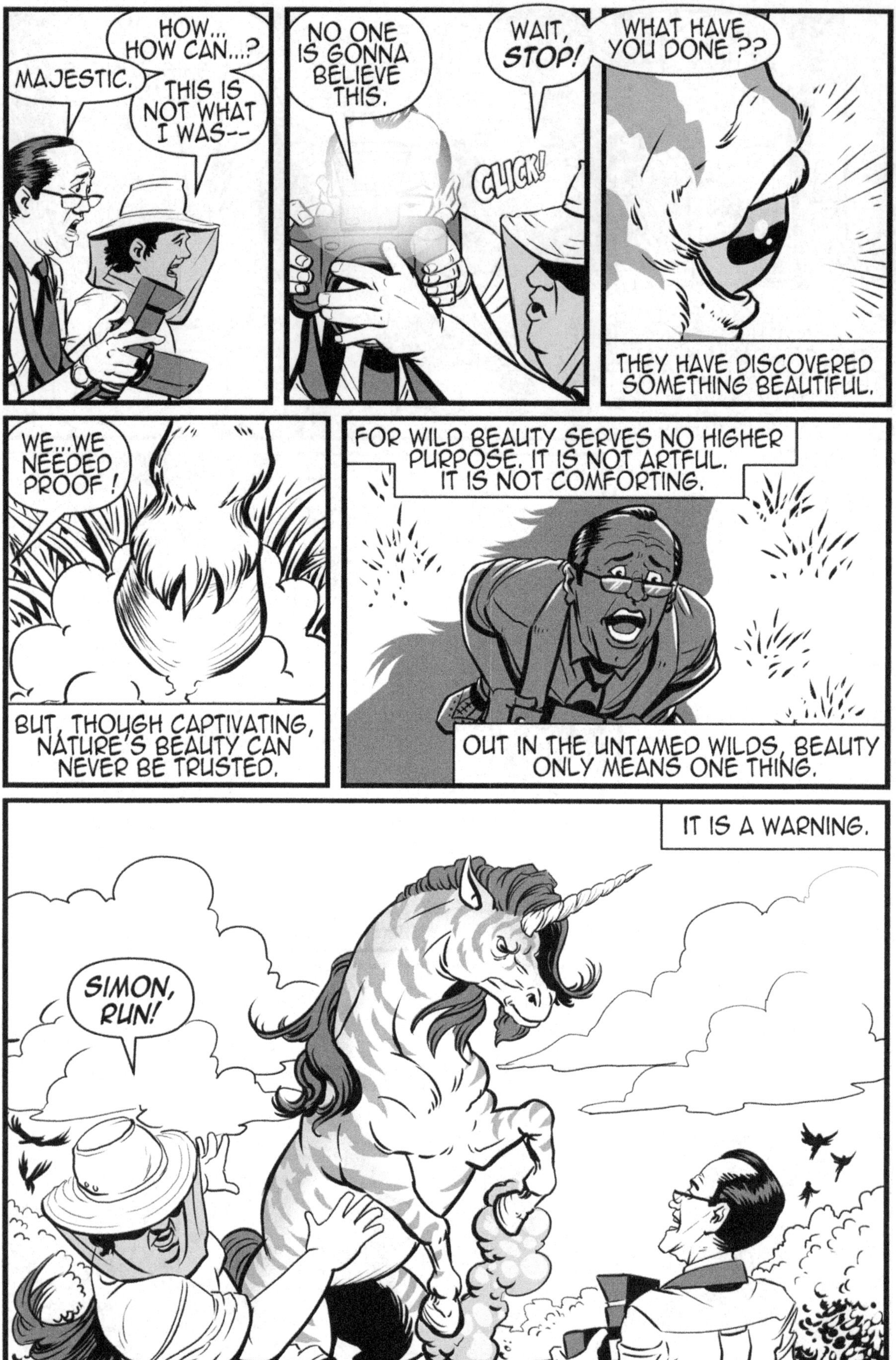
MAJESTIC.
HOW... HOW CAN...?
THIS IS NOT WHAT I WAS--
NO ONE IS GONNA BELIEVE THIS.
WAIT, STOP!
CLICK!
WHAT HAVE YOU DONE ??
THEY HAVE DISCOVERED SOMETHING BEAUTIFUL.
WE...WE NEEDED PROOF !
BUT, THOUGH CAPTIVATING, NATURE'S BEAUTY CAN NEVER BE TRUSTED.
FOR WILD BEAUTY SERVES NO HIGHER PURPOSE. IT IS NOT ARTFUL. IT IS NOT COMFORTING.
OUT IN THE UNTAMED WILDS, BEAUTY ONLY MEANS ONE THING.
IT IS A WARNING.
SIMON, RUN!

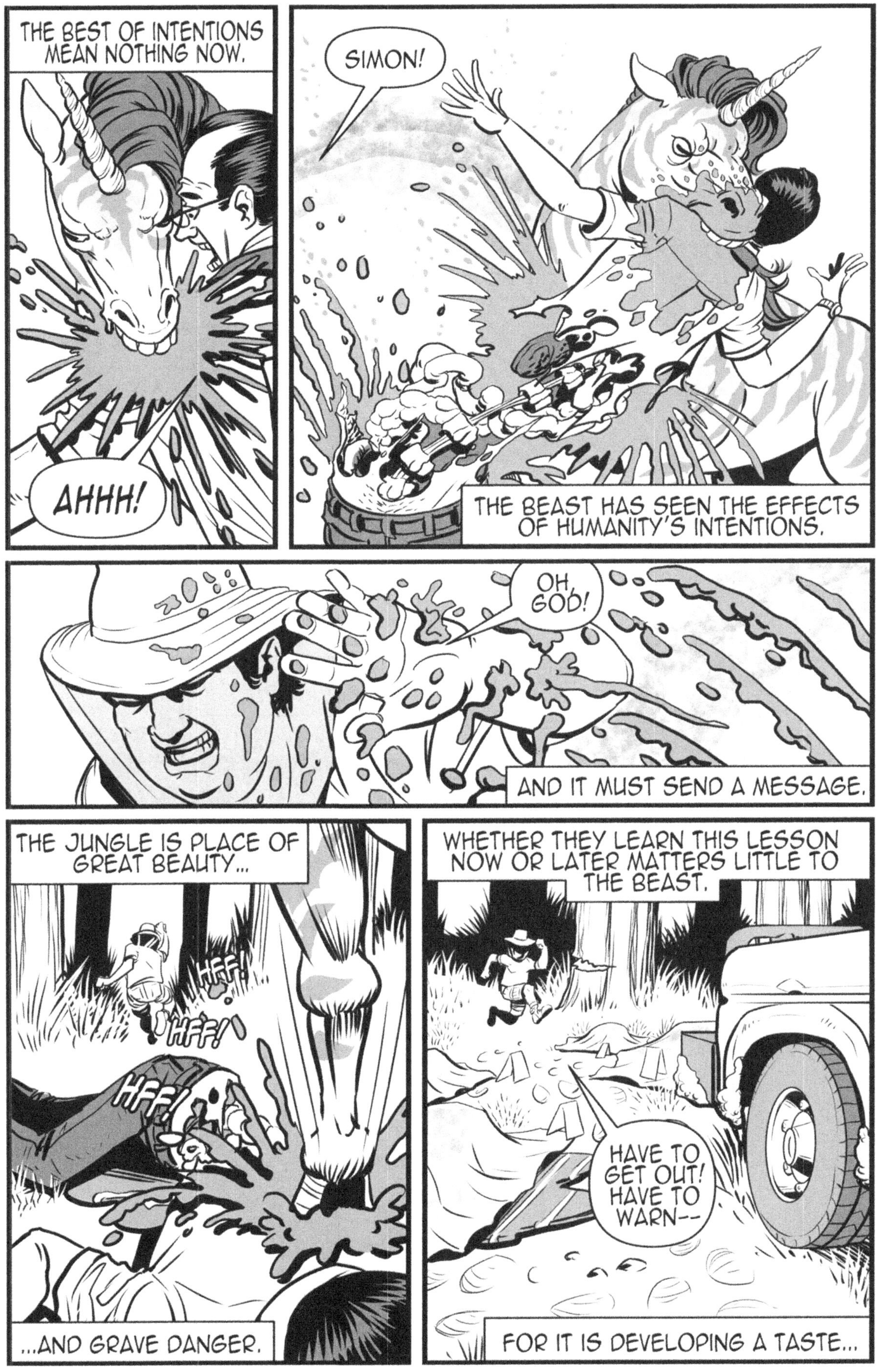

THE BEST OF INTENTIONS MEAN NOTHING NOW.
AHHH!
SIMON!
THE BEAST HAS SEEN THE EFFECTS OF HUMANITY'S INTENTIONS.
OH, GOD!
AND IT MUST SEND A MESSAGE.
THE JUNGLE IS PLACE OF GREAT BEAUTY...
HFF!
HFF!
HFF!
...AND GRAVE DANGER.
WHETHER THEY LEARN THIS LESSON NOW OR LATER MATTERS LITTLE TO THE BEAST.
HAVE TO GET OUT! HAVE TO WARN--
FOR IT IS DEVELOPING A TASTE...

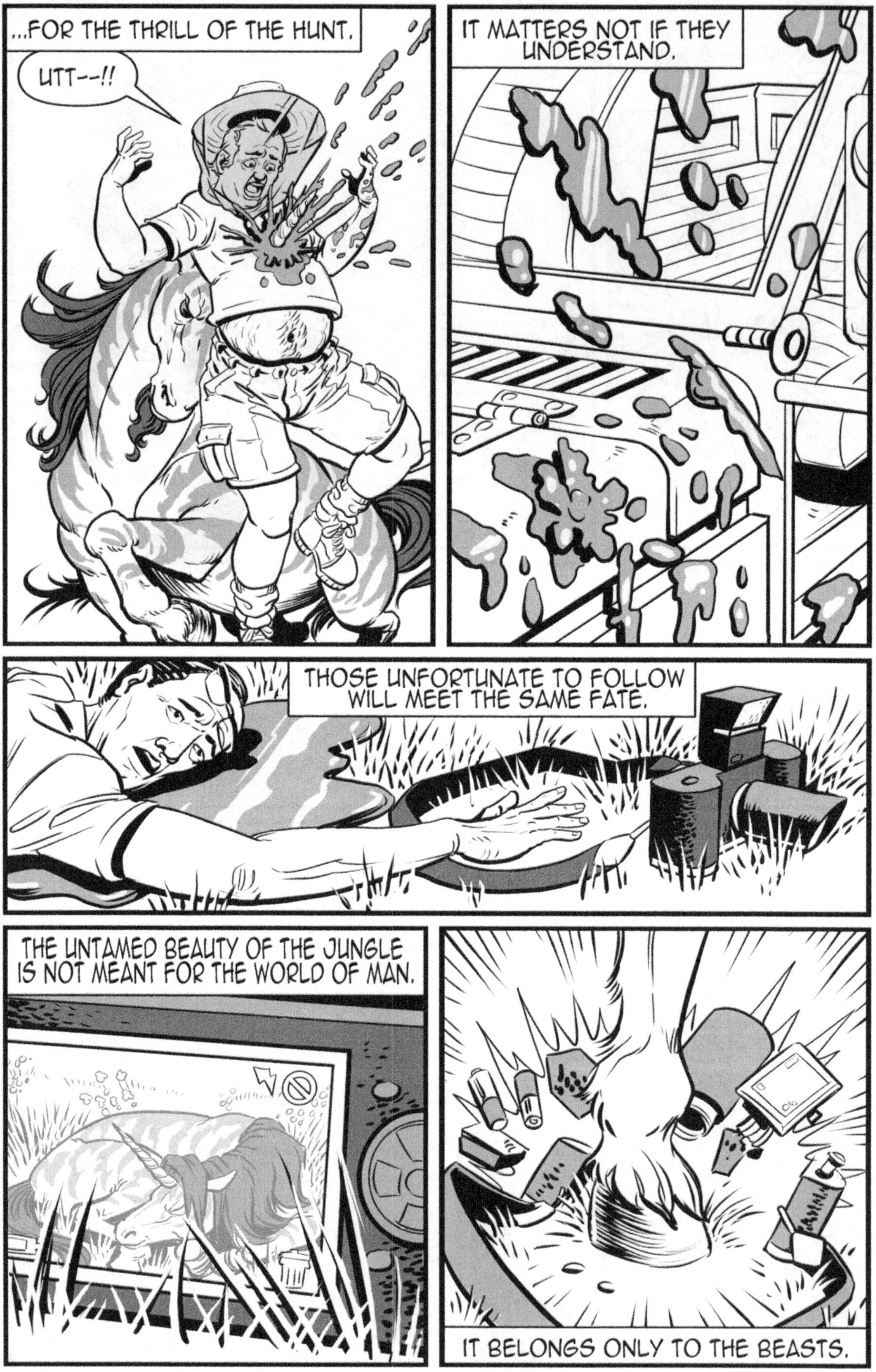

...FOR THE THRILL OF THE HUNT.
UTT--!!
IT MATTERS NOT IF THEY UNDERSTAND.
THOSE UNFORTUNATE TO FOLLOW WILL MEET THE SAME FATE.
THE UNTAMED BEAUTY OF THE JUNGLE IS NOT MEANT FOR THE WORLD OF MAN.
IT BELONGS ONLY TO THE BEASTS.

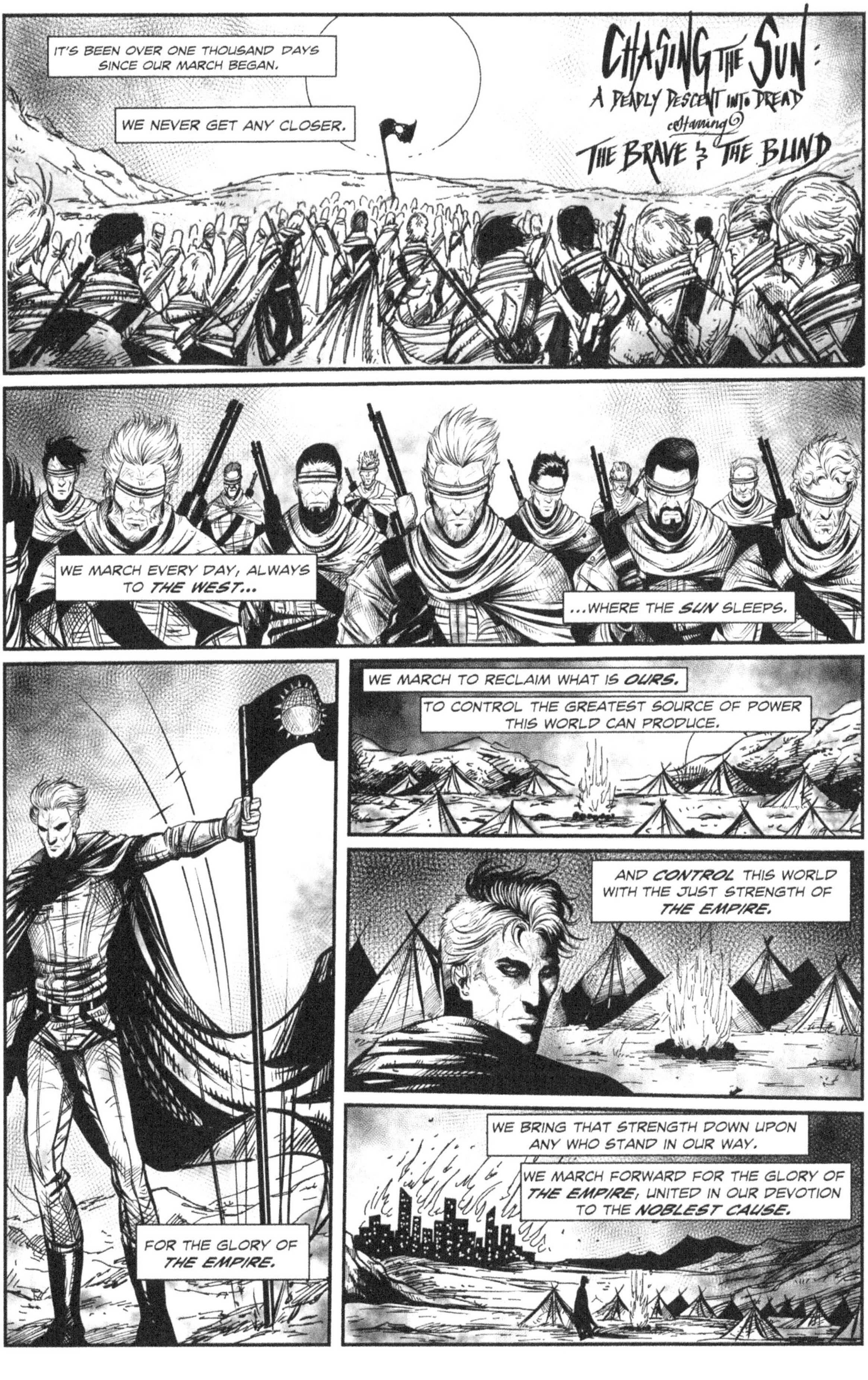
CHASING THE SUN: A DEADLY DESCENT INTO DREAD
starring
THE BRAVE & THE BLIND
IT'S BEEN OVER ONE THOUSAND DAYS SINCE OUR MARCH BEGAN.
WE NEVER GET ANY CLOSER.
WE MARCH EVERY DAY, ALWAYS TO THE WEST...
...WHERE THE SUN SLEEPS.
FOR THE GLORY OF THE EMPIRE.
WE MARCH TO RECLAIM WHAT IS OURS.
TO CONTROL THE GREATEST SOURCE OF POWER THIS WORLD CAN PRODUCE.
AND CONTROL THIS WORLD WITH THE JUST STRENGTH OF THE EMPIRE.
WE BRING THAT STRENGTH DOWN UPON ANY WHO STAND IN OUR WAY.
WE MARCH FORWARD FOR THE GLORY OF THE EMPIRE, UNITED IN OUR DEVOTION TO THE NOBLEST CAUSE.

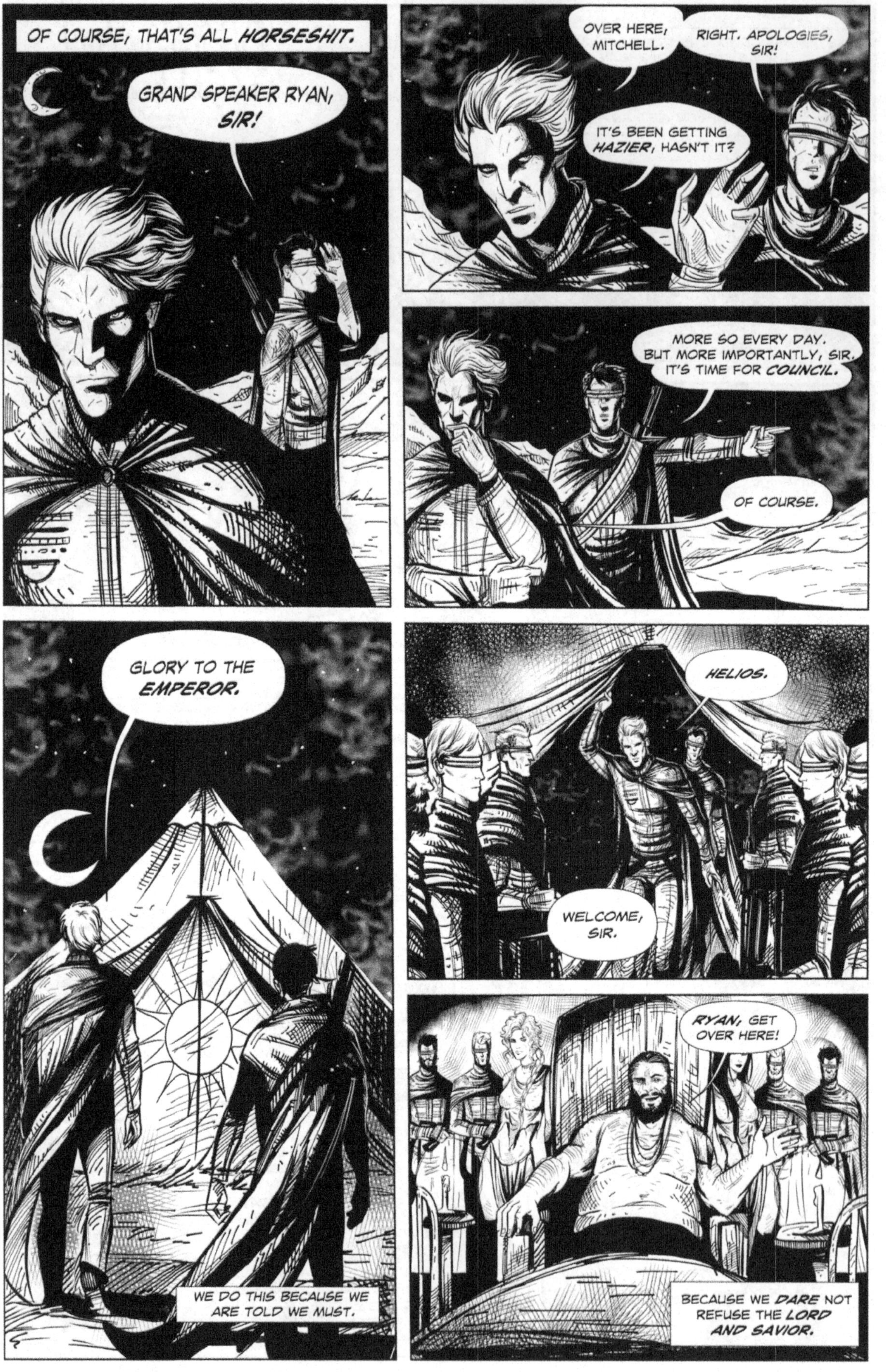
OF COURSE, THAT'S ALL HORSESHIT.
GRAND SPEAKER RYAN, SIR!
OVER HERE, MITCHELL.
RIGHT. APOLOGIES, SIR!
IT'S BEEN GETTING HAZIER, HASN'T IT?
MORE SO EVERY DAY. BUT MORE IMPORTANTLY, SIR. IT'S TIME FOR COUNCIL.
OF COURSE.
GLORY TO THE EMPEROR.
WE DO THIS BECAUSE WE ARE TOLD WE MUST.
HELIOS.
WELCOME, SIR.
RYAN, GET OVER HERE!
BECAUSE WE DARE NOT REFUSE THE LORD AND SAVIOR.

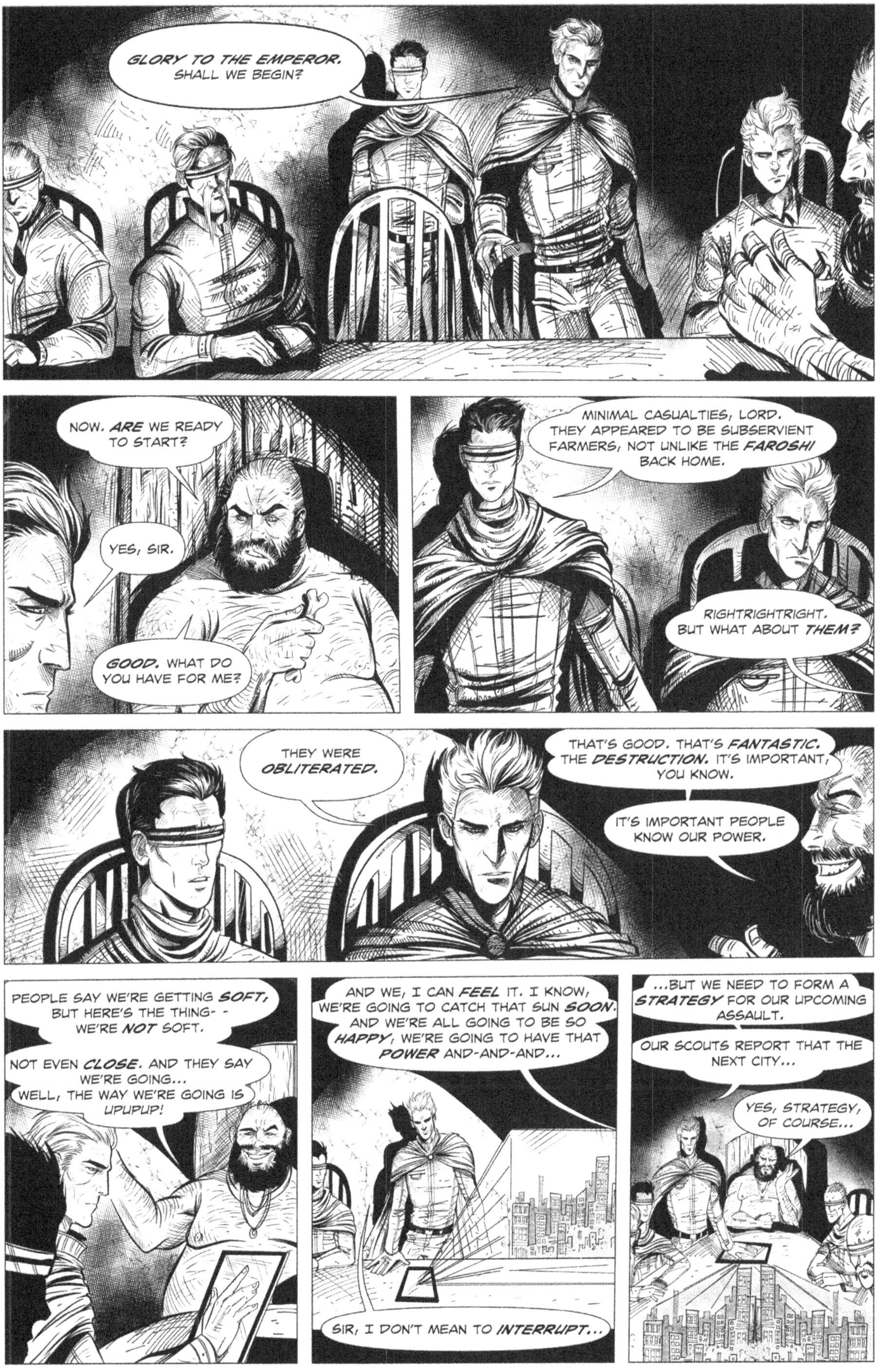
GLORY TO THE EMPEROR. SHALL WE BEGIN?
NOW. ARE WE READY TO START?
YES, SIR.
GOOD. WHAT DO YOU HAVE FOR ME?
MINIMAL CASUALTIES, LORD. THEY APPEARED TO BE SUBSERVIENT FARMERS, NOT UNLIKE THE FAROSHI BACK HOME.
RIGHTRIGHTRIGHT. BUT WHAT ABOUT THEM?
THEY WERE OBLITERATED.
THAT'S GOOD. THAT'S FANTASTIC. THE DESTRUCTION. IT'S IMPORTANT, YOU KNOW.
IT'S IMPORTANT PEOPLE KNOW OUR POWER.
PEOPLE SAY WE'RE GETTING SOFT, BUT HERE'S THE THING- - WE'RE NOT SOFT.
NOT EVEN CLOSE. AND THEY SAY WE'RE GOING... WELL, THE WAY WE'RE GOING IS UPUPUP!
AND WE, I CAN FEEL IT. I KNOW, WE'RE GOING TO CATCH THAT SUN SOON. AND WE'RE ALL GOING TO BE SO HAPPY, WE'RE GOING TO HAVE THAT POWER AND-AND-AND...
SIR, I DON'T MEAN TO INTERRUPT...
...BUT WE NEED TO FORM A STRATEGY FOR OUR UPCOMING ASSAULT.
OUR SCOUTS REPORT THAT THE NEXT CITY...
YES, STRATEGY, OF COURSE...

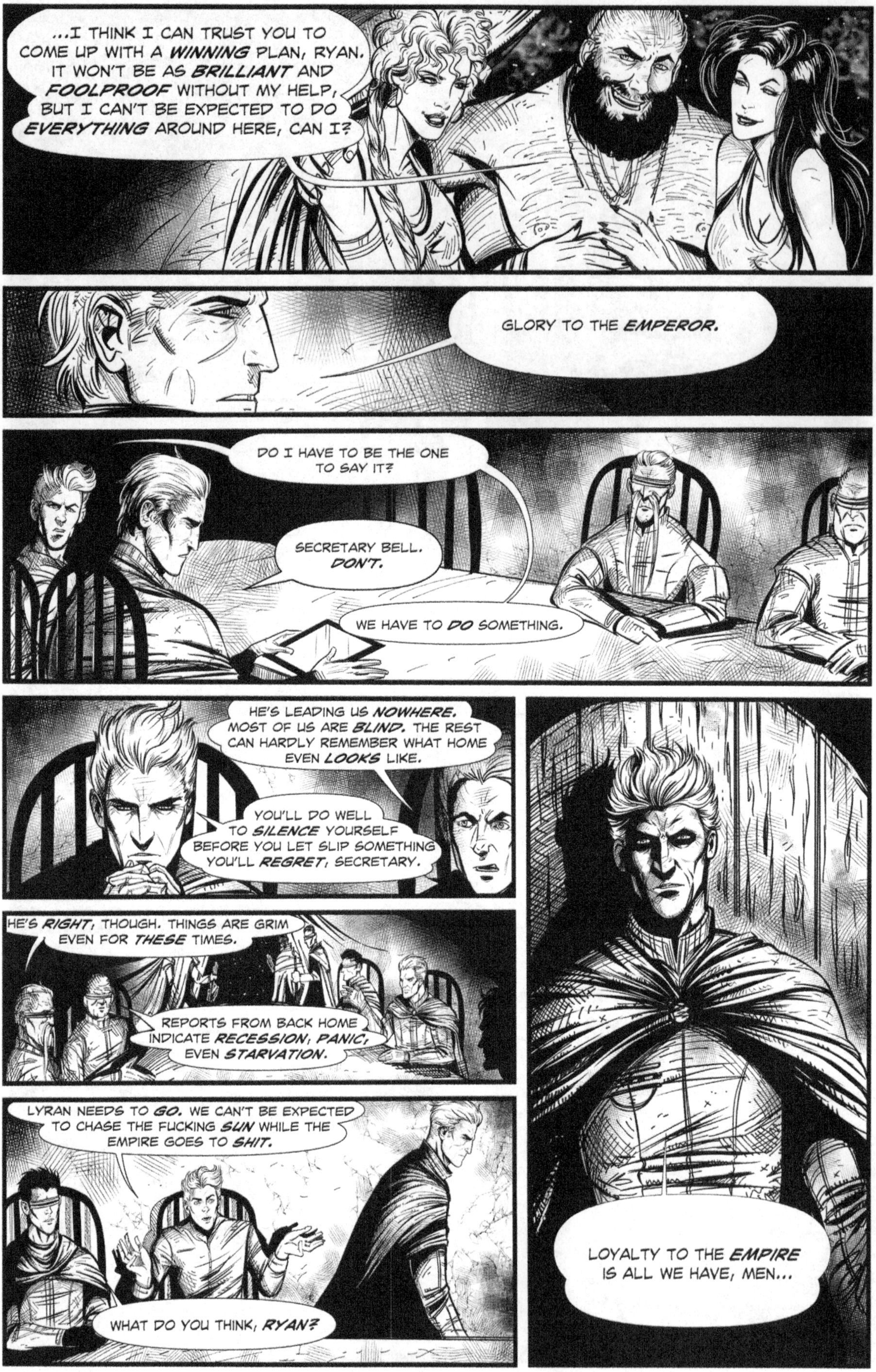
...I THINK I CAN TRUST YOU TO COME UP WITH A WINNING PLAN, RYAN. IT WON'T BE AS BRILLIANT AND FOOLPROOF WITHOUT MY HELP, BUT I CAN'T BE EXPECTED TO DO EVERYTHING AROUND HERE, CAN I?
GLORY TO THE EMPEROR.
DO I HAVE TO BE THE ONE TO SAY IT?
SECRETARY BELL. DON'T.
WE HAVE TO DO SOMETHING.
HE'S LEADING US NOWHERE. MOST OF US ARE BLIND. THE REST CAN HARDLY REMEMBER WHAT HOME EVEN LOOKS LIKE.
YOU'LL DO WELL TO SILENCE YOURSELF BEFORE YOU LET SLIP SOMETHING YOU'LL REGRET, SECRETARY.
HE'S RIGHT, THOUGH. THINGS ARE GRIM EVEN FOR THESE TIMES.
REPORTS FROM BACK HOME INDICATE RECESSION, PANIC, EVEN STARVATION.
LYRAN NEEDS TO GO. WE CAN'T BE EXPECTED TO CHASE THE FUCKING SUN WHILE THE EMPIRE GOES TO SHIT.
WHAT DO YOU THINK, RYAN?
LOYALTY TO THE EMPIRE IS ALL WE HAVE, MEN...

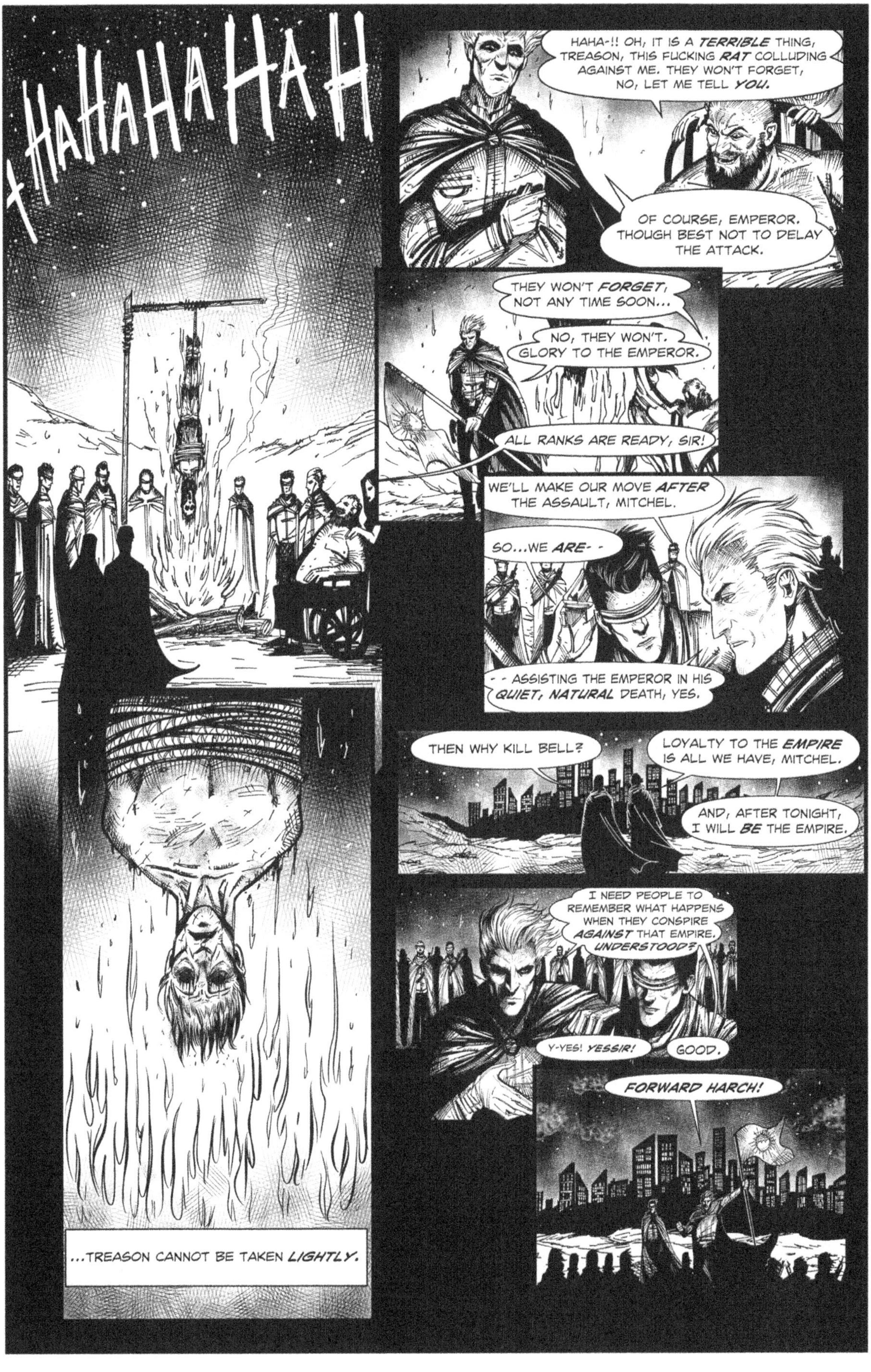
HAHAHAHAHAH
HAHA-!! OH, IT IS A *TERRIBLE* THING, TREASON, THIS FUCKING *RAT* COLLUDING AGAINST ME. THEY WON'T FORGET, NO, LET ME TELL *YOU.*
OF COURSE, EMPEROR. THOUGH BEST NOT TO DELAY THE ATTACK.
THEY WON'T *FORGET*, NOT ANY TIME SOON...
NO, THEY WON'T. GLORY TO THE EMPEROR.
ALL RANKS ARE READY, SIR!
WE'LL MAKE OUR MOVE *AFTER* THE ASSAULT, MITCHEL.
SO...WE *ARE*- -
- - ASSISTING THE EMPEROR IN HIS *QUIET, NATURAL* DEATH, YES.
THEN WHY KILL BELL?
LOYALTY TO THE *EMPIRE* IS ALL WE HAVE, MITCHEL.
AND, AFTER TONIGHT, I WILL *BE* THE EMPIRE.
I NEED PEOPLE TO REMEMBER WHAT HAPPENS WHEN THEY CONSPIRE *AGAINST* THAT EMPIRE. *UNDERSTOOD?*
Y-YES! *YESSIR!*
GOOD.
FORWARD HARCH!
...TREASON CANNOT BE TAKEN *LIGHTLY.*

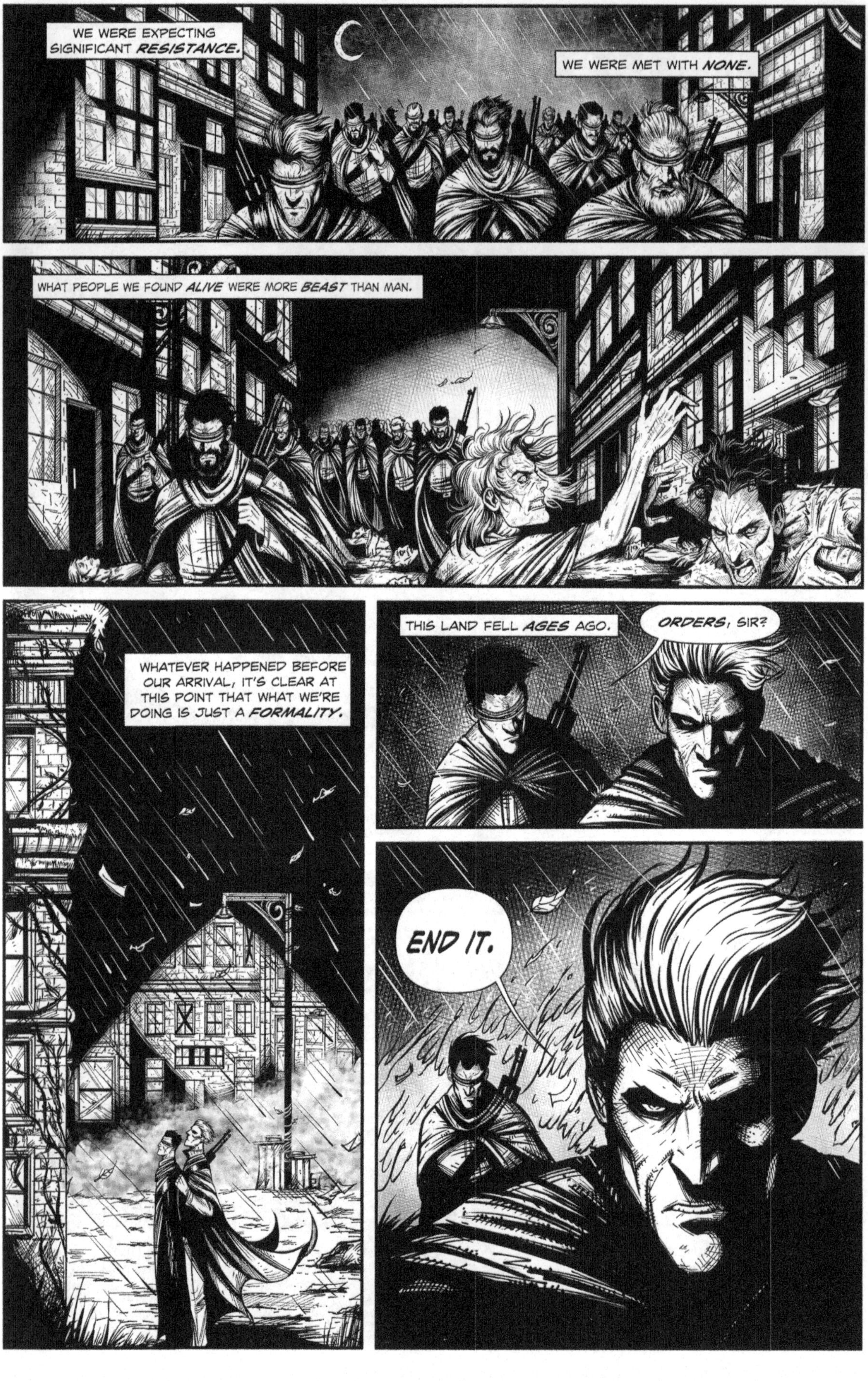
WE WERE EXPECTING SIGNIFICANT RESISTANCE.
WE WERE MET WITH NONE.
WHAT PEOPLE WE FOUND ALIVE WERE MORE BEAST THAN MAN.
WHATEVER HAPPENED BEFORE OUR ARRIVAL, IT'S CLEAR AT THIS POINT THAT WHAT WE'RE DOING IS JUST A FORMALITY.
THIS LAND FELL AGES AGO.
ORDERS, SIR?
END IT.

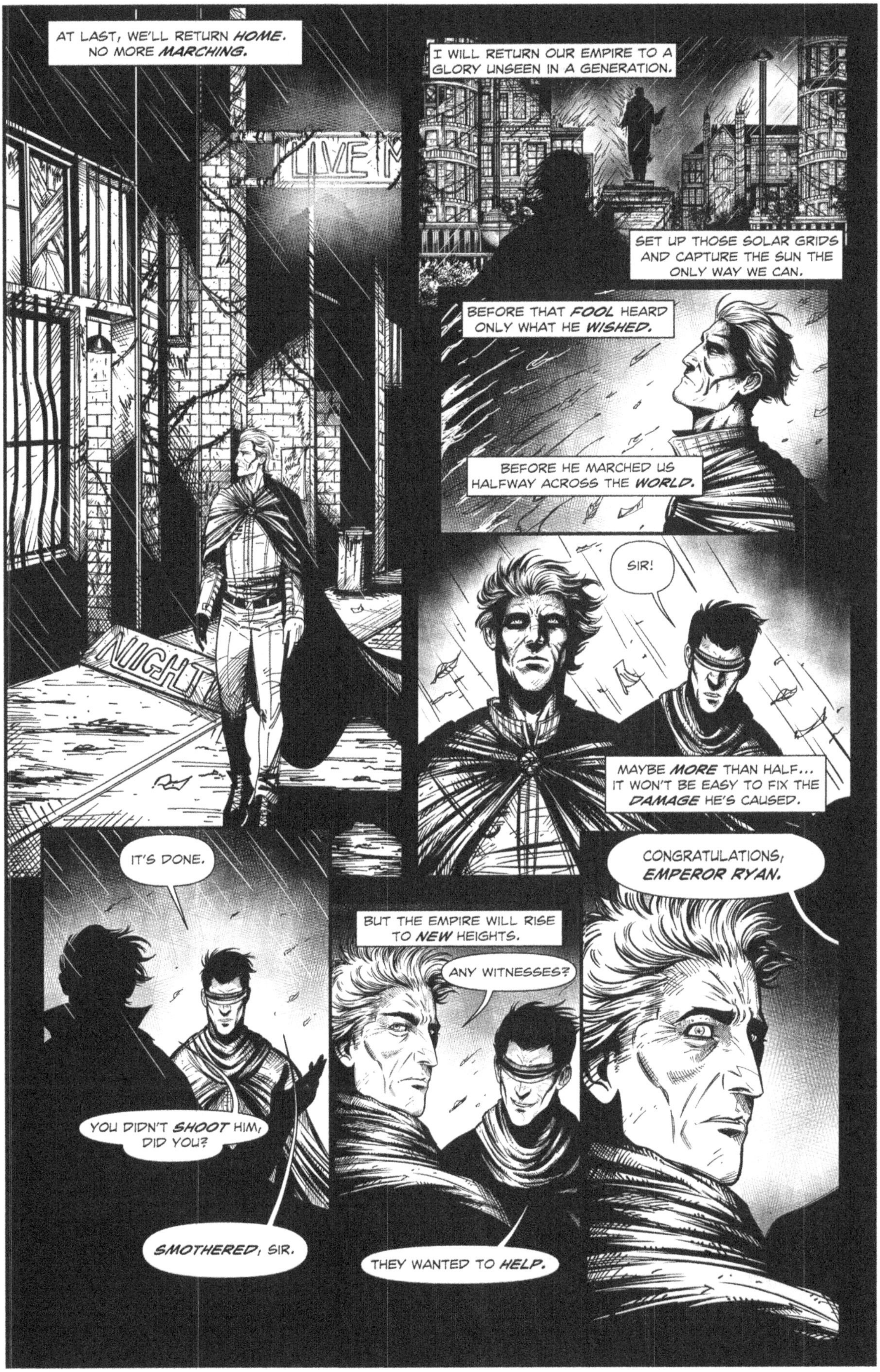
AT LAST, WE'LL RETURN HOME. NO MORE MARCHING.
LIVE M
NIGHT
I WILL RETURN OUR EMPIRE TO A GLORY UNSEEN IN A GENERATION.
SET UP THOSE SOLAR GRIDS AND CAPTURE THE SUN THE ONLY WAY WE CAN.
BEFORE THAT FOOL HEARD ONLY WHAT HE WISHED.
BEFORE HE MARCHED US HALFWAY ACROSS THE WORLD.
SIR!
MAYBE MORE THAN HALF... IT WON'T BE EASY TO FIX THE DAMAGE HE'S CAUSED.
IT'S DONE.
YOU DIDN'T SHOOT HIM, DID YOU?
SMOTHERED, SIR.
BUT THE EMPIRE WILL RISE TO NEW HEIGHTS.
ANY WITNESSES?
THEY WANTED TO HELP.
CONGRATULATIONS, EMPEROR RYAN.

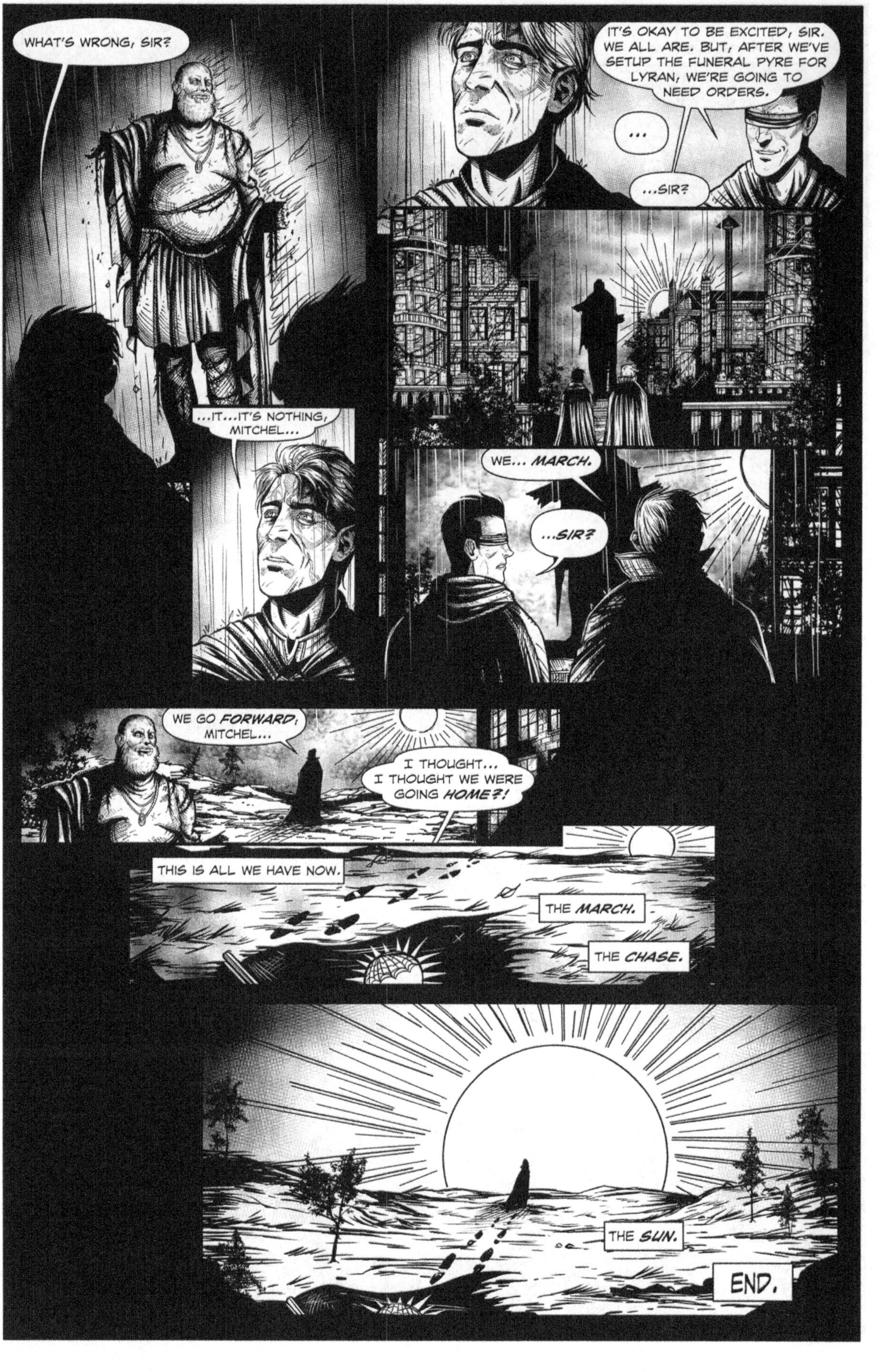

WHAT'S WRONG, SIR?
IT'S OKAY TO BE EXCITED, SIR. WE ALL ARE. BUT, AFTER WE'VE SETUP THE FUNERAL PYRE FOR LYRAN, WE'RE GOING TO NEED ORDERS.
...
...SIR?
...IT...IT'S NOTHING, MITCHEL...
WE... *MARCH.*
...*SIR?*
WE GO *FORWARD*, MITCHEL...
I THOUGHT... I THOUGHT WE WERE GOING *HOME?!*
THIS IS ALL WE HAVE NOW.
THE *MARCH.*
THE *CHASE.*
THE *SUN.*
END.

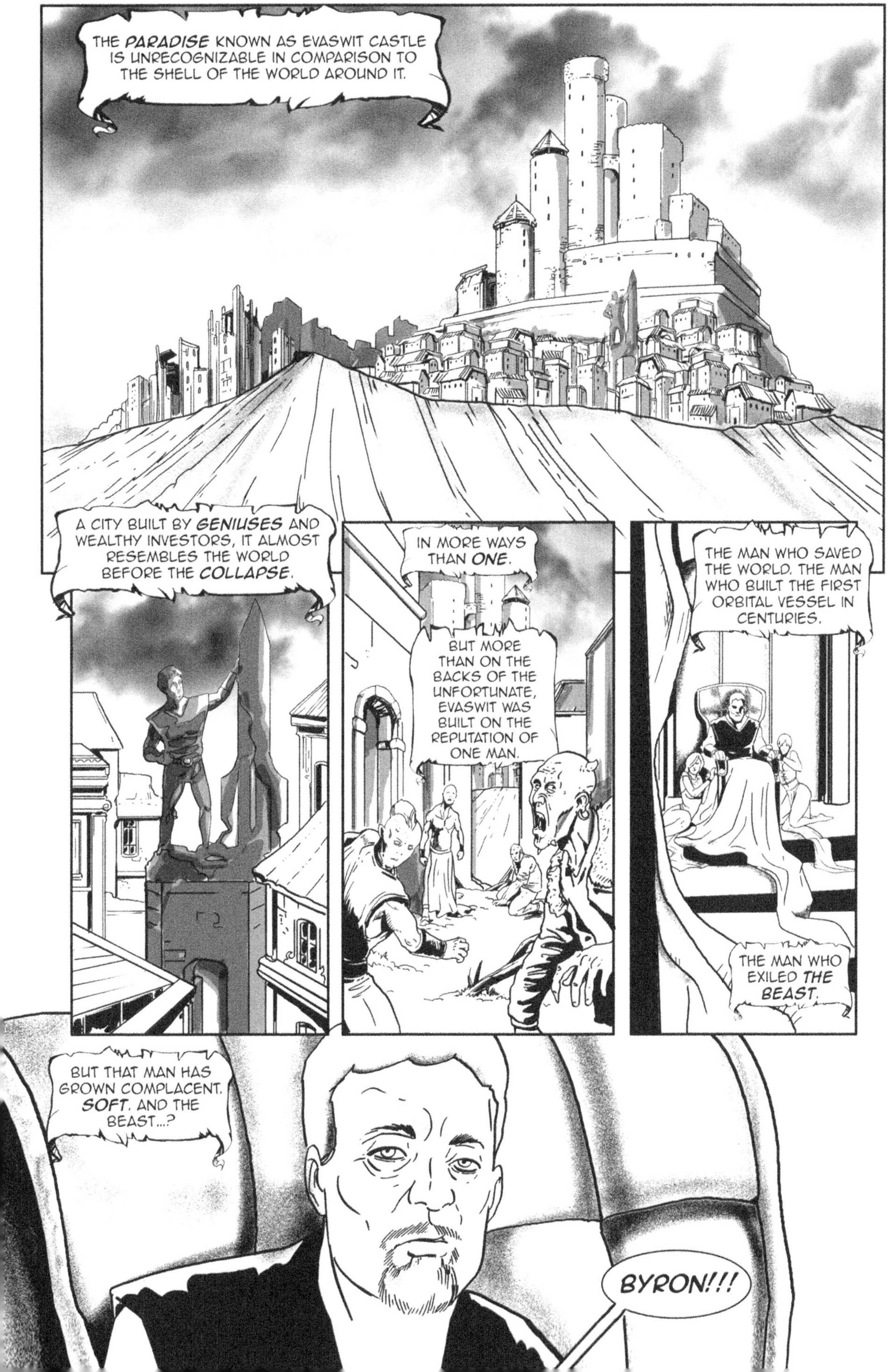
THE PARADISE KNOWN AS EVASWIT CASTLE IS UNRECOGNIZABLE IN COMPARISON TO THE SHELL OF THE WORLD AROUND IT.
A CITY BUILT BY GENIUSES AND WEALTHY INVESTORS, IT ALMOST RESEMBLES THE WORLD BEFORE THE COLLAPSE.
IN MORE WAYS THAN ONE.
BUT MORE THAN ON THE BACKS OF THE UNFORTUNATE, EVASWIT WAS BUILT ON THE REPUTATION OF ONE MAN.
THE MAN WHO SAVED THE WORLD. THE MAN WHO BUILT THE FIRST ORBITAL VESSEL IN CENTURIES.
THE MAN WHO EXILED THE BEAST.
BUT THAT MAN HAS GROWN COMPLACENT. SOFT. AND THE BEAST...?
BYRON!!!

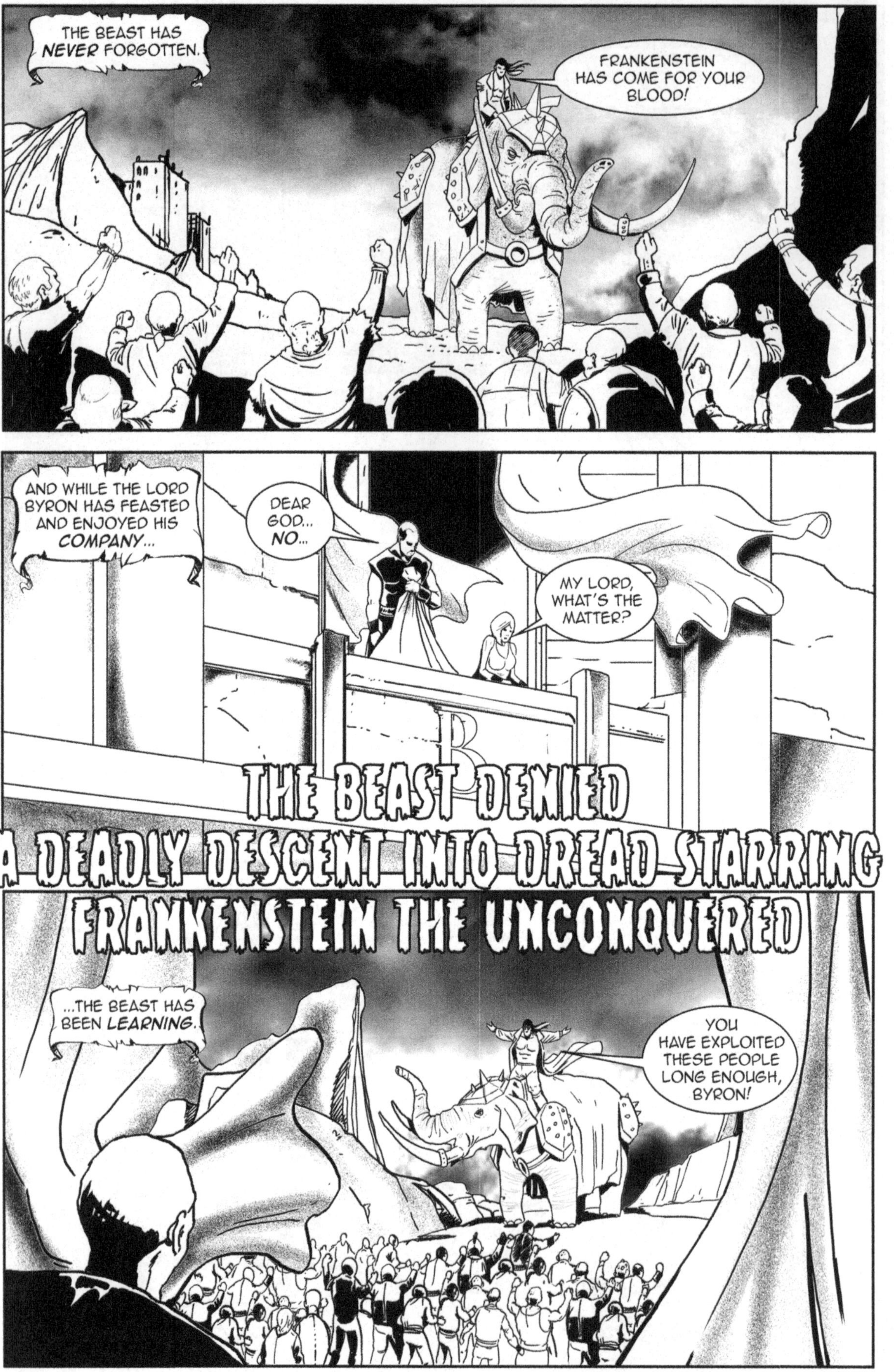
THE BEAST HAS NEVER FORGOTTEN.
FRANKENSTEIN HAS COME FOR YOUR BLOOD!
AND WHILE THE LORD BYRON HAS FEASTED AND ENJOYED HIS COMPANY...
DEAR GOD... NO...
MY LORD, WHAT'S THE MATTER?
THE BEAST DENIED
A DEADLY DESCENT INTO DREAD STARRING
FRANKENSTEIN THE UNCONQUERED
...THE BEAST HAS BEEN LEARNING.
YOU HAVE EXPLOITED THESE PEOPLE LONG ENOUGH, BYRON!

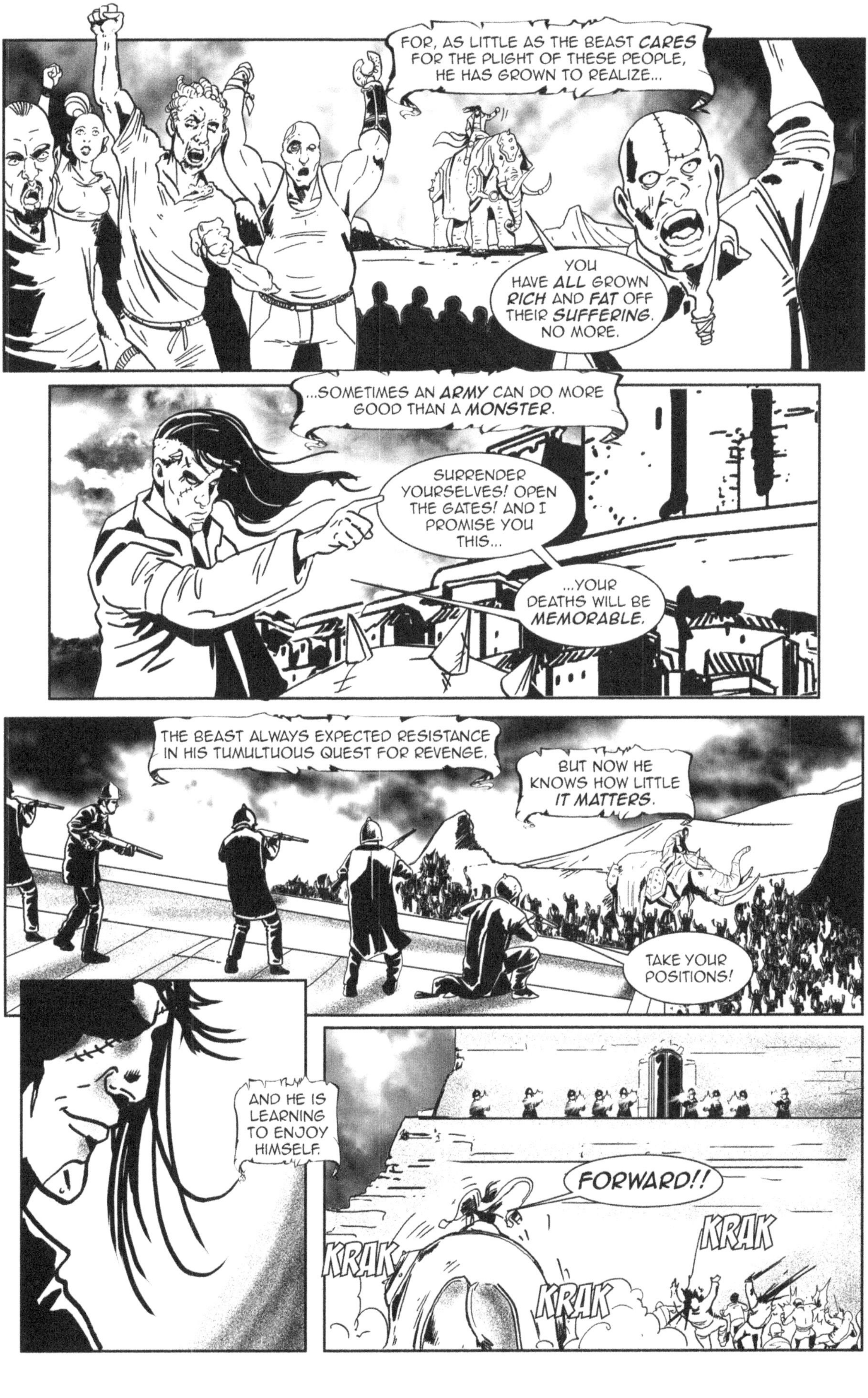
FOR, AS LITTLE AS THE BEAST CARES FOR THE PLIGHT OF THESE PEOPLE, HE HAS GROWN TO REALIZE...
YOU HAVE ALL GROWN RICH AND FAT OFF THEIR SUFFERING. NO MORE.
...SOMETIMES AN ARMY CAN DO MORE GOOD THAN A MONSTER.
SURRENDER YOURSELVES! OPEN THE GATES! AND I PROMISE YOU THIS...
...YOUR DEATHS WILL BE MEMORABLE.
THE BEAST ALWAYS EXPECTED RESISTANCE IN HIS TUMULTUOUS QUEST FOR REVENGE.
BUT NOW HE KNOWS HOW LITTLE IT MATTERS.
TAKE YOUR POSITIONS!
AND HE IS LEARNING TO ENJOY HIMSELF.
FORWARD!!
KRAK
KRAK
KRAK

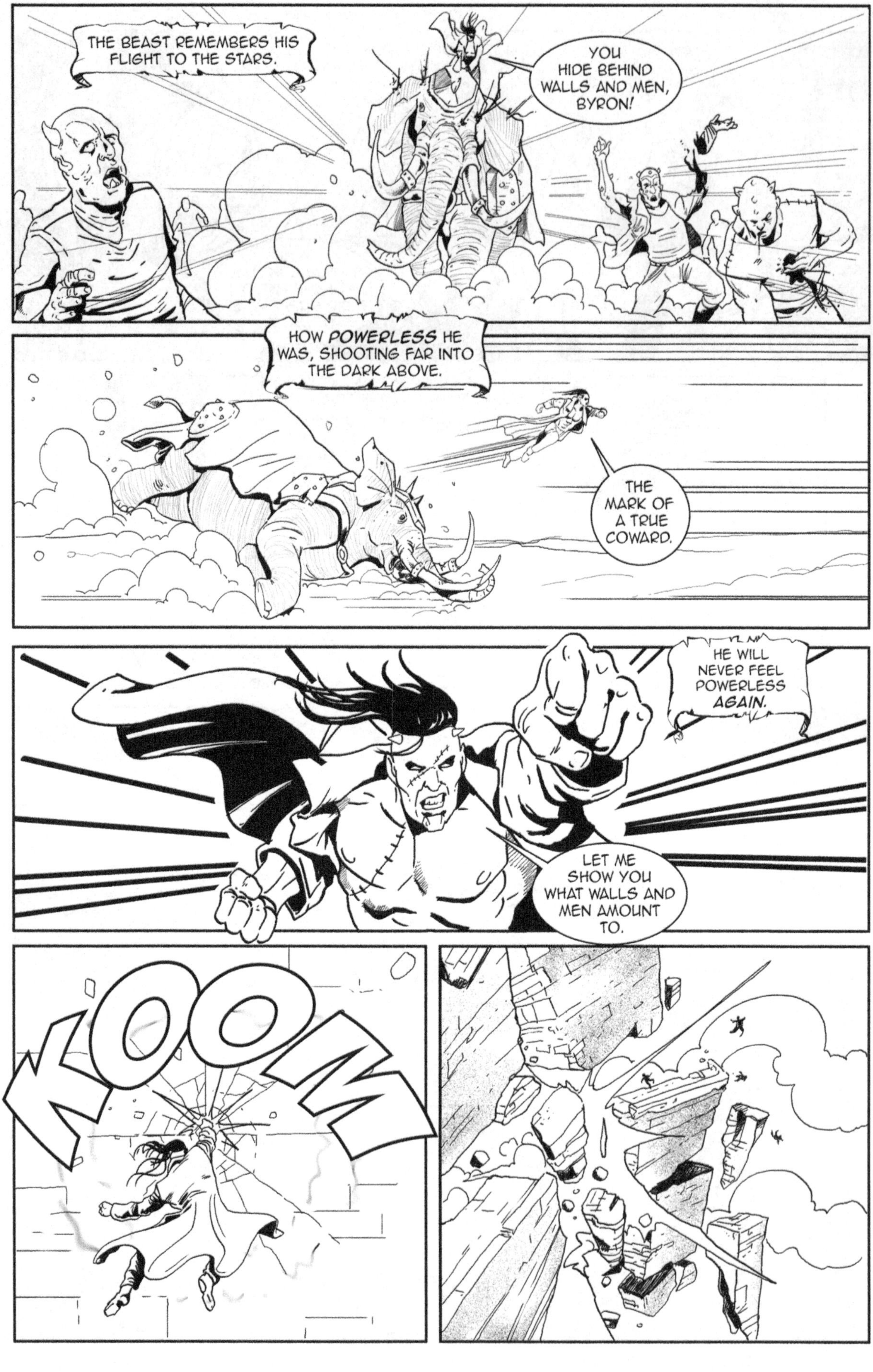
THE BEAST REMEMBERS HIS FLIGHT TO THE STARS.
YOU HIDE BEHIND WALLS AND MEN, BYRON!
HOW *POWERLESS* HE WAS, SHOOTING FAR INTO THE DARK ABOVE.
THE MARK OF A TRUE COWARD.
HE WILL NEVER FEEL POWERLESS *AGAIN.*
LET ME SHOW YOU WHAT WALLS AND MEN AMOUNT TO.
KOOM

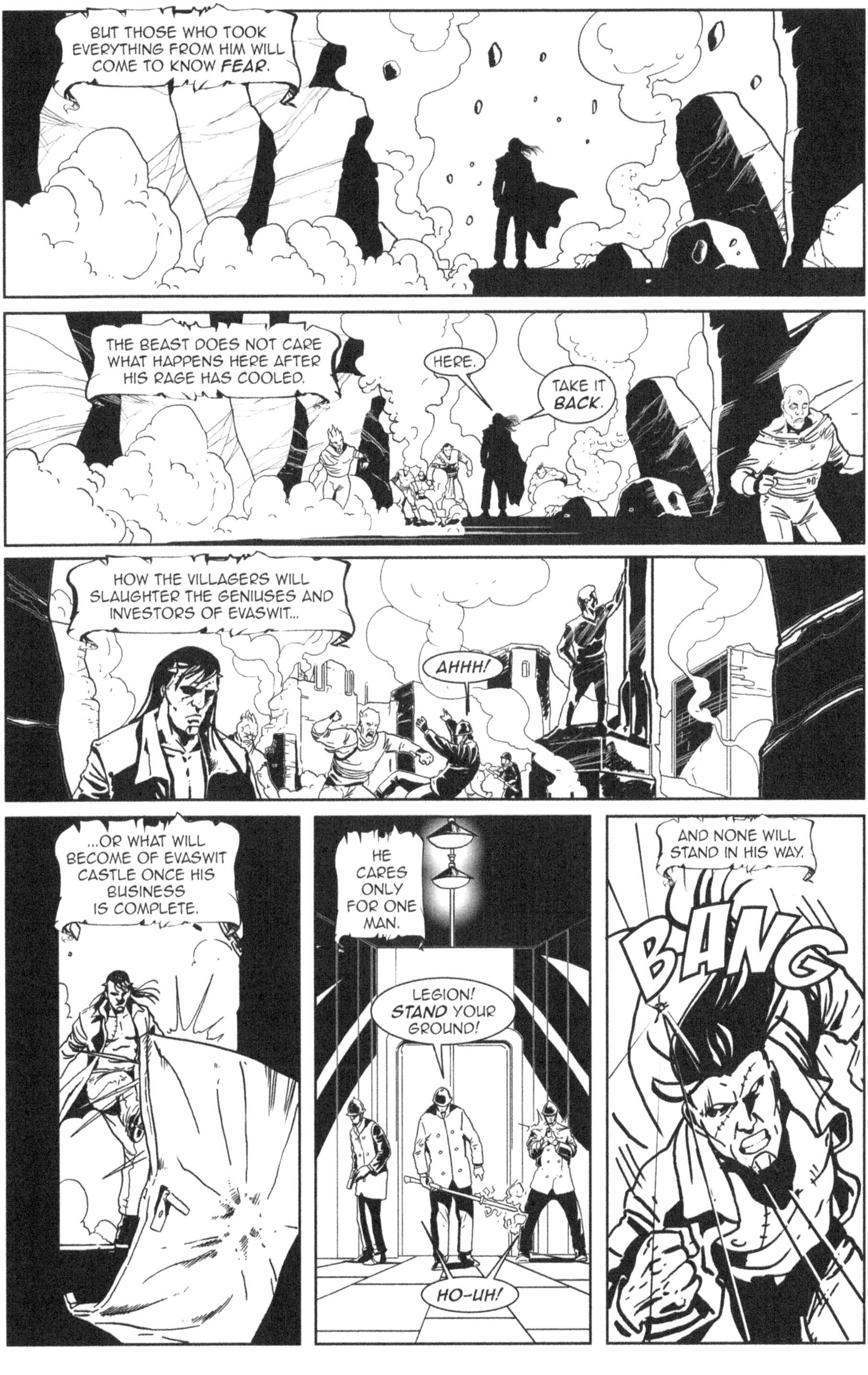
BUT THOSE WHO TOOK EVERYTHING FROM HIM WILL COME TO KNOW FEAR.
THE BEAST DOES NOT CARE WHAT HAPPENS HERE AFTER HIS RAGE HAS COOLED.
HERE.
TAKE IT BACK.
HOW THE VILLAGERS WILL SLAUGHTER THE GENIUSES AND INVESTORS OF EVASWIT...
AHHH!
...OR WHAT WILL BECOME OF EVASWIT CASTLE ONCE HIS BUSINESS IS COMPLETE.
HE CARES ONLY FOR ONE MAN.
LEGION! STAND YOUR GROUND!
HO-UH!
AND NONE WILL STAND IN HIS WAY.
BANG

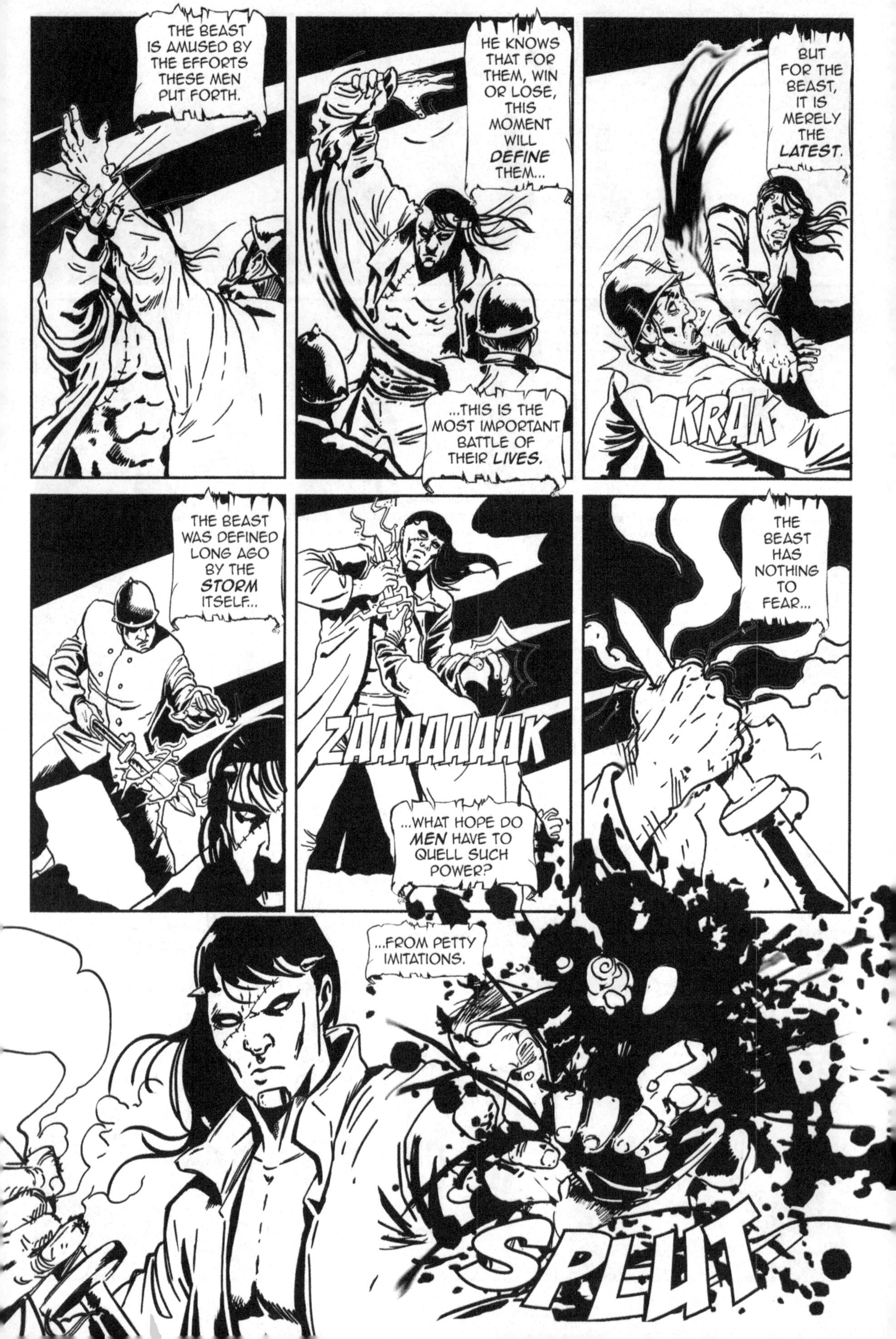
THE BEAST IS AMUSED BY THE EFFORTS THESE MEN PUT FORTH.
HE KNOWS THAT FOR THEM, WIN OR LOSE, THIS MOMENT WILL DEFINE THEM...
...THIS IS THE MOST IMPORTANT BATTLE OF THEIR LIVES.
BUT FOR THE BEAST, IT IS MERELY THE LATEST.
KRAK
THE BEAST WAS DEFINED LONG AGO BY THE STORM ITSELF...
ZAAAAAAAK
...WHAT HOPE DO MEN HAVE TO QUELL SUCH POWER?
THE BEAST HAS NOTHING TO FEAR...
...FROM PETTY IMITATIONS.
SPLUT

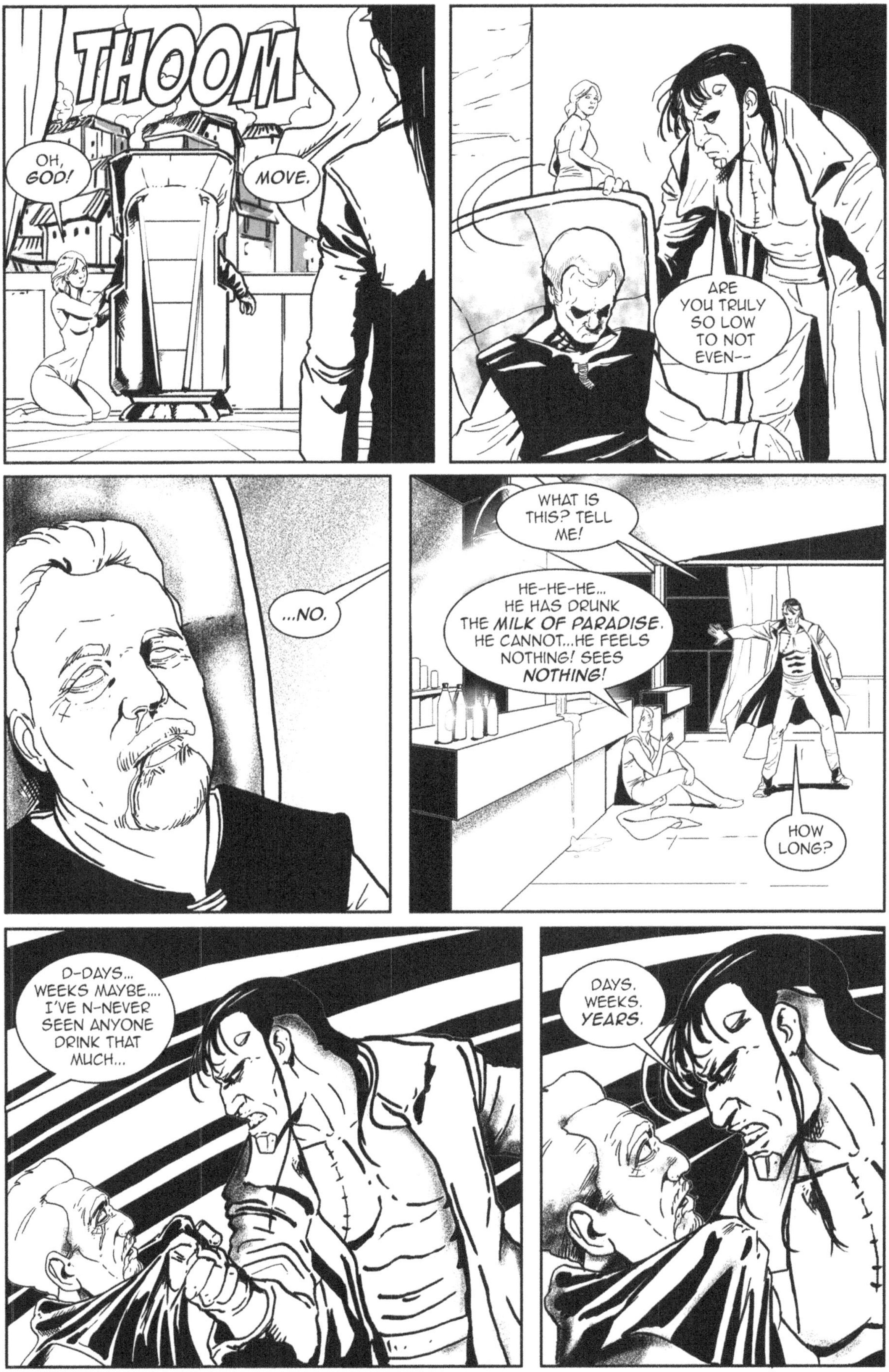
THOOM
OH, GOD!
MOVE.
ARE YOU TRULY SO LOW TO NOT EVEN--
...NO.
WHAT IS THIS? TELL ME!
HE-HE-HE... HE HAS DRUNK THE MILK OF PARADISE. HE CANNOT...HE FEELS NOTHING! SEES NOTHING!
HOW LONG?
D-DAYS... WEEKS MAYBE.... I'VE N-NEVER SEEN ANYONE DRINK THAT MUCH...
DAYS. WEEKS. YEARS.

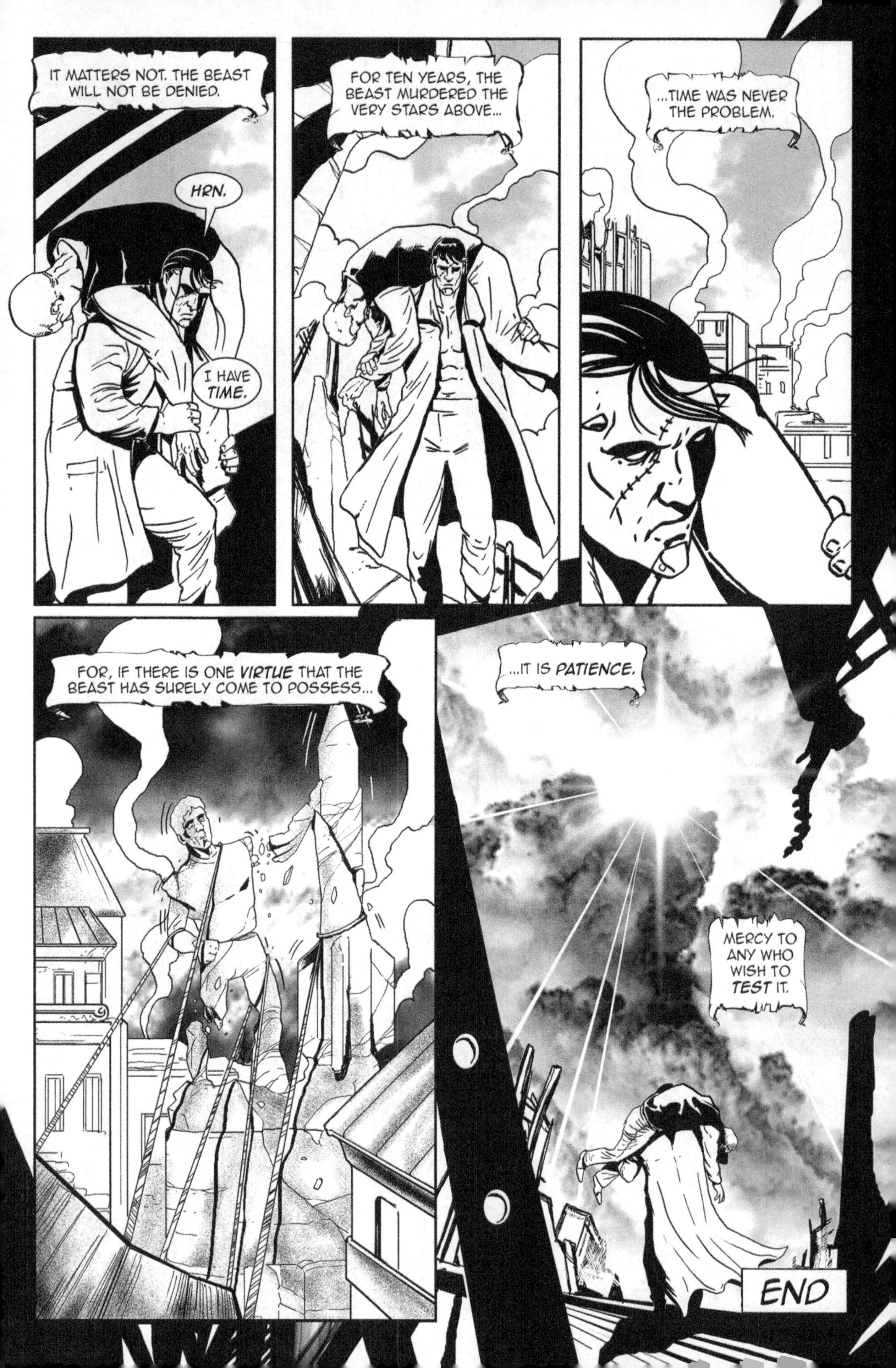
IT MATTERS NOT. THE BEAST WILL NOT BE DENIED.
HRN.
I HAVE TIME.
FOR TEN YEARS, THE BEAST MURDERED THE VERY STARS ABOVE...
...TIME WAS NEVER THE PROBLEM.
FOR, IF THERE IS ONE VIRTUE THAT THE BEAST HAS SURELY COME TO POSSESS...
...IT IS PATIENCE.
MERCY TO ANY WHO WISH TO TEST IT.
END

CREATOR BIOS

DALTON SHANNON HAS BEEN CREATING STORIES FOR ALMOST TWENTY YEARS, EVER SINCE HE FIRST CRACKED OPEN A COPY OF **CAPTAIN UNDERPANTS** AND NOTICED "HEY, IF THIS GUY CAN DO IT, MAYBE I CAN TOO!" HE HAS TAKEN PART IN NUMEROUS CREATIVE EXPLOITS, PRIMARILY WHILE ATTENDING THE UNIVERSITY OF CENTRAL ARKANSAS IN SERVICE OF RECIEVING A PIECE OF PAPER THAT TOLD EVERYONE "NO, REALLY, HE'S A WRITER." FINDING PUBLICATION IN THE UNIVERSITY'S **VORTEX MAGAZINE** AND CREATING THE WEBSERIES **HIGH AND MIGHTY**, HE GRADUATED WITHOUT HONORS, WITHOUT A GIRLFRIEND, AND WITHOUT ANY JOB OFFERS.

IN HIS SECRET IDENTITY, HE IS AN AVID KAIJU FANATIC, A STUDENT OF ANYTHING THAT HAS ABSOLUTELY ZERO REAL-WORLD APPLICATION, SUPERHERO SPOKESPERSON, AND A HUSBAND THAT SHOULD HAVE BEEN LEFT BEHIND AGES AGO FOR THE NEWER, BETTER MODEL. HE DIVIDES HIS TIME MOSTLY BETWEEN HIS HOME IN **ROGERS, ARKANSAS** AND HIS LIFE IN SUPERMAN'S METROPOLIS.

CHECK OUT HIS WORK ON HIS **WEBSITE:** FOURCOLOURMEDIA.COM

FOLLOW HIM ON HIS **TWITTER:** @DALTONKSHANNON AND @FOURCOLOURFUN AND ON HIS **INSTAGRAM:** DALTONKSHANNON AND FOURCOLOURCOMICS

WELLS THOMPSON STUDIED WRITING AND LITERATURE AT THE UNIVERSITY OF CENTRAL ARKANSAS WHERE HE MET **DALTON SHANNON** AND WROTE A BUNCH OF SHORT FILMS AND FICTION. HE'S A FREQUENT CONTRIBUTER TO **COMIC BOOK YETI,** A COMIC BOOK REVIEW WEBSITE, AND IS BEGINNING HIS JOURNEY INTO COMIC BOOK LETTERING BY FINISHING THIS SENTENCE.

A NATIVE OF ARKANSAS, WELLS NOW LIVES IN **NASHVILLE, TENNESSEE** WITH HIS FIANCÉE, **BRIANNA LEBOEUF**, WITHOUT WHOM THIS ANTHOLOGY WOULDN'T EXIST. IN HIS SPARE TIME, HE HELPS SOCIALIZE FERAL CATS, TENDS TO HIS STRAWBERRY AND SPICE GARDENS, AND CLEANS UP AFTER HIS CATS: **NOODLE, GILLY, BUG, CORNIFER,** AND **QUELAAG.** HE GAVE UP ON NAMING THEM HALFWAY THROUGH.

CHECK OUT HIS WORK ON HIS **WEBSITES:** WELLSTHOMPSON.COM AND FOURCOLOURMEDIA.COM

FOLLOW HIM ON **TWITTER:** @WELLSAFP AND @FOURCOLOURFUN

ANDREA MODUGNO BECAME A COMIC BOOK DESIGNER IN 2016 AT THE AGE OF 38 AND HAS SINCE WORKED INTERNATIONALLY IN FRANCE, THE U.S., AND HIS HOME COUNTRY OF ITALY TO CREATE SOME TRULY INSPIRING WORK. HE'S BEST KNOWN FOR HIS INDIE COMIC **DAREK**, A COLLABORATION WITH **MASSIMO PINI** THAT'S WORTH CHECKING OUT EVEN IF YOU CAN'T READ ITALIAN.

FOR TWENTY-FIVE YEARS, ANDREA HAS PRACTICED AND MASTERED WING CHUN, THE FOUNDATIONAL MARTIAL ART THAT INSPIRED BRUCE LEE. HIS WIFE AND TWO CHILDREN LIVE WITH HIM IN GENOA, IN A HOUSE NEAR THE SEA.

CHECK OUT HIS WORK ON **FACEBOOK** AND **INSTAGRAM:** ANDREAMODUGNO78, AND ON HIS **WEBSITE:** MODART78-BLOGSPOT.COM

ARTIST: THE BEAST RETURNED, THE BEAST AVENGED, THE BEAST DISPLAYED, THE BEAST DENIED

LEONARDO MARCELLO GRASSI HAS BEEN WORKING IN COMICS FOR TEN YEARS, DRAWING GRAPHIC NOVELS LIKE **ROTTAMI** AND WORKING AS A FINISHER FOR **UNDISCOVERED COUNTRY.**

HE LIVES IN REGGIO EMILIA IN NORTHERN ITALY WHERE HE COMPETES IN VARIOUS SPORTING EVENTS. HE OFTEN DRAWS SURREAL AND MORBID STILL-LIVES FOR HIS **INSTAGRAM** FOLLOWERS TO ENJOY.

CHECK OUT HIS WORK ON **INSTAGRAM:** LEONOVELS

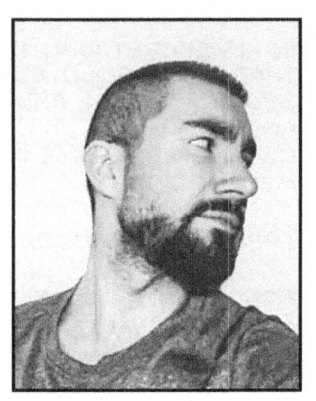

ARTIST AND LETTERER: DREAMS OF THE DROWNED

KATH LOBO IS A COSTARRICAN ARTIST THAT WORKS MAINLY ON SMALL INDIE PROJECTS (LIKE THIS ONE!) OR ON HER OWN WEBCOMIC **INVENTOR OF NOTHING.** SHE ALSO DOES OCCASIONAL COLORING WORK FOR BOOM! STUDIOS AND COMICS EXPERIENCE. SHE'S EXTREMELY ACTIVE ON SOCIAL MEDIA AND POSTS TONS OF FANART, DRAWINGS OF GIRLS, AND HER OWN ORIGINAL CHARACTERS.

SHE WORKS FROM HOME AND LIVES WITH HER TWO CHILDREN, DOGS, AND HUSBAND **SERG ACUÑA.** THERE, SHE FIGHTS AN EVER LOSING BATTLE WITH COFFEE ADDICTION AND STRUGGLES WITH ACCEPTING "GIFTS" FROM HER CAT **GATA** IN THE FORM OF MICE.

CHECK OUT HER WORK ON **INSTAGRAM:** KATH_LOBO, **TWITTER:** @KATHLOBO, AND ON HER **BLOG:** BEHANCE-NET/KATHRINELOBO

ARTIST AND LETTERER: RUBBING ELBOWS

DOCTOR FANTASTIC IS THE UNFORTUNATE RESULT OF EARLY AND LONGTERM EXPOSURE TO JOHN CARPENTER, JACK KIRBY, AND NINJA TURTLERY. HE DREW THE ART USED FOR THE BACK COVER OF THIS ANTHOLOGY AND CONTINUES TO DO COMMISSION WORK FULL TIME.

FOLLOW HIM ON **INSTAGRAM:** DOCFANTASTIC_

ANTONIO RUSSO TANTARO WORKS PREDOMINANTLY AS AN INKER FOR **AUREA EDITORIALE** IN BOLOGNA, ITALY. A GRADUATE OF THE INTERNATIONAL COMICS SCHOOL, HE DOES LOADS OF COMMISSION WORK, ANTHOLOGIES, AND OCCASIONALLY SOME PAGES FOR MARVEL.

AS A LIFELONG COMICS LOVER AND COMMUNITY MEMBER, HE CO-FOUNDED THE VOLUNTEER ASSOCIATION **COMIX DREAMLAND** WHICH HE OPERATED FOR 13 YEARS. HE LOVES PLAYING VIDEO GAMES AND BOARD GAMES WHENEVER HE CAN TEAR HIMSELF AWAY FROM DRAWING COMICS (WHICH WE'VE BEEN ASSURED IS NOT OFTEN).

ARTIST: THE MYTH OF TOMORROW

LETTERER: THE MYTH OF TOMORROW, THE BEAST RETURNED, THE BEAST AVENGED, THE BEAST DISPLAYED, THE BEAST DENIED, THE FLY TRAP

SLEIGHT IS A COMIC BOOK ARTIST AND ILLUSTRATOR FROM THE PHILIPPINES. HE LIKES POP PUNK MUSIC AND PLAYING **WORLD OF WARCRAFT.**

CHECK OUT HIS WORK ON HIS **WEBSITE:** SLEIGHT.XYZ

ARTIST AND LETTERER: THE FINAL SCREAM

MIA STRIZZI IS AN ILLUSTRATOR FROM LOS ANGELES THAT IS CURRENTLY LIVING IN NEW YORK CITY. THOUGH MOSTLY WORKING AS AN ARTIST FOR BAND POSTERS, SHE HAS A LIFELONG PASSION FOR COMICS AND INTENDS TO PUBLISH MANY MORE. THIS STORY IS HER FIRST COMIC IN THAT EFFORT.

SHE AFFECTIONATELY REFERS TO HER ART STYLE AS *"WATERCOLOR NIGHTMARE FUEL."* HER HOBBIES INCLUDE CAT SITTING, WATCHING OBSCURE HORROR MOVIES, SURFING, AND DAY DREAMING ABOUT SOMEDAY OWNING A TARANTULA.

CHECK OUT HER WORK ON **INSTAGRAM:** MIA_STRIZZI, **TWITTER:** @MIASTRIZZI, AND ON HER **WEBSITE:** MIASTRIZZI.COM

ARTIST: THE FLY TRAP

WALTER OSTLIE IS A COMIC ARTIST BEST KNOWN FOR HIS INDIE BOOK **METALSHARK BRO** AND HIS YOUTUBE SERIES WHERE HE PASSES ON COMICS INDUSTRY AND DRAWING ADVICE TO ASPIRING ARTISTS. HE DREW THE COVER FOR THIS ANTHOLOGY.

FOLLOW HIM ON **INSTAGRAM:** WALTEROSTLIE

MR. FISH LEE IS A FREELANCE COMIC WRITER AND ILLUSTRATOR BASED OUT OF CONWAY, ARKANSAS. HIS CROWNING WORK IS ***T-MAN & HYPERSTRIKE***, A COMIC ABOUT A SUPER HERO TEAM WITH TOURETTE'S SYNDROME AND ADHD.

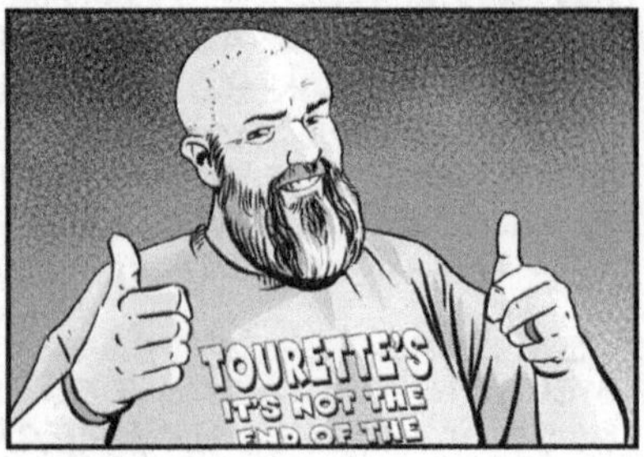
TOURETTE'S
IT'S NOT THE
END OF THE

HE FELT IT IMPORTANT TO GIVE REPRESENTATION TO THESE GROUPS SINCE HE GREW UP WITH BOTH DISORDERS AND DIDN'T HAVE THAT REPRESENTATION HIMSELF. HE ALSO FREQUENTLY WORKS ON KICKSTARTER PROJECTS FOR UP AND COMING COMIC WRITERS.

CHECK OUT HIS WORK ON ***TWITTER:*** @MRFISHLEE, ***INSTAGRAM:*** TOURETTESLIFE, AND ***DEVIANTART:*** @MRFISHLEE

ARTIST AND LETTERER: TERRITORIAL IMPERATIVE

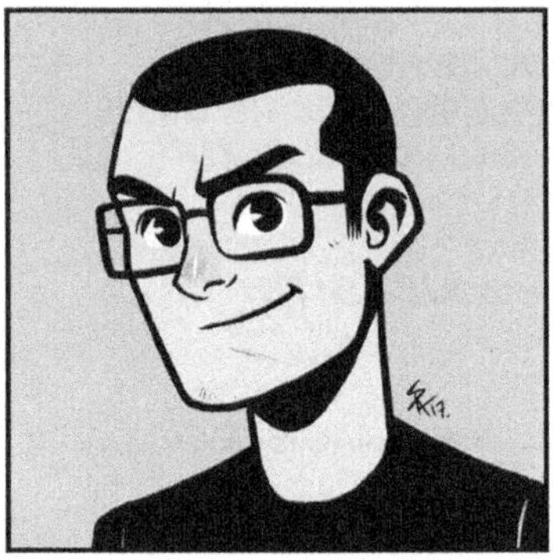

SERG ACUÑA GRADUATED FROM THE UNIVERSITY OF ***COSTA RICA*** WITH A DEGREE IN GRAPHIC DESIGN AND HAS BEEN WORKING AS A COMIC ARTIST AND GRAPHIC DESIGNER FOR THE LAST FOUR YEARS. BEST KNOWN FOR DRAWING BOOM! STUDIOS ***WWE*** SERIES, SERG HAS DONE WORK ON ***FIREFLY, BUFFY,*** AND SEVERAL INDIE PROJECTS IN HIS SHORT BUT PRODUCTIVE CAREER.

SERG SPENDS MUCH OF HIS FREE TIME IMPARTING HIS LOVE OF DINOSAURS AND EPIC FANTASY TO HIS CHILDREN, DRAWING BEAUTIFUL PORTRAITS OF HIS WIFE, ***KATH LOBO,*** HUNTING FOR THE BEST PIXEL ART IN VIDEO GAMES, AND EATING PIZZA...WAY TOO MUCH PIZZA.

CHECK OUT HIS WORK ON ***INSTAGRAM:*** SERGACUNA, ***TWITTER:*** @SERGACUNA, AND ON HIS ***BLOG:*** BEHANCE.NET/SERGCHAYOTE

ARTIST AND LETTERER: AWASH

MARY LANDRO IS AN ASPIRING COMIC BOOK ARTIST FROM THE MYSTERIOUS LAND OF CANADA. SHE RECENTLY BEGAN PURSUING ART AS HER FULL TIME CAREER BY ACCEPTING COMMISSIONS ON HER SOCIAL MEDIA AND WORKING ON HER OWN COMIC, ***LOCKE THEORY.***

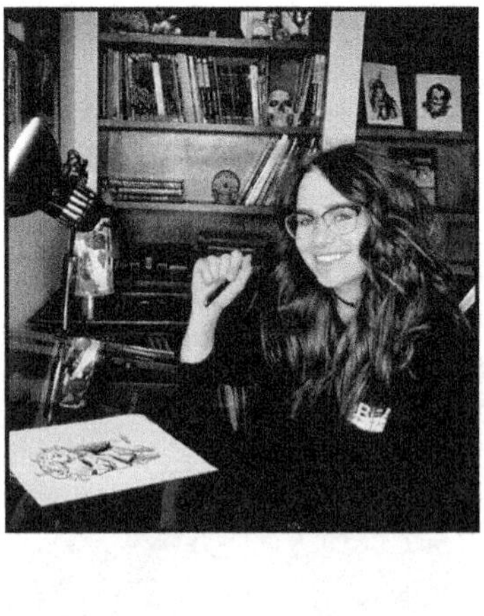

WHEN SHE'S NOT SHUT IN FOR A GLOBAL PANDEMIC, SHE OFTEN GOES SNOWBOARDING. NOWADAYS, SHE PRACTICES PLAYING MUSIC ON MULTIPLE INSTRUMENTS INCLUDING SAXOPHONE, GUITAR, AND PIANO. THESE PERFORMANCES ARE FOR THE BENEFIT OF HER CATS ***LILY*** AND ***HERMAN*** WHO APPLAUD HER MUSIC WITH A CHORUS OF MEOWS AND CRITICIZE HER ART BY SITTING ON IT.

CHECK OUT HER WORK ON ***INSTAGRAM:*** MLANDART, ***TWITTER:*** @MLANDART AND @LOCKETHEORYCOMIC

ARTIST AND LETTERER: CHASING THE SUN

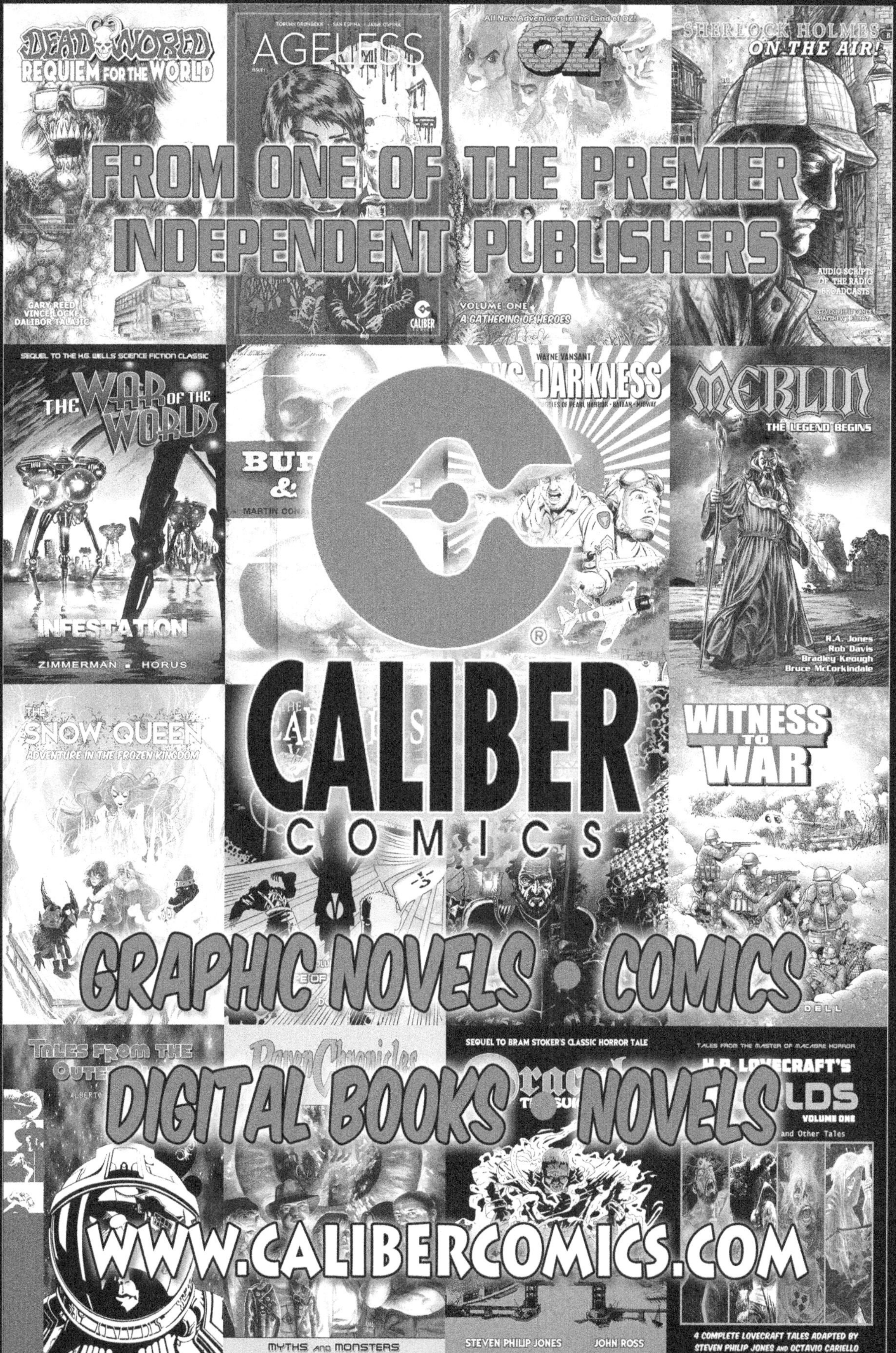
DEADWORLD
REQUIEM FOR THE WORLD
GARY REED
VINCE LOCKE
DALIBOR TALAJIC
AGELESS
All New Adventures in the Land of OZ!
OZ
VOLUME ONE
A GATHERING OF HEROES
SHERLOCK HOLMES
ON THE AIR!
AUDIO SCRIPTS OF THE RADIO BROADCASTS
FROM ONE OF THE PREMIER
INDEPENDENT PUBLISHERS
SEQUEL TO THE H.G. WELLS SCIENCE FICTION CLASSIC
THE WAR OF THE WORLDS
INFESTATION
ZIMMERMAN • HORUS
WAYNE VANSANT
DARKNESS
MERLIN
THE LEGEND BEGINS
R.A. Jones
Rob Davis
Bradley Keough
Bruce McCorkindale
CALIBER
COMICS
THE SNOW QUEEN
ADVENTURE IN THE FROZEN KINGDOM
WITNESS TO WAR
GRAPHIC NOVELS • COMICS
SEQUEL TO BRAM STOKER'S CLASSIC HORROR TALE
TALES FROM THE MASTER OF MACABRE HORROR
H.P. LOVECRAFT'S
VOLUME ONE
and Other Tales
DIGITAL BOOKS • NOVELS
WWW.CALIBERCOMICS.COM
MYTHS AND MONSTERS
STEVEN PHILIP JONES
JOHN ROSS
4 COMPLETE LOVECRAFT TALES ADAPTED BY
STEVEN PHILIP JONES AND OCTAVIO CARIELLO

Made in the USA
Coppell, TX
29 June 2020